LEGAL WRITING, LEGAL PRACTICE

Program in Judaic Studies
Brown University
Box 1826
Providence, RI 02912

BROWN JUDAIC STUDIES

Edited by

David C. Jacobson
Saul M. Olyan
Rachel Rojanski
Michael L. Satlow
Adam Teller

Number 370
LEGAL WRITING, LEGAL PRACTICE

by
Yael Landman

LEGAL WRITING, LEGAL PRACTICE

THE BIBLICAL BAILMENT LAW AND DIVINE JUSTICE

by
Yael Landman

Brown Judaic Studies
Providence, Rhode Island

Library of Congress Control Number: 2021946651

Contents

Acknowledgments

In 2011, I took a course at Yeshiva University about the Covenant Code, the main legal portion of the book of Exodus, with my eventual dissertation advisor Barry Eichler. Per the assigned final project, I wrote a commentary on the laws of bailment in Exod 22:6–14, but I misunderstood the assignment and wrote the wrong kind of paper. This misstep led to extra hours working on and developing a fascination with these laws, to my 2017 dissertation, "The Biblical Law of Bailment in Its Ancient Near Eastern Contexts," and now, finally, to this book. The moral of the story is that if you tell me I did something incorrectly, I will spend a decade writing about the subject of my errors.

I thank my wonderful dissertation advisor, Barry Eichler, and committee members, Shalom Holtz and Chaim Saiman, for their guidance both while I wrote my dissertation and as I thought about how I would shape this book. Shalom Holtz in particular has remained a constant source of support and friendship. I also thank David Berger, Moshe Bernstein, Aaron Koller, Richard Steiner, Sheniagia Washington, and the Gottesman Library staff, who supported my work at Yeshiva. I am grateful for the generous funding I received while earning my PhD from the Mozes S. Schupf Fellowship, the Dr. Monique C. Katz Fellowship, the Center for Jewish Law and Contemporary Civilization at Benjamin N. Cardozo School of Law, the Tikvah Center for Law and Jewish Civilization at New York University School of Law, the Memorial Foundation for Jewish Culture Doctoral Scholarship Grant, and the Association for Jewish Studies Dissertation Completion Fellowship.

I wrote this book while serving as a fellow in the Judaic Studies department at Brooklyn College and then as an affiliated fellow at the Katz Center for Judaic Studies at the University of Pennsylvania, and I completed revisions while teaching in Penn's Department of Near Eastern Languages and Civilizations. Thank you to my colleagues at both institutions for believing in this project. I am also grateful to Gorgias Press, where I am fortunate to work alongside colleagues who are both brilliant and kind. In 2017–2018, I participated in the Paula E. Hyman Mentoring Program through the Association for Jewish Studies. Thank you to the phenomenal women scholars who created and led this program, and especially to Christine Hayes, who has continued to mentor me since then.

I am grateful to colleagues and friends who have discussed aspects of my work with me, shared resources, and offered encouragement. In particular, thank you to Pamela Barmash, Binyamin Goldstein, Chumie Juni, Mayer Juni, Ze'ev Sudry, Jacqueline Vayntrub, Bruce Wells, Tali Arbit Winkler, Meira Wolkenfeld, Shlomo Zuckier, and members of the SBL Biblical Law section. To my dear friends Rachel Allon, Neesa Berezin-Bahr, Louise Cohen, Alana Ebin, Pamela Kaplan, Reena Ribalt Papir, Yaffa Setton, and Jessica Zimble, who sustain me via Whatsapp throughout the day (and night), and to Dani, Sarah, Hillel, Rachel, and Ahuva Landman, thank you for lifting me up always. The COVID-19 pandemic, which is ongoing at the time of this writing, has posed particular challenges for conducting research, and I thank members of the Facebook groups Hebrew Bible Resources in the Times of Corona and ANE Researcher Quarantine "Library" for their kindness. Thank you also to Saul Olyan, Maurya Horgan, and the team at Brown Judaic Studies for expertly shepherding this book to publication.

I am grateful for the steadfast support of my parents and parents-in-law, Leorah and David Landman and Jeanette and Neil Wermuth, without whom I cannot imagine having completed this book. To Noam, Meirav, and Yoav, thank you for adding color to my life, if also to my laptop and furniture. I love you more than anything, whether you are jaguars or microraptors or actual human children. Finally, I thank David Wermuth, my life partner and inspiration, for supporting my dreams and for dreaming with me. I dedicate this book to him with love.

Abbreviations

A	Tablets in the collections of the Oriental Institute, University of Chicago
AASOR	Annual of the American Schools of Oriental Research
AB	Anchor Bible
AbB	Altbabylonische Briefe

    1 F. R. Kraus, *Briefe aus dem British Museum (CT 43 and 44)*, AbB 1 (Leiden: Brill, 1964)

    4 F. R. Kraus, *Briefe aus dem Archive des Šamaš-Ḥāzir in Paris and Oxford (TCL 7 und OECT 3)*, AbB 4 (Leiden: Brill, 1968)

    7 F. R. Kraus, *Briefe aus dem British Museum (CT 52)*, AbB 7 (Leiden: Brill, 1977)

    9 Marten Stol, *Letters from Yale: Transliterated and Translated*, AbB 9 (Leiden: Brill, 1981)

ABL	R. F. Harper, *Assyrian and Babylonian Letters Belonging to the Kouyunjik Collections of the British Museum* (Chicago: University of Chicago Press, 1892–1914)
AfO	*Archiv für Orientforschung*
Ai	Lexical series ana ittišu. *See* MSL 1
AIL	Ancient Israel and Its Literature
AOAT	Alter Orient und Altes Testament
AOS	American Oriental Series
AP	A. E. Cowley, *The Aramaic Papyri of the Fifth Century B.C.* (Oxford: Clarendon, 1923; repr., Osnabrück: Zeller, 1967)
ARM	Archives royales de Mari

    8 Georges Boyer, *Textes juridiques*, ARM 8 (Paris: Impr. Nationale, 1958)

   10 G. Dossin, *La correspondance féminine*, 2 vols., ARM 10 (Paris: P. Guethner, 1978)

Asb.	Maximilian Streck, *Assurbanipal und die letzten assyrischen Könige bis zum Untergange Niniveh's*, Vorderasiatische Bibliotek 7 (Leipzig: Hinrichs, 1916)
AT	D. J. Wiseman, *The Alalakh Tablets* (London: British Institute of Archaeology at Ankara, 1953)
AuOr	*Aula Orientalis*
b	Babylonian Talmud

BA   *Biblical Archaeologist*
BASOR   *Bulletin of the American Schools of Oriental Research*
BATSHDK   Berichte der Ausgrabung Tall Seh Hamad Dur-Katlimmu
BBR   *Bulletin for Biblical Research*
BE   Babylonian Expedition of the University of Pennsylvania:
          Series A: Cuneiform Texts
              6.1 Hermann Ranke, *Babylonian Legal and Business Doc-*
              uments from the Time of the First Dynasty of Babylon,
              Chiefly from Sippar, BE 6.1 (Philadelphia: Department
              of Archaeology, University of Pennsylvania, 1906)
              6.2 Arno Poebel, *Babylonian Legal and Business Docu-*
              ments: From the Time of the First Dynasty of Babylon,
              Chiefly from Nippur, BE 6.2 (Philadelphia: Department
              of Archaeology, University of Pennsylvania, 1909)
              8   Albert Tobias Clay, *Legal and Commercial Transac-*
              tions Dated in the Assyrian, Neo-Babylonian and Persian
              Periods … Chiefly from Nippur, BE 8 (Philadelphia:
              Department of Archaeology, University of Pennsyl-
              vania, 1908)
BGU   Aegyptische Urkunden aus den Königlichen Museen zu Ber-
          lin, Griechische Urkunden
BH   Biblical Hebrew
BIN   *Babylonian Inscriptions in the Collection of James. B. Nies* (New
          Haven: Yale University Press, 1918–1987)
BJS   Brown Judaic Studies
BM   tablets in the collections of the British Museum
BWL   W. G. Lambert, *Babylonian Wisdom Literature* (Oxford: Claren-
          don, 1960)
BZABR   Beihefte zur Zeitschrift für altorientalische und biblische
          Rechtsgeschichte
BZAW   Beihefte zur Zeitschrift für die alttestamentliche Wissen-
          schaft
CAD   *The Assyrian Dictionary of the Oriental Institute of the University*
          of Chicago, 21 vols. (Chicago: Oriental Institute of the Univer-
          sity of Chicago, 1956–2011)
CBET   Contributions to Biblical Exegesis and Theology
CBQ   *Catholic Biblical Quarterly*
CC   Covenant Code
CHANE   Culture and History of the Ancient Near East
COS   William W. Hallo and K. Lawson Younger Jr., eds., *The Con-*
          text of Scripture, 4 vols. (Leiden: Brill, 1997–2016)
CT   Cuneiform Texts from Babylonian Tablets in the British
          Museum

DL	Deuteronomic laws
DN	Divine Name
EA	Die El-Amarna-Tafeln; El Amarna letters
EN	Excavations at Nuzi
	9.2 Martha A. Morrison, *The Eastern Archives of Nuzi*, EN 9.2, SCCNH 4.1 (Winona Lake, IN: Eisenbrauns, 1993)
FAT	Forschungen zum Alten Testament
FLP	Free Library of Phildadelphia
GKC	W. Gesenius, *Gesenius' Hebrew Grammar*, ed. Emil Kautzsch, trans. A. E. Cowley, 2nd ed. (Oxford: Clarendon, 1910)
HCOT	Historical Commentary of the Old Testament
HdO	Handbuch der Orientalistik
HL	Hittite Laws
HSS	Harvard Semitic Studies
	9 R. H. Pfeiffer, *Excavations at Nuzi II: The Archives of Shilwateshub, Son of the King (1932)*, HSS 9 (Leiden: Brill, 2019)
	13 R. H. Pfeiffer and E. R. Lacheman, *Excavations at Nuzi IV: Miscellaneous Texts from Nuzi, Part I (1942)*, HSS 13 (Leiden: Brill, 2019)
HTR	*Harvard Theological Review*
HUCA	*Hebrew Union College Annual*
IMMP	L. E. Pearce and C. Wunsch, *Into the Midst of Many People: Judaean and West Semitic Exiles in Mesopotamia*, Cornell University Studies in Assyriology and Sumerology 18 (Bethesda, MD: CDL, forthcoming)
IUSS	Istituto Universitario di Studi Superiori
JANES	*Journal of the Ancient Near Eastern Society*
JAOS	*Journal of the American Oriental Society*
JBL	*Journal of Biblical Literature*
JCS	*Journal of Cuneiform Studies*
JEN	Edward Chiera, ed., *Joint Expedition with the Iraq Museum at Nuzi*, 6 vols., Publications of the Bagdad School; Publications of the American Schools of Oriental Research (Paris: P. Guethner, 1927–1939)
JESHO	*Journal of the Economic and Social History of the Orient*
JLH	*Journal of Legal History*
JNES	*Journal of Near Eastern Studies*
JNSL	*Journal of Northwest Semitic Languages*
Josephus	
Ant.	*Antiquities*
JPS	Jewish Publication Society

JSJ	*Journal for the Study of Judaism*
JSOT	*Journal for the Study of the Old Testament*
JSOTSup	Journal for the Study of the Old Testament Supplement Series
JSS	*Journal of Semitic Studies*
JTSA	Jewish Theological Seminary of America
JWB	Cornelia Wunsch, *Judeans by the Waters of Babylon: New Historical Evidence in Cuneiform Sources from Rural Babylonia*, Babylonische Archive 6 (Dresden: ISLET, forthcoming in 2022)
K	tablets in the Kouyunjik collection of the British Museum
KAJ	E. Ebeling, *Keilschrifttexte aus Assur juristischen Inhalts, Ausgrabungen der Deutschen Orient-Gesellschaft in Assur: E, Inschriften 4*; Wissenschaftliche Veröffentlichung der Deutschen Orient-Gesellschaft 50 (Leipzig: Hinrichs, 1927)
KJV	King James Version
KUB	Keilschrifturkunden aus Boghazköi
LAOS	Leipziger Altorientalistischen Studien
LE	Laws of Eshnunna
LH	Laws of Hammurabi
LHBOTS	Library of Hebrew Bible/Old Testament Studies
LIH	L. W. King, ed., *The Letters and Inscriptions of Hammurabi, King of Babylon, about B.C. 2200 to Which Are Added a Series of Letters of Other Kings of the First Dynasty of Babylon*, 3 vols. (London: Luzac, 1898–1900)
LL	Laws of Lipit-Ištar
LNB	Neo-Babylonian Laws
LOx	Laws about Rented Oxen. M. Civil, "New Sumerian Law Fragments," in *Studies in Honor of Benno Landsberger on His Seventy-Fifth Birthday, April 21, 1965*, ed. H. G. Güterbock and T. Jacobsen, AS 16 (Chicago: University of Chicago Press, 1965)
LTBA	Lubor Matouš and Wolfram von Soden, *Die lexikalischen Tafelserien der Babylonier und Assyrer in den Berlin Museen*, 2 vols. (Berlin: Staatlichen Museen, 1933)
LXX	Septuagint
m	Mishnah
MA	Middle Assyrian
MAL	Middle Assyrian Laws
MB	Middle Babylonian
MDP	Mémoires de la Délégation en Perse
	22 V. Scheil, *Actes juridiques susiens*, MDP 22 (Paris, 1930)
MSL	*Materialien zum sumerischen Lexikon / Materials for the Sumerian Lexicon*, ed. Benno Landsberger, 17 vols., Scripta

Pontificii Instituti Biblici (Rome: Pontifical Biblical Institute, 1937–2004)

    1 Benno Landsberger, *Die Serie ana ittišu*, MSL 1 (Rome: Pontificium Institutum Biblicum, 1937)

   12 Miguel Civil, ed., *The Series lú = ša and Related Texts*, MSL 12 (Rome: Pontificium Institutum Biblicum, 1969)

MT   Masoretic Text

MVAG   Mitteilungen der Vorderasiatisch-Ägyptischen Gesellschaft

   10 W. F. von Landau, *Vorläufige Nachrichten über die im Eshmuntempel bei Sidon gefundenen phönizischen Altertümer*, MVAG 10 (Berlin: Wolf Peiser, 1905)

   33 G. Eisser and J. Lewy, *Die altassyrischen Rechturkunden vom Kültepe*, MVAG 33 (Leipzig: Hinrichs, 1930)

  35.3 G. Eisser and J. Lewy, *Die altassyrischen Rechturkunden vom Kültepe*, MVAG 35.3 (Leipzig: Hinrichs, 1935)

NA   Neo-Assyrian

NB   Neo-Babylonian

Nbn.   Johann N. Strassmaier, *Inschriften von Nabonidus, König von Babylon (555–538 v. Chr.) von den Throntafeln des Britischen Museums*, Babylonische Texte (Leipzig: Eduard Pfeiffer, 1889)

NIV   New International Version

NJPS   New Jewish Publication Society of America Tanakh (1985)

NKJV   New King James Version

NRSV   New Revised Standard Version

O.   M. Sandowicz, *Oaths and Curses: A Study of Neo- and Late Babylonian Legal Formulary* (Münster: Ugarit-Verlag, 2012)

OA   Old Assyrian

OB   Old Babylonian

OBO   Orbis Biblicus et Orientalis

OECT   Oxford Editions of Cuneiform Texts

    3 G. R. Driver, *Letters of the First Babylonian Dynasty*, OECT 3 (London: Oxford University Press, 1924)

OLA   Orientalia Lovaniensia Analecta

OTL   Old Testament Library

P. Catt. Papyrus Cattaoui

PBS   Publications of the Babylonian Section, University of Pennsylvania

   1/2 Henry Frederick Lutz, *Selected Sumerian and Babylonian Texts*, PBS 1, no. 2 (Philadelphia: University Museum, 1919)

	7 Arthur Ungnad, *Babylonian Letters of the Hammurapi Period*, PBS 7 (Philadelphia: University Museum, 1915)
PL	Priestly laws
PN	Personal Name
RA	*Revue d'assyriologie et d'archéologie orientale*
RS	Ras Shamra
RSV	Revised Standard Version
SAOC	Studies in Ancient Oriental Civilization
SBL	Society of Biblical Literature
SBLAIL	Society of Biblical Literature Ancient Israel and Its Literature
SBLWAW	Society of Biblical Literature Writings from the Ancient World
SCCNH	Studies on the Civilization and Culture of Nuzi and the Hurrians
SHCANE	Studies in the History and Culture of the Ancient Near East
SLEx	Sumerian Laws Exercise Tablet. A. T. Clay, "A Sumerian Prototype of the Hammurabi Code," *Orientalische Literaturzeitung* 17 (1914): 1–3; Clay, *Miscellaneous Inscriptions in the Yale Babylonian Collection*, YOS 1 (New Haven: Yale University Press, 1915)
SLHF	Sumerian Laws Handbook of Forms. M. T. Roth, "Scholastic Tradition and Mesopotamian Law: A Study of FLP 1287, a Prism in the Collection of the Free Library of Philadelphia" (PhD diss., University of Pennsylvania, 1979)
STDJ	Studies on the Texts of the Desert of Judah
t	Tosefta
TCL	Textes cunéiformes, Musées du Louvre (Paris, 1910–1967)
	12 Georges Contenau, *Contrats néo-babyloniens*, vol. 1: *De Téglath-phalasar III à Nabonide*, TCL 12 (Paris: P. Guethner, 1927)
	18 George Dossin, *Lettres de la première dynastie babylonienne*, TCL 18 (Paris: P. Guethner, 1934)
TDOT	G. Johannes Botterweck and Helmer Ringgren, eds., *Theological Dictionary of the Old Testament*, trans. John T. Willis et al., 17 vols. (Grand Rapids: Eerdmans, 1974–2018)
Tg.	Targum
TJA	Émile Szlechter, ed., *Tablettes juridiques et administratives de la IIIe dynastie d'Ur et de la Ire dynastie de Babylone conservées au Musée de l'Université de Manchester et, à Cambridge, au Musée Fitz-William, à l'Institut d'études orientales et à l'Institut d'egyptologie*, Publications de l'Institut de droit romain de l'Universitéde Paris 21a (Paris: Recueil Sirey, 1963)
TLB	Rintje Frankena, William W. Hallo, and Wilhelmus F. Leemans, *Tabulae cuneiformes a F.M. Th. de Liagre Böhl collectae*, 4

Introduction

Prescriptive law writings rarely mirror a society's law in practice, a fact that raises special problems for the social and legal historian. Law codes or legal collections offer only a partial view of the law of a group of people in a given time or place.[1] To reconstruct "law in practice," historians must examine other documents, such as contracts, trial records, and private letters.

Scholars who wish to reconstruct the legal landscape of biblical Israel and Judah face certain special challenges. First, the very nature of the biblical "law codes"—the Covenant Code in Exodus; the Holiness Code in Leviticus; the Priestly laws in Exodus, Leviticus, and Numbers; and the Deuteronomic laws in Deuteronomy—is hotly debated, with scholars questioning whether these laws, and indeed ancient Near Eastern legal writings in general, were intended to bear prescriptive force at all, or to serve an altogether different purpose.[2] Second, the near-absence of documents attesting to legal practice makes it difficult to reconstruct that practice and to contextualize the law writings in the Bible.

This book probes the relationship between the so-called "law codes" of the Hebrew Bible and "law in practice" in biblical Israel, through close analysis of the law of bailment in Exod 22:6–14. This law refers to arrangements such as deposits of goods and animal herding, in which one person gives property to another person for temporary safekeeping or use. Standing at the crossroads of law, religion, and economics, the institution of bailment offers an underexploited window into the conceptual underpinnings of biblical law and legal practice in ancient Israel. Employing philological analysis and interdisciplinary legal theory, I draw conclusions about the institution of bailment specifically and biblical law generally.

---

1. Regarding inevitable discrepancies between written law and legal practice, see Aryeh Amihay, *Theory and Practice in Essene Law* (Oxford: Oxford University Press, 2017), 187.

2. For example, were the laws primarily scholastic texts or royal apologia? For an overview of this debate, see Bruce Wells, "What Is Biblical Law? A Look at Pentateuchal Rules and Near Eastern Practice," *CBQ* 70 (2008): 223–43.

With respect to bailment, I argue that the law in Exodus concerns not just safekeeping but also fact-finding; that the law's treatment of fact-finding advances a conception of divine justice based on such concerns as protecting the vulnerable (as defined by the law) and ascertaining the innocence of the accused to the satisfaction of the plaintiff; and that ancient Near Eastern bailment laws exhibit continuity with postbiblical Jewish law. With respect to biblical law more generally, I advance an approach to the study of operative law in ancient Israel that connects pentateuchal law, biblical narrative and prophecy, and Mesopotamian legal documents. This multidimensional approach generates a reconstructed "law in practice" that can then be compared with pentateuchal law writings. The application of this approach to the law of bailment demonstrates that pentateuchal law can be descriptively accurate for the most part, even when it serves the apologetic purpose of advancing a particular conception of divine justice.

Guiding the course of this study is Exod 22:6–14, the biblical law of bailment in the collection of laws known as the Covenant Code or the Book of the Covenant. Although the term *bailment* is obscure to most non-legal specialists, I have chosen to use it here because it is the most accurate English word available. The term *bailment* encapsulates all the subtopics of this law, which include deposits of goods, herding, and animal borrowing and rental. In contrast, the term *deposit*, the choice of some other scholars who have addressed these laws, does not accurately account for all of the cases that Exod 22:6–14 treats.[3] The criterion for determining the relevance of other biblical and extrabiblical sources in this book is not whether they fall under the umbrella of the Anglo-Saxon legal term *bailment* per se but whether they pertain to the situations that Exod 22:6–14 envisions.[4]

---

3. On the disadvantages of the term *deposit* in this context, see Bernard S. Jackson, *Wisdom-Laws: A Study of the Mishpatim of Exodus 21:1–22:16* (Oxford: Oxford University Press, 2006), 332 n. 2. For *deposit*, see, e.g., Ira M. Price, "The Laws of Deposit in Early Babylonia and the Old Testament," *JAOS* 47 (1927): 250–55; Eckart Otto, "Die rechtshistorische Entwicklung des Depositenrechts in altorientalischen und altisraelitischen Rechtskorpora," *Zeitschrift der Savigny-Stiftung für Rechtsgeschichte: Romanitische Abteilung* 105 (1988): 1–31; reprinted in Otto, *Kontinuum und Proprium: Studien zur Sozial- und Rechtsgeschichte des Alten Orients und des Alten Testaments*, Orientalia Biblica et Christiana 8 (Wiesbaden: Harrassowitz, 1996), 139–63; Horst Seebass, "Noch einmal zum Depositenrecht Ex 22, 6–14," in *Gottes Recht als Lebensraum: Festschrift für Hans Jochen Boecker*, ed. Peter Mommer, Werner H. Schmidt, and Hans Strauss (Neukirchen-Vluyn: Neukirchener Verlag, 1993), 21–31; Raymond Westbrook, "The Deposit Law of Exodus 22, 6–12," *ZAW* 106 (1994): 390–403; reprinted in *Law from the Tigris to the Tiber: The Writings of Raymond Westbrook*, ed. Bruce Wells and F. Rachel Magdalene, 2 vols. (Winona Lake, IN: Eisenbrauns, 2009), 2:361–77.

4. Thus, for example, this study will exclude pledges, a form of bailment in which the bailee is a creditor holding onto the bailor-debtor's personal property as security for a debt. See Bryan A. Garner, ed., *Black's Law Dictionary*, 9th ed. (Saint Paul, MN: Thomson Reuters, 2009), s.v. "pledge."

Although this study makes wide use of the term *bailment*, it also questions throughout the extent to which there existed a unified concept of bailment in biblical and/or cuneiform law, and repeatedly returns to the problem of defining the term with fidelity to the ancient sources. This line of questioning further informs an account of the development of legal thinking in ancient Israel as it emerges with respect to bailments.

Though as a legal topic bailment lacks the allure of homicide or adultery, I hope that readers will see past the unfamiliarity of the word and appreciate that, as an institution, bailment was extremely ordinary—and therefore, to historians and Bible scholars interested in daily life in ancient Israel, should be a highly valuable topic of study. Bailments were deeply embedded in the socioeconomic fabric of ancient Israel. By tugging at this thread, we uncover numerous strands worth following.

The biblical bailment law appears in the Covenant Code, a set of laws from the book of Exodus. The name "Covenant Code" is a conventional rendering of the Hebrew ספר הברית (Exod 24:7) and, although I prefer the term *law collection* to *law code* to describe biblical and cuneiform legal writings, I continue to use this name because it is conventional.[5] Most scholars accept a preexilic date for the Covenant Code and consider it the earliest of the pentateuchal law collections.[6] There is no consensus, however, regarding the compositional and redactional history of the Covenant Code.[7] While the composition and editing of the Covenant Code are important, I am more interested in the final form of Exod 22:6–14 than in how it came to look the way it does.[8] I choose to adopt a synchronic

---

5. For discussion of the terms *law code* and *law collection*, including views for and against the term *law code*, see Pamela Barmash, *Homicide in the Biblical World* (Cambridge: Cambridge University Press, 2005), 6–7; S. J. [Van Wyk] Claassens, "The So-Called 'Mesopotamian Law Codes': What's in a Name?," *JSem* 19 (2010): 461–78.

6. A notable exception is John Van Seters, who has argued that the Covenant was composed during the Neo-Babylonian period when Judeans lived in exile in Babylonia, and that it postdates the other biblical law collections (*A Law Book for the Diaspora: Revision in the Study of the Covenant Code* [Oxford: Oxford University Press, 2003]). For a response to Van Seters, see Bernard M. Levinson, "Is the Covenant Code an Exilic Composition? A Response to John Van Seters," in *In Search of Pre-Exilic Israel: Proceedings of the Oxford Old Testament Seminar*, ed. John Day, JSOTSup 406 (London: T&T Clark, 2004), 272–325.

7. For an overview of positions, see Barmash, *Homicide in the Biblical World*, 74–76; cf. David P. Wright, *Inventing God's Law: How the Covenant Code of the Bible Used and Revised the Laws of Hammurabi* (Oxford: Oxford University Press, 2009), 17–20.

8. Scholars favoring a diachronic approach to this pericope have suggested a number of reconstructions of its history of composition. In Eckart Otto's view, for example, an original law included only verses 6, 7aα, 9a, 11, 12, 13, and 14a; later additions sought to correct this original law in the interests of justice and of systematization. Otto thus proposes a legal history of bailment, and of the legal system more broadly, internal to Exod 22:6–14: an older law simply defined when a person had to pay single compensation and what circumstances exempted the person from payment. Additions to the law reflect increasing systematization, imposing sanctions to discourage wrongdoing and affording the court more expansive

approach to this individual legal pericope, valuing an internally consistent understanding of the law over one that views the final form of the text
as contradicting itself. This approach does not invalidate diachronic analysis or its results but instead focuses on the text in front of us, including
how to interpret and contextualize it and how to use it critically as one
limited, methodologically thorny piece of evidence for the reconstruction
of legal practice and thinking in the ancient world.[9]

The reader of biblical and cuneiform law will find it difficult to ignore
how frequently the two corpora share cases, details, and even linguistic
forms. In light of these similarities, as well as many cultural and societal
affinities, scholars have posited a historical connection between the societies in which biblical and ancient Near Eastern law emerged.[10] Meir Malul
in particular articulates a well-defined historical-comparative approach,
which posits that the connections between biblical and ancient Near Eastern law are rooted in a common source or influence of one society over the
other, rather than a typological approach, which compares societies with
no temporal or geographical relationship.[11] Despite the relative consensus
regarding the existence of a connection between biblical and cuneiform
law, however, debate concerning the origin of this connection persists.[12] In
the case of the Covenant Code in particular, a minority of scholars, including most recently John Van Seters and David Wright, have argued for
direct literary dependence of the biblical law collection upon cuneiform
forebears.[13] Most scholars reject this premise, instead adopting one of

---

means of trying parties whose guilt might otherwise remain indeterminable (see Otto, "Die
rechtshistorische Entwicklung," 139–63).

9. On the merits of adopting a synchronic approach to biblical law before turning to
diachronic analysis, see Moshe Greenberg, "Some Postulates of Biblical Criminal Law," in
Yehezkel Kaufmann Jubilee Volume, ed. M. Haran (Jerusalem: Magnes, 1960), 5–28, here 7–8. Cf.
Westbrook, "Deposit Law," 362: "in a legal text, the sole criterion for resolving ambiguities
of language is the most appropriate legal meaning. For that purpose it must be assumed that
the law is coherent, and only if all attempts fail should recourse be had to explanations based
upon error, inelegant editing, or unresolved difficulties arising from the historical development of legal conceptions."

10. A bibliography on this subject would exceed the parameters of a footnote, but, as
Wells has noted, Westbrook's work on this matter has strongly articulated and bolstered the
argument. See citations in Bruce Wells, *The Law of Testimony in the Pentateuchal Codes*, BZABR
4 (Wiesbaden: Harrassowitz, 2004), 7 n. 19.

11. Meir Malul, *The Comparative Method in Ancient Near Eastern and Biblical Legal Studies*,
AOAT 227 (Kevelaer: Butzon & Bercker; Neukirchen-Vluyn: Neukirchener Verlag, 1990).

12. For a minority view rejecting a relationship between biblical and cuneiform law, see
A. Van Selms, "The Goring Ox in Babylonian and Biblical Law," *ArOr* 18 (1950): 321–30.

13. See especially Van Seters, *Law Book for the Diaspora*, 98–99; David P. Wright, "The
Laws of Hammurabi as a Source for the Covenant Collection (Exodus 20:23–23:19)," *Maarav*
10 (2003): 11–87; Wright, "The Laws of Hammurabi and the Covenant Code: A Response to
Bruce Wells," *Maarav* 13 (2006): 211–60; Wright, *Inventing God's Law*. Other scholars have
argued for a direct connection between the biblical and ancient Near Eastern law collections

many versions of a traditions argument, which involves the indirect absorption of features of the Mesopotamian legal tradition into biblical law.[14] Such models identify points of contact or conduits allowing for the influence of Mesopotamian editorial techniques and legal problems on the Covenant Code, while generally excluding the possibility of textual dependence.[15] This study situates itself in this latter camp, without seeking to identify precise origins of commonality.

While consideration of biblical law in its own context should always precede comparative analysis, scholars have long recognized the benefits of employing a comparative methodology as an interpretative aid.[16] A comparative approach accompanies all other methods of analysis in this study, with an eye toward convergences and divergences between sources, where one text raises questions about another, and how one can illuminate the other's difficulties. The comparative investigation aims not only to fulfill an exegetical and elucidatory purpose but, further, to explore whether one should explain similarities and differences in terms of underlying conceptions or ideologies, legal institutions, social or economic models, or other factors.

Although the comparative approach offers invaluable fodder for the study of biblical law, methodological blunders may neutralize its efficacy. These blunders include primarily variations on a single theme, namely, generalization. The history of comparative biblical and ancient Near Eastern studies has shifted back and forth between two trends, from viewing

---

while asserting that the means of transmission cannot be identified; see, e.g., J. J. Finkelstein, *The Ox That Gored*, TAPS 71.2 (Philadelphia: American Philosophical Society, 1981), 20.

14. See especially Raymond Westbrook, *Studies in Biblical and Cuneiform Law*, CahRB 26 (Paris: Gabalda, 1988), 1–4; Reuven Yaron, *The Laws of Eshnunna*, 2nd rev. ed. (Jerusalem: Magnes; Leiden: Brill, 1988), 294–95; Ludger Schwienhorst-Schönberger, *Das Bundesbuch (Ex 20,22–23,33): Studien zu seiner Entstehung und Theologie*, BZAW 188 (Berlin: de Gruyter, 1990), 240–68; Ralf Rothenbusch, *Die kasuistische Rechtssammlung im "Bundesbuch" (Ex 21,2–11.18–22,16) und ihr literarischer Kontext im Licht altorientalischer Parallelen*, AOAT 259 (Münster: Ugarit-Verlag, 2000), 394–98; Bruce Wells, "The Covenant Code and Near Eastern Legal Traditions: A Response to David P. Wright," *Maarav* 13 (2006): 85–118.

15. Suggestions for points of contact or possible intermediary conduits have included Akkadian scribal schools in second-millennium Canaan (Westbrook, *Studies in Biblical and Cuneiform Law*, 2–3); Mesopotamian influence on the west during the Middle Bronze and Late Bronze Ages, mediated to Israel and Judah in the first millennium through a Phoenician intermediary (Rothenbusch, *Die kasuistische Rechtssammlung*, 398); and an Amorite common tradition to which both cuneiform law and the Covenant Code were heir (W. G. Lambert, "Interchange of Ideas between Southern Mesopotamia and Syria-Palestine as Seen in Literature," in *Mesopotamien und seine Nachbarn: Politische und kulturelle Wechselbeziehungen im alten Vorderasien vom 4. bis 1. Jahrtausend v. Chr.*, ed. Hans-Jörg Nissen and Johannes Renger [Berlin: D. Reimer, 1982], 312–13).

16. On the illuminative capacity of the comparative approach, see Malul, *Comparative Method*, 23–25. This is one of six uses of the comparative method that Malul identifies in the history of scholarship on biblical and cuneiform studies.

the Bible as continuous with the rest of the ancient Near East to viewing it as a unique break from the latter. The tendency to view biblical law in opposition to "cuneiform law," the latter conceived of as a single entity, is arbitrary unless justified and risks ignoring differences between ancient Near Eastern cultures and societies that covered a vast span of time and space. Nor should one assume a monolithic "biblical law" without internal divergences, unless coherence has been demonstrated. Every primary source demands analysis in its own right before comparison with other texts, and, despite many observable cultural similarities in the ancient Near East over time, one must be sensitive to diversities amid the uniformity. This study will attempt to avoid such errors by considering each text in its own context, by studying a substantial number of texts in order to penetrate each culture's laws more deeply, and by highlighting and exploring variety as well as uniformity, especially where cuneiform texts diverge from one another.[17]

In addition to exploring legal texts external to the biblical corpus, I make extensive use of nonlegal texts from within the Bible, in order to glean information that may help us approach a reconstruction of legal practice in ancient Israel and to identify a range of perspectives on justice and equity. We thus enter the tricky realm of law and literature, a school of thought whose methodologies have gained currency among scholars both of law and of literature, including biblical and Judaic studies scholars.[18] Whereas some scholars once understood references to law in biblical

---

17. On the pitfalls of the comparative method and suggested correctives, see Barmash, *Homicide in the Biblical World*, 3–4.

18. In biblical studies, recent examples include Pamela Barmash, "Achieving Justice through Narrative in the Hebrew Bible: The Limitations of Law in the Legal Potential of Literature," *ZABR* 20 (2014): 181–99; Barmash, "The Narrative Quandary: Cases of Law in Literature," *VT* 54 (2004): 1–16; F. Rachel Magdalene, *On the Scales of Righteousness: Neo-Babylonian Trial Law and the Book of Job*, BJS 348 (Providence, RI: Brown Judaic Studies, 2007); Assnat Bartor, "The 'Juridical Dialogue': A Literary-Judicial Pattern," *VT* 53 (2003): 445–64; and see chapters in Klaus-Peter Adam, Friedrich Avemarie, and Nili Wazana, eds., *Law and Narrative in the Bible and in Neighbouring Ancient Cultures*, FAT 2/54 (Tübingen: Mohr Siebeck, 2012). In Judaic studies, recent examples include Moshe Simon-Shoshan, *Stories of the Law: Narrative Discourse and the Construction of Authority in the Mishnah* (Oxford: Oxford University Press, 2012); Chaya T. Halberstam, *Law and Truth in Biblical and Rabbinic Literature* (Bloomington: Indiana University Press, 2010); Suzanne Last Stone, "On the Interplay of Rules, 'Cases,' and Concepts in Rabbinic Legal Literature: Another Look at the Aggadot on Ḥoni the Circle-Drawer," *Dine Israel* 24 (2007): 125–55; Steven D. Fraade, "'The Torah of the King' (Deut. 17:14–20) in the Temple Scroll and Early Rabbinic Law," in *The Dead Sea Scrolls as Background to Postbiblical Judaism and Early Christianity: Papers from an International Conference at St. Andrews in 2001*, ed. James R. Davila, STDJ 46 (Leiden: Brill, 2003), 25–62; Fraade, "Navigating the Anomalous: Non-Jews at the Intersection of Early Rabbinic Law and Narrative," in *The Other in Jewish Thought and History: Constructions of Jewish Thought and Identity*, ed. Laurence J. Silberstein and Robert L. Cohn, New Perspectives on Jewish Studies (New York: New York University Press, 1994), 145–65. A recent conference hosted by the Jewish Law

narrative as essentially accurate depictions of law in ancient Israel, recent scholarship has identified numerous methodological problems with such an approach.[19] Because literature uses the law to advance its own literary and theological program, it may skew aspects of the law and depict the legal system inaccurately.[20] Therefore, law and literature scholarship has moved toward an approach that does not see literature as mirroring law per se, but instead as reflecting upon it. In the landmark essay "*Nomos* and Narrative," Robert Cover argues that "[law] may be viewed as a system or a bridge linking a concept of a reality to an imagined alternative—that is, as a connective between two states of affairs, both of which can be represented in their normative significance only through the devices of narrative."[21] A narrative may distort details of the law in order to create a better story but may also do so to expose flaws in the law—for example, in cases where the law enables one person to exploit another's vulnerability, thereby behaving legally and yet immorally—and may further imagine an alternative to the flawed law that rectifies its deficiencies.

Ultimately, though they may deviate from reality, literary texts draw from the real world, including how the law functioned and what people thought about it. Indeed, without resonance with the "real," the text would have failed to make sense to its intended audience. Therefore, with the appropriate caveats in place, I utilize extralegal biblical texts to cull data about history, social contexts, and perceptions in ancient Israel.[22] In particular, I build on recent scholarship by Bruce Wells regarding the reconstruction of operative law in ancient Israel and its relationship to the pentateuchal law collections, in the absence of practice documents from ancient Israel. Wells has proposed that, if one can identify connections in the forms of similar legal issues, similar legal reasoning, and similar legal remedies between the pentateuchal law collections and ancient Near Eastern practice documents, then one can also posit a connection between the pentateuchal law collections and Israelite legal practice.[23] To this I add a third source of data: biblical narrative and prophecy.[24] If one can identify

Association also centered on the theme of "Judaism, Law and Literature" (Antwerp, 14–17 July 2014).

19. For references to numerous works adopting such a methodology in biblical studies, see Barmash, "Narrative Quandary," 1.

20. Magdalene, *Scales of Righteousness*, 11, 51; Barmash, "Narrative Quandary," 2–3.

21. Robert M. Cover, "*Nomos* and Narrative," *Harvard Law Review* 97 (1983): 4–68, here 9.

22. Compare the methodology of F. Rachel Magdalene, "Trying the Crime of Abuse of Royal Authority in the Divine Courtroom and the Incident of Naboth's Vineyard," in *The Divine Courtroom in Comparative Perspective*, ed. Ari Mermelstein and Shalom E. Holtz (Leiden: Brill, 2014), 167–245, here 169.

23. Wells, "What Is Biblical Law?," 231–32.

24. For discussion of both biblical narrative and Mesopotamian practice documents in relation to biblical law, see Barmash, *Homicide in the Biblical World*, 4–6.

connections between ancient Near Eastern practice texts (i.e., documents pertaining to legal practice) and pentateuchal law, between ancient Near Eastern practice texts and biblical narrative and/or prophecy, and also between biblical narrative and/or prophecy and the pentateuchal law collections, then one can make an even stronger and richer case for the connection between the pentateuchal law collections and Israelite legal practice.

When a narrative appears to reflect a legal reality rather than fiction, a methodologically thorny question arises: What reality? Is it a reality contemporaneous with the composition—the reality of an author or editor, or of others living during their time (or during any of their times), in the same or different geographical or social setting—or a past reality known to an author or editor? Should affinities between the legal reality of a biblical narrative and the details of the Covenant Code be used as evidence of either text's date? The abundance of confounding variables, such as the tendency of biblical and ancient Near Eastern texts to mask continuous adaptations that would have occurred in reality, and the gap between the socioeconomic status(es) of authors and editors of biblical texts and others living throughout Israel and Judah, allows for too wide a margin of error for these questions to be answered meaningfully.[25] Without dated or datable legal documents such as contracts, trial records, and letters from ancient Israel, similar to those from the cuneiform record, the enterprise of reconstructing operative law requires restraint, with an appreciation of both the possibilities and the limitations posed by an imperfect corpus of evidence. At the same time, we can point cautiously to the generally conservative nature of biblical and ancient Near Eastern law and posit a reconstruction of aspects of bailment practice in ancient Israel that likely would not have seen drastic change over time, including details such as who could be a bailee or bailor, wrongdoings that might incur liability, and motivations underlying the initiation of bailments.[26] Biblical narrative and prophecy unfortunately do not offer clues regarding aspects of the Covenant Code's bailment law that feature in discussions of legal changes in ancient Israel, such as the character of associated legal procedures.[27] When a practice is demonstrably specific to a particular setting, I discuss

---

25. See recently Roland Boer, *The Sacred Economy of Ancient Israel*, LAI (Louisville: Westminster John Knox, 2015), 102–3.

26. For the conservative nature of ancient Near Eastern law, see Bruce Wells, "Law and Practice," in *A Companion to the Ancient Near East*, ed. Daniel C. Snell, Blackwell Companions to the Ancient World: Ancient History (Malden, MA: Blackwell, 2005), 183–95; Raymond Westbrook, "The Laws of Biblical Israel," in *The Hebrew Bible: New Insights and Scholarship*, ed. Frederick E. Greenspahn, Jewish Studies in the 21st Century (New York: New York University Press, 2008), 99–119.

27. See, e.g., Bernard M. Levinson, *Deuteronomy and the Hermeneutics of Legal Innovation* (New York: Oxford University Press, 1997), 113–30, regarding changes in location (from local

the historical contours of that practice, and its inapplicability to other settings.[28] My goal in reconstructing bailment in practice in ancient Israel is not to present a complete picture of the institution at one time or at all times but rather to paint in broad strokes a sketch of the institution throughout ancient Israel's history, to the extent that the available sources allow. The use of nonlegal biblical texts as sources for actual legal practice faces the same potential pitfall as the comparative method discussed above: generalization. Certainly, just as the legal reality of Babylon in the eighteenth century BCE should not be superimposed onto the reality of a sixth-century BCE Mesopotamian city, we ought not to flatten the periods and regions of the biblical world into a single, unchanging "ancient Israel." And yet, to the extent that it is possible, and without wishing to commit any flattening, I do indeed generalize, by looking for the primary features of an institution that could have traversed these particularities of time and space.

Beyond exploring the relationship between the law of Exod 22 and law in practice, I return to the conclusions emerging from the primary sources and reexamine them from a legal perspective, to address the question, What do our ancient texts tell us about how their writers thought about law? Despite the risk of anachronistically misapplying modern thought to ancient texts,[29] engaging modern legal theory may help to illuminate this material with a sophistication that would otherwise be impossible.[30] The modern legal discourse surrounding bailments facilitates an understanding of the full range of conceptual problems that a bailment may create in its distinction between possession and ownership, in particular, and further informs an account of biblical and ancient Near Eastern jurisprudence.[31] Beyond the results of exegetical and comparative examination, legal analysis yields insights into the following: the organization and details of the biblical and cuneiform bailment laws, including how and to what extent these laws conceive of "bailments"; concepts of liability and the circumstances under which opportunities for exoneration are allowed or curtailed; a notion of duty and how it manifests differently in

---

sanctuaries to the central temple in Jerusalem) for resolving ambiguous cases between the time of the Covenant Code and the Deuteronomic laws.

28. E.g., herding practices relating to wool in Ezek 34, discussed in chapter 2 below.

29. On this, see, e.g., Bernard S. Jackson, *Studies in the Semiotics of Biblical Law*, JSOTSup 314 (Sheffield: Sheffield Academic, 2000), 171.

30. See further Amihay, *Theory and Practice in Essene Law*, 187–88.

31. For the conceptual complexity of bailments and its ramifications, see, e.g., Oliver Wendell Holmes, *The Common Law*, ed. Paulo J. S. Pereira and Diego M. Beltran (Toronto: University of Toronto Law School Typographical Society, 2011 [originally published, 1881]), 146: "The test of the theory of possession which prevails in any system of law is to be found in its mode of dealing with persons who have a thing within their power, but do not own it, or assert the position of the owner for themselves with regard to it, bailees in a word."

the Covenant Code and the Laws of Hammurabi; and a model of justice as distinct from truth. Biblical and cuneiform law collections reflect what Raymond Westbrook has called an "archaic legal system," which deals with narrow examples of cases rather than spelling out principles of the law;[32] the jurisprudential underpinnings of these texts are therefore difficult to uncover. In the face of these challenges, legal analysis provides a usable set of tools for accessing and talking about the legal thinking that shaped our ancient texts.

Summary of the Chapters

Chapter 1 focuses on the creation of bailments, including the persons who would have created bailments, why they might have wanted or needed to create them, and how they would go about doing so. Exodus 22:6–14 serves as a starting point for consideration of deposits of goods, herding arrangements, animal borrowing, and animal rental, while ancient Near Eastern law collections and documents of legal practice, as well as biblical narrative and prophecy, offer a means of fleshing out possible parameters of bailments in ancient Israel. In particular, legal documents from Mesopotamia shed light on various commercial functions of bailments that the Bible does not address, while biblical narrative points to the usefulness of bailments in a range of military contexts.

The second chapter addresses the ways in which a bailment may go awry. Biblical law envisions a range of possible mishaps, most of which find cuneiform parallels: the theft of deposited goods; death, injury, capture, predation, and theft of animals entrusted to a shepherd; and death and injury of borrowed and rented animals. In addition to mapping out the various things that can go wrong in a bailment, this chapter explores levels of human fault, including fraudulent, deliberate wrongdoing; acts of negligence; and "acts of God" that go beyond the scope of human responsibility. A new interpretation of the Hebrew verbal idiom שלח יד ("to lay a hand on") in Exod 22:7, 10 [Eng. 8, 11] as an expression for negligence yields a novel understanding of the biblical bailment law.

When a bailment goes wrong, the accuser may seek justice from the accused. The third chapter examines the range of judicial procedures that may follow in order to establish the facts of the case, such as examination of physical evidence, hearing eyewitness testimony, and allowing the accused to undertake a cultic judicial procedure. This chapter further investigates how justice is established through the determination of liabil-

---

32. Raymond Westbrook, ed., *A History of Ancient Near Eastern Law*, 2 vols., HdO 1.72 (Leiden: Brill, 2003), 1:21–22.

ity and penalties for wrongdoing, including what happens when someone swears falsely to their innocence but later acknowledges their wrongdoing. In some cases, biblical narrative and Mesopotamian legal documents diverge from biblical and cuneiform law collections in the penalties they establish. Differences between the Laws of Hammurabi and Exod 22:6–14 help to clarify the interests of the biblical law, which are not limited to the topic of bailment.

Chapter 4 shifts from the use of primarily exegetical and comparative methodologies in the previous three chapters to the application of legal analysis to the primary sources. This analysis offers a means of interrogating the ways in which the drafters of ancient law collections thought about law, apart from how the law may have operated in practice. With an eye toward culling modern legal studies for precise terminology and useful frames for conceptualizing ancient laws—the risks of anachronism notwithstanding—this chapter examines how the ancient law collections treat methods of fact-finding and variations in fault and liability, as well as whether bailments in these sources may be understood using the modern categories of contract, tort, and property.

The fifth chapter moves from a reconstruction of legal practice and thought in ancient Israel to what came next in postbiblical Jewish contexts. Early Jewish legal texts include documents of legal practice from Jewish communities at Elephantine and in the Judean Desert, as well as law writings from the Tannaitic period, such as the Mishnah and Midrash. These texts offer a window into the afterlife of areas of law in communities that viewed themselves as heirs to the Bible, while also sharing aspects of other legal traditions. In particular, this chapter demonstrates continuities between ancient Near Eastern and early Jewish bailment law, with features exclusive to these bodies of law and legal practice, without parallels in biblical or Greco-Roman law. I propose different ways in which these commonalities might have arisen.

Taken together, the chapters in this book speak to overarching questions that cut at the heart of the human experience of law: What is the connection between law in the books and law on the ground? How do humans respond to the law? What does "justice" entail? By fusing close readings of primary sources with interdisciplinary humanistic analysis, I offer answers that have ramifications not only for the fields of Hebrew Bible, Assyriology, and Jewish studies but for other disciplines that involve the intersection of law, literature, and religion. Through the lens of a single legal institution, this project illuminates broader questions of definitions of justice, aspects of everyday life in ancient societies, the interaction of law and literature, and the earliest articulations of a legal practice whose relevance has persisted into the modern era.

1

The Creation of a Bailment

Who created bailments in the ancient world, and why? How did people enter into bailments? To answer these questions, I bring together sources beginning with the law in Exod 22 and including relevant texts from cuneiform law, biblical narrative and prophecy, and Mesopotamian legal documents. Following the structure of Exod 22:6–14, this chapter addresses the formation of four kinds of bailments: a deposit of goods, herding arrangements, animal borrowing, and animal rental.

Deposits of Goods

Exodus 22:6a offers little information about the creation of a bailment:

כי יתן איש אל רעהו כסף או כלים לשמר

When a man gives to another silver or goods to watch ...[1]

One person gives property to another person to watch. The continuation of the verse introduces a scenario where the property is stolen from the house of the bailee who watches the property—וגנב מבית האיש, "but it is stolen from that man's house"—indicating that it was kept in that person's home. Yet the Covenant Code offers no further information about who these parties might be; whether or not any procedural formality, restrictions, or conditions accompany the "giving" of the property; or why a person might wish to initiate such an arrangement. The Laws of Eshnunna (LE) 36–37, on the other hand, discuss a case where the bailee, who receives the property for safekeeping, is identified specifically as a *napṭaru*:

36. If a man gives his goods to a *napṭaru* for safekeeping, and he [the *napṭaru*] then allows the goods which he gave to him for safekeeping to become lost—without evidence that the house has been broken into, the doorjamb scraped, the window forced—he shall replace his goods for him.

---

1. All translations are my own except where noted.

13

37. If the man's house has been burglarized, and the owner of the house incurs a loss along with the goods which the depositor gave to him, the owner of the house shall swear an oath to satisfy him at the gate of (the temple of) the god Tishpak: "My goods have been lost along with your goods; I have not committed a fraud or misdeed"; thus shall he swear an oath to satisfy him and he will have no claim against him.[2]

The specific identity of the bailee in LE 36–37 raises a series of questions: What is a *napṭaru*? Does the law apply only to deposit in the care of a *napṭaru*, or does it apply to any bailee–bailor relationship? How is the *napṭaru* connected to the *bīt napṭarim* ("house of the *napṭaru*") which bears its name elsewhere in cuneiform literature? Can the inclusion of the *napṭaru* among two other terms—the *ubāru* and *mudû*—in another law, LE 41, illuminate its meaning in LE 36? An understanding of the *napṭaru* is critical for determining whether the institution of bailment that the Laws of Eshnunna envision requires a particular kind of person to function as bailee.[3]

The napṭaru as Bailee

Studies of the *napṭaru* have yielded a range of interpretations. J. J. Finkelstein has argued that the *napṭaru* was a person of high status who resided in a *bīt napṭarim*, whose status afforded both himself and his house immunity from search and seizure. The *bīt napṭarim* bore various functions, the common denominator of which was that responsibility for the safety of persons and things fell upon the shoulders of the *napṭaru*.[4] Meir

---

2. For this translation, see Martha T. Roth, *Law Collections from Mesopotamia and Asia Minor*, 2nd ed., SBLWAW 6 (Atlanta: Scholars Press, 1997), 64–65.

3. Although Albrecht Goetze initially suggested that the *napṭaru* in LE 36 might be a location, a consensus has since emerged among scholars that the *napṭaru* must be a person. See Goetze, "The Laws of Eshnunna," *AASOR* 31 (1951–1952): 1–197, here 99; note that he also considers the possibility that the noun that originally referred to a location might have developed the more concrete meaning of a professional custodian. In LE 41, Goetze translates *napṭaru* as "one awaiting redemption" ("Laws of Eshnunna," 107). Although most scholars have accepted that the *napṭaru* must be a person, F. R. Kraus has maintained that it most likely refers to a location ("Akkadische Wörter und Ausdrücke, X–XI," *RA* 70 [1976]: 165–79). Scholars who agree that the *napṭaru* is a person draw on the following data as evidence: LE 41's mention of the *napṭaru* together with the *ubāru* and *mudû*, two other terms referring to people; various references to the *bīt napṭarim*, understood as a house, the function of which is debated, that belongs to or is managed by a person called the *napṭaru*; the verb *paṭāru*; synonym lists citing equivalents to *napṭaru*, including *anzanīnu* and *susapinnu* in Akkadian and GA.AN.URÌ, GAN.AN.DU₈, and ŠEŠ.E.NE in Sumerian, all of which refer to people; and mention of the *napṭaru*, evidently also a person, at Ugarit. For the use of the term *napṭaru* in Ugaritic, see Raymond Westbrook, "The Naptaru at Ugarit," *JCS* 60 (2008): 53–55.

4. J. J. Finkelstein, "Some New *Misharum* Material and Its Implications," in *Studies in*

Malul, focusing on an equation made between the *napṭaru* and bridal paranymph in another cuneiform text, arrives at a similar conclusion in a different way:[5] Just as the bridal paranymph provides friendship and protection to a bride, the *napṭaru* provides friendship and protection in the form of preserving the well-being of the persons or things in his care.[6] Sumerian equivalents to *napṭaru* on lexical lists further corroborate this protective aspect of the *napṭaru*.[7]

Challenging Finkelstein's exhaustive characterization of the *bīt napṭa-rim*, F. R. Kraus has argued that the *bīt napṭarim* simply functioned as an inn or guest lodging.[8] Numerous scholars have favored this view, consequently interpreting the *napṭaru* as a person connected to the *bīt napṭarim* in some capacity, whether as guest or as host (i.e., innkeeper).[9] Raymond Westbrook has argued that although in theory, based on all of the evidence, the term *napṭaru* could refer either to an innkeeper or to a visitor, LE 36 itself proves that the latter must be true. While an innkeeper might frequently encounter the situation of having to watch over guests' possessions, and thus might seem a logical choice of bailee for the law to treat,

---

Honor of Benno Landsberger on His Seventy-Fifth Birthday, April 21, 1965, ed. Hans Gustav Güterbock and Thorkild Jacobsen, Assyriological Studies 16 (Chicago: University of Chicago Press, 1965), 233–46, here 238; Finkelstein, "On Some Recent Studies in Cuneiform Law," *JAOS* 90 (1970): 243–56, here 252–53. Benno Landsberger ("Jungfräulichkeit: Ein Beitrag zum Thema 'Beilager und Eheschliessung,'" in *Symbolae Iuridicae et Historicae Martino David Dedicatae*, ed. J. A. Ankum, R. Feenstra, and W. F. Leemans, 2 vols. [Leiden: Brill, 1968], 2:41–105, here 98) adapted Finkelstein's view, identifying the word *napṭaru* as a professional title and describing him as "ein Immuner," but arguing that the privileged status of the *napṭaru* applied primarily to his residence (the *bīt napṭarim*) rather than to his person. *CAD* has cautiously defined *napṭaru* as a "person with certain privileges," leaning in the direction of Finkelstein and Landsberger but without fleshing out any details of the *napṭaru*'s character.

5. Meir Malul, "*Susapinnu*: The Mesopotamian Paranymph and His Role," *JESHO* 32 (1989): 241–78, citing the cuneiform text LTBA 2 2.

6. Ibid., 274–75; and see 274 n. 127 for citations of the view he disputes, namely, that the *susapinnu* (bridal paranymph) is primarily friend to the groom. The latter view is also adopted by *CAD* S, s.v. "*susapinnu*." Regardless of whether the *susapinnu* is defined in terms of the bride or groom, he retains the same basic function of providing friendship and protection.

7. Malul, "Mesopotamian Paranymph," 175 n. 131, citing MSL 12 141–42. The synonyms GA.AN.URI₃ and ŠEŠ.E.NE both contain ŠEŠ (= URI₃), the equivalent of the Akkadian *naṣāru*. For an alternate interpretation of ŠEŠ.E.NE, see Raymond Westbrook, "The Old Babylonian Term *napṭarum*," *JCS* 46 (1994): 41–46.

8. Kraus, "Akkadische Wörter und Ausdrücke," 165–79.

9. Wolfram Von Soden understands the *napṭaru* as a "Gastfreund" — a foreigner acting as both guest and host ("Kleine Beiträge zum Verständnis der Gesetze Hammurabis und Bilalamas," *ArOr* 17 [1949]: 359–73). Kraus argues that, if the *napṭaru* refers to a person (and not to a location, as he deems correct), then it must mean "host" ("Akkadische Wörter und Ausdrücke," 171). In a similar vein, Emile Szlechter translates the word *napṭaru* as "aubergiste," or innkeeper (*Les Lois d'Ešnunna: Transcription, traduction et commentaire* [Paris: Recueil Sirey, 1954], 84).

that is precisely the situation that the law does not discuss. The moment a guest deposits goods with the innkeeper, the innkeeper becomes a simple bailee with the same responsibilities as any other bailee; one's status as innkeeper does not in any way affect one's liability. The "special category" of innkeeper adds nothing of consequence to the law; therefore, it is unlikely that the law would have the innkeeper per se in mind. On the other hand, if the *napṭaru* is a guest, then the law's focus on physical signs of a break-in takes on new significance, such that the law makes the following point: the security of a building stands outside the scope of a visitor's responsibility; therefore, if there is physical evidence of a break-in, the visitor is not liable, but if there is no such evidence, then the visitor bears all responsibility for theft.[10]

Westbrook's reading of LE 36–37 identifies physical evidence of a break-in as the determining factor in the law. In his view, the liability of the *napṭaru* hinges on whether the building shows signs of forced entry. Yet LE 37 presents as paramount the criterion of joint loss, wherein the bailee suffers a loss of property together with the bailor, thus rendering the bailee eligible for an oath of innocence. Signs of forced entry receive no mention at all in LE 37. In fact, it appears that LE 36's enumeration of evidence serves merely to heighten the sense of suspicion surrounding the bailee, rather than as proof of the bailee's guilt.[11]

Moreover, Westbrook's contention that the *napṭaru* cannot be an innkeeper, because this "special category" of the innkeeper as bailee would add nothing of consequence to the law, need not pose a difficulty if one views the innkeeper as a paradigmatic bailee: a person with whom others might realistically leave their goods for safekeeping. The drafters' choice of the *napṭaru* as bailee would thus be an empirical one, drawing on typical experiences of daily life.[12] In this case, one would not expect any legal distinction between the *napṭaru* and any other bailee; the *napṭaru*, as a per-

---

10. Westbrook, "Old Babylonian Term *napṭarum*," 41–46. Note that Westbrook explains the identification of the *napṭaru* with the *susapinnu* on the basis of their temporary visits. Westbrook's view has been accepted by Sophie Lafont, "Le roi, le juge et l'étranger à Mari et dans la Bible," *RA* 92 (1998): 161–81, here 174–75.

11. Cf. Finkelstein, "On Some Recent Studies in Cuneiform Law," 254: "The decisive factor here is not whether or not there are visible signs of forced entry as specified in §36, but rather the fact that in that section the only goods lost are those of the bailor. The fact that there were no visible signs of forced entry … simply adds to the circumstances pointing to suspicion of the bailee for malfeasance." See also Yaron, *Laws of Eshnunna*, 249: "It does not follow that if there had been evidence to that effect he would necessarily have been absolved."

12. This criterion, which has been called "empirical choice in the selection of the legal situation" (see Barry L. Eichler, "Literary Structure in the Laws of Eshnunna," in *Language, Literature, and History: Philological and Historical Studies Presented to Erica Reiner*, ed. Francesca Rochberg-Halton, AOS 67 [New Haven: American Oriental Society, 1987], 71–84, here 72), was discussed by J. J. Finkelstein, "Sex Offenses in Sumerian Laws," *JAOS* 86 (1966): 355–72, here 368.

son likely to become a bailee, simply stands in for any bailee of no special category.

In fact, when one considers the law from the perspective of everyday life, it hardly seems likely that the *napṭaru* would refer to a visitor: Why would a person entrust goods for safekeeping with a visitor whom one does not know well and whose stay is temporary? On the other hand, an innkeeper is an excellent candidate for the safekeeping of goods, whether belonging to guests or to others, who trust them to care for the things in their possession. The *bīt napṭarim* served as temporary lodging for private individuals and troops; it appears to have been a place of higher repute than other guest houses, such as the *bīt sābî* and the *aštammu*, where men also enjoyed entertainment and met prostitutes.[13] As the proprietor of a more respectable manner of inn, the *napṭaru* would have been viewed with higher regard than other innkeepers. Malul's characterization of the *napṭaru* as friend and protector is apt: the *napṭaru* was an innkeeper in whom one could place the highest degree of trust. Although not a bailee by profession, the *napṭaru*'s reputation as a professional who could protect the people and things under the inn's respectable roof would have made such a person a likely choice of bailee.

LE 36–37 treats a scenario where a person gives property in bailment to an innkeeper, who might frequently be asked by guests to watch their possessions, and so earn a reputation as a trusted guardian for any would-be bailor. The law selects the *napṭaru* because the innkeeper is a likely choice for a bailee in daily life; however, it may easily apply to any scenario of bailment, regardless of the bailee's identity or profession. Moreover, while the term *napṭaru* is the professional title of an innkeeper, it does not denote a bailee by profession; the professional innkeeper just happens to be a natural choice for a bailee. The Laws of Eshnunna choose a more specific bailee to highlight than the "man" of the Covenant Code, but there is no compelling evidence that it has in mind only a person who meets this description.

Setting Up Deposits

Neither the Covenant Code nor the Laws of Eshnunna touch upon the procedure for creating a deposit beyond one party "giving" the property

---

13. See citations in *CAD* S, s.v. "*sābû*" in *bīt sābî*; A/2, s.v. "*aštammu*"; and see Rivkah Harris, *Gender and Aging in Mesopotamia: The Gilgamesh Epic and Other Ancient Literature* (Norman: University of Oklahoma Press, 2000), 228 n. 27; Harry A. Hoffner, "The Arzana House," in *Anatolian Studies Presented to Hans Gustav Güterbock on the Occasion of His 65th Birthday*, ed. K. Bittel, Ph. H. J. Houwink ten Cate, and E. Reiner, Publications de l'Institut historique et archéologique néerlandais de Stamboul 35 (Istanbul: Nederlands Historisch-Archaeologisch Instituut, 1974), 113–21, here 113.

to another. The Laws of Hammurabi (LH), in contrast, focus on these matters with regard to deposits both of grain and of goods. LH 120–121 address a case of grain storage and specify an annual storage fee of 5 silas of grain per kur. LH 122 then transitions into the requisite procedure to effect a legally valid deposit of silver, gold, or goods:

> 122. If a man gives silver, gold, or anything else to another man for a deposit, whatever he gives he shall show to witnesses; he shall set forth contractual stipulations [*riksātim*]; (thus) he shall give (it) for a deposit.

According to this law, the deposit must occur before witnesses, and a contractual arrangement must accompany the bailment. LH 7 also highlights the requirement of witnesses and a contract to effect a deposit legally, though within a specific context: a person who accepts anything for a deposit from a dependent son or slave without following the appropriate procedure is considered a thief and is consequently killed.[14] The term *riksātum* refers to oral contractual stipulations, rather than to a written contract.[15] Whereas witnesses served to prove the existence of a deposit, the oral contract had no evidentiary function; rather, it served a procedural role in the deposit's creation.[16] This distinction forms the basis of Samuel Greengus's explanation of the apparent contradiction between LH 122 and 123, which mention both witnesses and a contractual arrangement, and LH 124, which mentions only witnesses:

> 124. If a man gives silver, gold, or anything else to another man for a deposit before witnesses and then he denies it, they shall convict that man; whatever he denied he shall give back double.

Because LH 124 deals specifically with a case of fraud where proof is necessary to establish the existence of a deposit, it mentions only witnesses, who play an evidentiary role, and not the contract, which, as an oral agreement, could not constitute evidence. According to the Laws of Hammurabi, then, both witnesses and contractual stipulations ought to accompany the formation of a deposit; the witnesses could later verify the details of the transaction, should any problems arise, while the contractual stipula-

---

14. For the interpretation of *mār awīlim* in LH 7 as a son, rather than any (free) man or a man of a particular social status, see, e.g., G. R. Driver and John C. Miles, *The Babylonian Laws*, 2 vols. (Oxford: Clarendon, 1968), 1:84–86; Bernard S. Jackson, *Essays in Jewish and Comparative Legal History*, SJLA 10 (Leiden: Brill, 1975), 66; Yaron, *Laws of Eshnunna*, 146–47.

15. This is the view of Samuel Greengus ("The Old Babylonian Marriage Contract," *JAOS* 89 [1969]: 505–32), which has been widely accepted. For further discussion of this argument, see, e.g., Yaron, *Laws of Eshnunna*, 201. I disagree here with the translation of Roth (*Law Collections*, 104) of *riksātum* in LH 122 as "a written contract."

16. Greengus, "Old Babylonian Marriage Contract," 505–32.

tions would define the contours of the arrangement, without serving any evidentiary function at a later time.

LH 121 establishes a rate at which the owner of grain should pay a bailee for storage of that grain, while LH 122 requires witnesses and contractual stipulations in order to set up a deposit of gold, silver, or anything else. Are these two separate laws, and are they mutually exclusive? That is, is there one law of grain deposits, and a separate law treating deposits of goods (gold, silver, etc.)? Does only one require a fee to the bailee, and only the other involve witnesses and a contract? The sections in which these laws occur (120–121 and 122–125) appear to diverge further with respect to liability; LH 120 establishes a penalty of double compensation for a bailee when a loss occurs, irrespective of whether the bailee bears any fault. LH 124–125, on the other hand, distinguish between the liability of a fraudulent and negligent bailee: the fraudulent bailee must pay twofold, while the negligent bailee must pay single compensation. Does the difference in the object of bailment—grain in LH 120 and silver, gold, or anything else in LH 124–125—account for this disparity in liability and, if so, why? Alternatively, do other factors play a contributing role in the distinct standards of liability in LH 120 and 124–125?

While the Laws of Hammurabi themselves do not clarify these matters, legal documents from Mesopotamia can shed light on aspects of deposits of grain and goods. Documents from Nuzi and Mari, for example, record the deposit of grain and precious metals as part of a single arrangement, without any distinction between how they are deposited or between expectations of the bailee for the different objects.[17] Moreover, while grain storage may have taken on different forms, numerous texts and archaeological findings point to the storage of grain and other provisions in sealed containers.[18] A trial record from Nuzi, for example, specifies that deposited grain was stored in sealed jars with the seals rolled.[19] These seals served to prevent tampering and theft but also indicate that the bailee's responsibilities in such arrangements could not have extended beyond watching the jars. Archaeological evidence bears out the ancient Near Eastern practice of storing grain in jars;[20] findings in domestic storage facilities from the third millennium site of Tell Bderi, for example, include jars of various sizes, corresponding lids and stoppers made of clay and gypsum "used to protect the contents from dirt, evaporation and

---

17. See, e.g., JEN 545, regarding a deposit of twenty minas of bronze and eight imers of grain; ARM 8 74, regarding 3.25 sheqels of silver and x ugars and 6 gurs of barley in pots.

18. E.g., HSS 9 108, cited below; TJA p. 153 UMM G 45:3; ARM 10 136; JEN 381.

19. HSS 9 108. See the translation of Raymond Westbrook and Bruce Wells, *Everyday Law in Biblical Israel: An Introduction* (Louisville: Westminster John Knox, 2009), 48.

20. Andrew T. Creekmore, "Kazane Höyük and Urban Life Histories in Third Millennium Upper Mesopotamia" (PhD diss., Northwestern University, 2008), 258.

predators," and seals.[21] The duties of the bailee of stored and sealed grain thus would not have differed from those of a bailee watching storage jars bearing any contents, such as silver, gold, tablets, or any goods one might store in a sealed jar.[22] At the same time, this was not the only possible form of grain storage, and a bailee of unsealed grain might have been expected to take care of the bailment in additional ways (for example, to separate fresh grain from old grain).[23]

Although the Laws of Hammurabi specify payment for grain storage and not for storage of goods, Mesopotamian legal texts demonstrate that, in practice, one could give grain and goods as part of the same bailment transaction. Likewise, there need not have been any distinction between the duties of the bailee of grain and the bailee of goods. There would thus have been no difference between the primary beneficiary in LH 120 and in LH 124–125, nor any difference between the expectations of the bailees in these laws, to account for the variation in liability.

While it certainly is possible that the Mesopotamian legal texts and archaeological evidence cited here reflect a reality different from the one that the Laws of Hammurabi portray, an alternative understanding of the Laws of Hammurabi may explain how sections 120–121 and 122–125 relate to each other. Mesopotamian practice documents indicate that bailees of grain and of goods might bear identical responsibilities. Thus, a bailor might find a bailee to watch both silver and grain without creating two separate arrangements, and a bailee might watch grain in sealed jars just as they would watch goods or silver in sealed jars. The primary difference emerging from LH 120–121 and 122–125 is not the object of bailment, but whether the bailee receives payment for services rendered. A paid bailee bears a higher degree of liability, including double compensation even in the absence of fraud. Although LH 120–121 specifically speaks of grain, while LH 122–125 speaks of silver, gold, or anything else, it is

---

21. Peter Pfälzner, "Modes of Storage and the Development of Economic Systems in the Early Jezireh-Period," in *Of Pots and Pans: Papers on the Archaeology and History of Mesopotamia and Syria Presented to David Oates in Honour of His 75th Birthday,* ed. Lamia al-Gailani Werr et al. (London: NABU, 2002), 259–86, here 276–78.

22. ARM 8 74, on the other hand, treats the bailment of silver and of barley in pots (*karpat*), which may or may not have been sealed. This leaves open the options for duties expected of the bailee, though none are specified in this document.

23. For general duties of granary supervisors, which might be applied to any person responsible for watching grain, see Tina Breckwoldt, "Management of Grain Storage in Old Babylonian Larsa," *AfO* 42/43 (1995/1996): 64–88, here 78. For other forms of grain storage, such as in bags or directly on the protective plastered floor, see Creekmore, "Kazane Höyük," 253. Early Jewish law includes examples of produce storage in what must have been unsealed containers in m. B. Meṣ. 3:6–7 and t. B. Meṣ. 3:8. These passages discuss the duties of a bailee vis-à-vis produce in his care that rots or is eaten by mice. Presumably, the bailee would not know that the produce was ruined if it was sealed away, nor would mice have been likely to penetrate sealed containers.

possible that the drafters chose these objects of bailment as representative rather than determinative. In fact, the words *mimma šumšu*, which LH 122 and 124 use to refer to "anything else" that is deposited aside from gold or silver, could easily include grain.[24] If this reading is correct, then LH 120–121 and 122–125 ought to be labeled not laws of "deposits of grain" and "deposits of goods" respectively, but "non-gratuitous deposits" (for which a bailee receives compensation) and "gratuitous deposits" (for which a bailee receives no compensation).[25] Such a reading also has ramifications for consideration of bailment categories in early Jewish law, and will be discussed further in chapter 5.

The Laws of Hammurabi address a number of concerns pertaining to the procedure for setting up deposits: If one person wished to deposit property (including grain, gold, silver, or any other goods) with another person, the two parties would require witnesses and contractual stipulations. These stipulations might include whether the bailee would receive payment for watching the owner's property, or whether the owner could count on the bailee to watch that property gratis. Although some have read similar concerns and distinctions into the law of Exod 22, the biblical text ignores the issue of payment for services; the gratuitous/non-gratuitous distinction is not the biblical law's concern.[26]

Herding Arrangements

Like the law of deposits, the law of herding in Exod 22:9a offers little information about the details of the arrangement:

כי יתן איש אל רעהו חמור או שור או שה וכל בהמה לשמר

When a man gives to another a donkey, or an ox, or a sheep, or any animal to watch …

As in the previous verses, the law goes on to address what might go wrong in a case of herding (in this case, not only theft but also death, injury, capture, or predation) and how to proceed under these various circumstances,

---

24. See, e.g., MVAG 33, no. 209, where *mimma šumšu* collocates with barley (as well as silver); Maximilian Streck, *Assurbanipal und die letzten assyrischen könige bis zum untergange Niniveh's*, Vorderasiatische Bibliothek 7 (Leipzig: Hinrichs, 1916), 264 iii, where *mimma šumšu* is brought for a meal; Jørgen Laessøe, *Studies on the Assyrian Ritual and Series bît rimki* (Copenhagen: Munksgaard, 1955), 38, where a person has eaten *mimma šumšu*.

25. These categories apply specifically to goods (including grain), as distinct from a herding arrangement (which is clearly non-gratuitous in LH, but treated separately).

26. This is the view of traditional Jewish commentaries adopting the categories of the rabbis in m. B. Meṣ. 7:8, accepted with modifications also by Umberto Cassuto, *A Commentary on the Book of Exodus*, trans. Israel Abrahams (Jerusalem: Magnes, 1967), 287.

without attending to the identity of the parties involved or why and how one might give to the other a donkey, ox, or sheep to watch in the first place. The Laws of Hammurabi 261 and 264 offer more information in their treatment of such transactions:

> 261. If a man [*awīlum*] hires a herdsman [*nāqidam*] to herd the cattle or the sheep and goats, he shall give him 2,400 silas of grain per year.

This law envisions a scenario wherein the bailee is a herdsman (*nāqidum*), as opposed to a standard shepherd (*rēʾûm*).[27] The role of the herdsman typically exceeded that of a shepherd, involving tasks such as managing the palace's livestock and mediating between the palace and shepherds. Yet the Laws of Hammurabi offer no indication that they envision an institutional context of any sort, whether palace or temple: A "man" (*awīlum*) hires and pays the herdsman, and, as the continuation of the law indicates (263), if the herdsman causes the loss of an animal in his care, he compensates that man directly. More likely, the owner envisioned by the Laws of Hammurabi is a wealthy individual who, like the temple or palace, would have owned flocks sufficiently large to require hiring multiple shepherds.[28] A *nāqidum* would have been in charge of these shepherds. In LH 261, then, the parties to the transaction are the flock-owner, a wealthy individual, and a herdsman who subcontracts with shepherds. The flock-owner initiates the transaction because he requires multiple shepherds to manage his flocks. In order to effect the bailment, he hires the herdsman in exchange for a set annual rate of 2,400 silas of grain per year.

Immediately following their treatment of the herdsman, the Laws of Hammurabi move on to a case where a regular shepherd (*rēʾûm*) is hired:

> 264. If a shepherd [*rēʾûm*], to whom cattle or sheep and goats were given for shepherding, is in receipt of his complete hire to his satisfaction, then allows the number of cattle to decrease, or the number of sheep and goats to decrease, or the number of offspring to diminish, he shall give for the (loss of) offspring and by-products in accordance with the terms of his contract [*riksātišu*].[29]

---

27. The *nāqidum*, here translated "herdsman," has also been called an "Oberhirt" (F. R. Kraus, *Staatliche Viehhaltung im altbabylonischen Lande Larsa* [Amsterdam: Noord-Hollandsche, 1966], 16), "herding-contractor" (J. N. Postgate, *Early Mesopotamia: Society and Economy at the Dawn of History* [London: Routledge, 1994], 160–61), or "flock-master" (Postgate, *Bronze Age Bureaucracy: Writing and the Practice of Government in Assyria* [Cambridge: Cambridge University Press, 2013], 304).

28. See Rivkah Harris, *Ancient Sippar: A Demographic Study of an Old Babylonian City (1894–1595 B.C.)*, Uitgaven van het Nederlands Historisch-Archaeologisch Instituut te Istanbul 36 (Leiden: Nederlands Historisch-Archaeologisch Instituut te Istanbul, 1975), 253.

29. This translation appears in Roth, *Law Collections*, 129–30.

A need for herding motivates the creation of this bailment. In this case, the bailee is a shepherd, but the law does not clarify whether the bailor who delivers the animals for herding is the flock-owner or a hired herdsman.

Setting Up Herding Arrangements

LH 264 requires the oral utterance of contractual stipulations (*riksā-tum*) to create and shape the contours of a herding transaction, without mentioning witnesses as in the case of deposits. Although the Laws of Hammurabi do not refer to recording these agreements in writing, many written herding contracts have survived from a range of ancient Near Eastern contexts. In the Old Babylonian period, during which the Laws of Hammurabi were written, herding contracts typically included all or most of the following elements:

1. Composition of the flock (i.e., number and kind of flock animal)
2. Shepherd's liability for losses
3. Shepherd's compensation
4. Clause concerning subcontracted shepherd (if relevant)
5. Witnesses
6. Date formula[30]

Among the various herding records from Nuzi are consignment texts recording only the composition of the flock and the name of the shepherd, as well as debt statements recording deficits in the flock, which offer a window into the shepherd's liability.[31] Similar records to those found at Nuzi have also survived from Durkatlimmu during the Middle Assyrian period.[32] A single extant Neo-Babylonian private herding contract between a herdsman and small flock-owner states the composition of the flock, the herdsman's annual compensation, and the division of shares and responsibility (e.g., for taxation) between the owner and herdsman for the duration of the contract.[33]

---

30. For examples, see J. J. Finkelstein, "An Old Babylonian Herding Contract and Genesis 31:38f," *JAOS* 88 (1968): 30–36.

31. A detailed discussion of these records and of herding at Nuzi is found in M. A. Morrison, "Evidence for Herdsmen and Animal Husbandry in the Nuzi Documents," in *Studies on the Civilization and Culture of Nuzi and the Hurrians in Honor of Ernest R. Lacheman on His Seventy-Fifth Birthday*, ed. M. A. Morrison and D. I. Owen (Winona Lake, IN: Eisenbrauns, 1981), 257–96.

32. Postgate, *Bronze Age Bureacracy*, 303–5, 350.

33. See BE 8 63, discussed by G. van Driel, "Neo-Babylonian Sheep and Goats," *Bulletin of Sumerian Agriculture* 7 (1993): 219–58, here 224. Van Driel cites many more contracts involving institutions rather than private owners but also notes that "[smaller] private herding

The requirement for *riksātum* in LH 264, and the many written records from Mesopotamia pointing to how flock-owners, herdsmen, and shepherds formulated these *riksātum*, speak to a concern that the Covenant Code does not consider in its law of herding. However, the use of contractual stipulations finds a parallel in the biblical narrative of Jacob and Laban in Gen 29–31. In this story, Jacob works for his uncle Laban for one month without compensation before Laban says, "Because you are my brother, should you work for me without pay? Tell me your wage" (Gen 29:15). Typical compensation for a shepherd in the ancient Near East could include a share of the flock's offspring and by-products, a flat fee of grain, or a clothing allowance.[34] Jacob, however, arranges with Laban to work seven years in exchange for the latter's younger daughter, Rachel, in marriage. At the end of this term, Laban gives Jacob his older daughter, Leah, instead, and Jacob agrees to work an additional seven years for Rachel. During these fourteen years, Jacob receives no sheep as compensation.[35] Upon completion of these arrangements, Jacob and Laban renegotiate, with Jacob apparently stipulating the terms once again.[36] The two agree to compensation in the form of a variety of flock animals of particular colors, and Jacob, through a process of animal breeding he devises, amasses great wealth.

Six years later, Jacob flees Laban's household with his family. When Laban catches up to him, hurling a number of accusations his way, Jacob responds with a detailed defense of his shepherding that depicts a number of herding practices and duties (Gen 31:36–41).[37] The patriarch ends his counteraccusation with the claim that, despite his incredible diligence and the grueling conditions he suffered in order to grow Laban's wealth, Laban "switched [his] wage ten times over!" (Gen 31:41).

Of what, precisely, does Jacob accuse his uncle? Was Laban not entitled to change Jacob's wage repeatedly? M. A. Morrison has argued that, in fact, Laban's repeated adjustments of Jacob's wages cohere with ancient Near Eastern herding practices. Herding followed an annual cycle, and at

---

arrangements may easily remain hidden between debtnotes, as so many other transactions are."

34. See M. A. Morrison, "The Jacob and Laban Narrative in Light of Near Eastern Sources," *BA* 46 (1983): 155–64, here 156–57.

35. See Gen 30:30, where Jacob indicates that, despite having accrued great wealth for Laban, he has not yet gained financially himself.

36. In contrast to Gen 31:7–8, in which Jacob, speaking to his wives, depicts Laban as setting (and repeatedly changing) his wages. Source-critical analysis has attributed Gen 30:25–43 to J and 31:4–13 to E, distinguishing between the former narrative in which Jacob amasses his own wealth through clever breeding tactics, and the latter, which attributes his success to the revelation of an angel of God.

37. These are discussed further in chapter 2.

the end of each cycle, new contracts were drawn up.[38] Laban would annually change the terms of Jacob's contract based on his previous year's successes: if Jacob bred many of a particular variety of sheep, Laban would set the next year's wages in a different variety. Jacob grew wealthy despite Laban's concerted efforts at undermining him; each time Laban chose a failing breed for Jacob's payment, that breed would suddenly have a successful year (Gen 31:7–8).

It was Laban's right to change Jacob's contract annually, and Laban honored the terms of each contract he set up with his nephew. Jacob's gripe was not that Laban withheld his wages or deceived him, but that he did everything in his power to ensure that Jacob could not succeed financially. Still, Laban exercised his rights—if adversely for Jacob—within the workings of an ancient Near Eastern herding arrangement. We can characterize Jacob and Laban's various agreements throughout the narrative as contractual; the two men set their terms (i.e., *riksātum*), which are subject to change with each renegotiation and do not appear to be predetermined. In the ancient Near East, the period of shearing was also the time when shepherds and flock-owners would settle accounts and negotiate new contracts. Indeed, Laban is at the shearing when Jacob decides to flee with his family (Gen 31:19), indicating that Jacob left honorably from a contractual perspective (if not from the perspective of his father-in-law), after settling accounts but before entering into a new contract.

Despite affinities between the Jacob–Laban narrative and herding practices from Mesopotamia, several details in the narrative not only deviate from details of ancient Near Eastern texts, but lack verisimilitude altogether: Jacob first works in exchange for wives, rather than for flock animals, their by-products, a clothing allowance, or a flat fee. When after fourteen years he begins to work in exchange for flock animals, he does so not for a set percentage of the flock, but for all animals of a particular hue. These peculiarities might constitute pure fantasy, meant to paint a picture of the underdog forefather who bests his evil foreign father-in-law with help from the god of Israel. However, they also serve an evaluative and implicitly normative purpose. As Pamela Barmash has amply demonstrated, building on insights from the law and literature school, biblical narrative may distort details of the law in order to expose its inadequacies and thereby demand a more just law.[39] Through its use of implausible contractual stipulations patently intended to disadvantage Jacob, the Jacob–Laban narrative offers a commentary on inequitable practices in herding, warning the naïve to reject irregular terms when drawing up contracts, and highlighting the importance of enabling a financially

---

38. Morrison, "Jacob and Laban Narrative," 158.

39. Barmash, "Achieving Justice through Narrative," 181–99; Barmash, "Narrative Quandary," 1–16.

inferior party in a commercial relationship to grow self-sufficient. Honoring a contract, as Laban does, is not the same as creating an honorable contract. Ideally, this narrative suggests, the law would not condone a contract such as Laban's with Jacob. But within the reality that the narrative begrudgingly acknowledges, a shepherd should avoid entering an abusive contractual relationship, even if it is legally sound. Beyond supporting the hypothesis that, as in Mesopotamia, in ancient Israel contractual stipulations were employed in setting up herding arrangements, the Jacob–Laban narrative further exposes the potential for injustice stemming from the ability to customize these stipulations.

Reasons for Deposits and Herding Arrangements

Exodus 22 introduces a scenario where a deposit occurs and then focuses on what happens when that deposit goes awry. What Exodus does not address is the reason a deposit might arise in the first place. LE 36's mention of the *napṭaru* points to one possible situation in which a person might deposit goods: a traveler may require safe storage of personal belongings and so prevail upon the innkeeper at the place of lodging to execute this task. Beyond this, however, the biblical and cuneiform law collections are by and large lacking when it comes to the *why* of deposits. Instead, biblical narrative and Mesopotamian documents of legal practice may provide insight into why people might have availed themselves of these arrangements.

Deposits for Storage

CT 4 30a is a record of deposit listing various household objects and furnishings that were deposited with a third person:[40]

> Two beds, one basket, one "household" basket … one basket without a lid, one grinding stone together with its upper stone, one sideboard (of a bed) together with one footboard, one perforated sieve, one perforated box, one wooden box, one [household furnishing] … that PN the shepherd, together with one […] belonging to PN₂, deposited [*paqdū*] with PN₃.

Although this text mostly reads as a list, it also provides clues for uncovering the reason for the transaction it records. The bailor who deposits the

---

40. See MVAG 10 40; Josef Kohler and Arthur Ungnad, *Hammurabis Gesetz*, 6 vols. (Leipzig: Pfeiffer, 1904–1923), 3:41.

majority of the property is a shepherd, the property he deposits primarily consists of household items, and the date, which appears at the end of the contract following the names of witnesses, is the 5th day of the 9th month of the 12th year of Ammiṣaduqa's reign. The 9th month, Kislimu (approximately November/ December), is when sheep would begin to make their way to the winter pasture, where they would remain for approximately half a year for the main period of lambing, until returning to their owner's hometown for the shearing and lamb harvesting.[41] Based on this information, we can reconstruct the following background. A shepherd, about to embark on a half-year migration with his flock, required safe storage of the household items and furniture that could not accompany him on his travels. He therefore deposited them with a bailee for safekeeping until his return.

CT 4 30a points to one social background for bailment: persons traveling for work might require storage of their belongings, if they were not leaving behind households that would continue to function in their absence.[42] Bailments for storage facilitated an economic system involving migratory work; a person could leave home for extended periods to accomplish tasks that required travel without permanently forfeiting personal property. The text also offers fodder for considering the contiguity of Exod 22's first two bailment scenarios, deposits of goods and animal herding. Beyond sharing basic legal principles, these two scenarios may have frequently occurred in tandem in practice. A shepherd without an established household might act as a bailee for a long stretch of the year (i.e., during the migratory stage of the herding cycle), while also requiring a bailee for safe storage of personal belongings during that time.

The need for temporary safekeeping might also arise over the course of a business venture. AbB 9 117 is a letter from the Old Babylonian period instructing two men to go to a specific location to receive fronds on behalf of Elmeštum, who would be away in Sippar.[43] The men were to ship the fronds elsewhere, but if they were unable to do this, they were instructed to store the fronds securely in one house (*ina bītim ištēn piḫiašunūti*). AbB 9 117 thus presents a commercial context in which a person might require a bailee. When a delay would occur between receiving and shipping out products, immediate temporary storage could become necessary. One can imagine how an innkeeper—such as the *napṭaru* of LE 36—might end up

---

41. For details about the herding cycle and calendar, see Morrison, "Jacob and Laban Narrative," 158; Michael Kozuh, *The Sacrificial Economy: Assessors, Contractors, and Thieves in the Management of Sacrificial Sheep at the Eanna Temple of Uruk (ca. 625–520 B.C.)*, Explorations in Ancient Near Eastern Civilizations 2 (Winona Lake, IN: Eisenbrauns, 2014), 15.

42. Examples of travel-related occupations, aside from the shepherd, could include merchants and diplomats.

43. For an edition and translation of this text, see Marten Stol, *Letters from Yale: Transliterated and Translated*, AbB 9 (Leiden: Brill, 1981), 76–77.

acting as a bailee in such a situation, in which people traveling for business find themselves in need of a place to stay the night as well as a place to store the goods in their possession.

LIH 79, also from the Old Babylonian period, sheds light on a further scenario in which bailment provides a solution to a temporary need for storage.[44] According to this letter, a family that owed barley in taxes was allowed the opportunity to settle the debt through payment of three cows and one-half mina of silver. Although they were required to pay this amount immediately, it would take some time for a messenger to arrive in order to transport the cows and silver to Babylon. In the interim, the debt was to be entrusted for safekeeping (*ana maṣṣarūtim paqādu*) with a specific third party.

LIH 79 reflects one important function of bailments, that is, to place property in escrow with a third party for a temporary period, after which it would be transferred to a designated recipient.[45] The property required immediate delivery to avoid creditor risk, but the creditor could not collect the property immediately; therefore, it had to be placed in escrow for temporary storage. Similar bailment arrangements commonly arose in cases of disputes, and will be treated in more detail presently.

Escrow and Sequestration

LIH 79 is just one example of a bailment wherein property is put into escrow. TCL 12 120, a Neo-Babylonian text, points to another situation in which a person might decide to deposit silver in order to avoid trouble with a creditor: Bēl-aḫḫē-iddin purchased a house from Bēl-rēmanni. In order to prevent Bēl-rēmanni's creditor from laying claim to the house, Bēl-aḫḫē-iddin did not pay Bēl-rēmanni directly, but instead placed into safekeeping a bag containing the remainder of the price of the house in silver. Years later, after the buyer and original bailee had died, the seller was able to lay claim to the deposited silver only when the high priest of Esangila declared that neither the temple nor anyone else, to his knowledge, had a claim to it.[46]

---

44. See the early edition and translation of this text in L. W. King, ed., *The Letters and Inscriptions of Hammurabi, King of Babylon, about B.C. 2200 to Which Are Added a Series of Letters of Other Kings of the First Dynasty of Babylon*, 3 vols. (London: Luzac, 1898–1900), 3:124–25.

45. See Garner, *Black's Law Dictionary*, s.v. "escrow": "A legal document or property delivered by a promisor to a third party to be held by the third party for a given amount of time or until the occurrence of a condition, at which time the third party is to hand over the document or property to the promisee."

46. For discussion of this text, along with the related texts Nbn. 1047 and Nbn. 1048, see Michael Jursa, "Economic Change and Legal Innovation: On Aspects of Commercial Interaction and Land Tenure in Babylonia in the First Millennium BC," in *I diritti del mondo cunei-*

Similar to bailments in which property is put into escrow with a third party, numerous documents reflect scenarios wherein contested property is placed with a neutral third party for a temporary period, pending the outcome of a dispute.[47] These bailments for sequestration functioned as a mechanism to ease the process of dispute resolution, by removing the property from its possessor until its status had been clarified.[48]

OECT 3 82, for example, is a letter detailing a conflict over a field.[49] According to the complainant, he had cultivated the field for five years before the person now claiming to be its owner came and seized it by force. The letter writer instructs his addressee to work with Šamaš-mušallim, to whom he has also written, and investigate the case. In the meantime, he orders that the barley from the field be placed in safekeeping (*ana maṣṣar-tim*) pending the results of the investigation. This case differs from a simple bailment in that a bailment is ordered, rather than chosen by its owner, because at the time of the bailment there is no agreement as to who is the legitimate owner. Therefore, the investigators stand in for the owner as bailor in the initial stage of the bailment: delivering the property to a bailee. When the status of the property has been clarified and its owner determined, that owner would automatically replace the investigators as bailor and could rightfully reclaim his property, thereby terminating the bailment.

In legal terms, the sequestration of OECT 3 82 is specifically judicial rather than conventional: the bailment is ordered by a judicial authority, rather than entered voluntarily by the parties to the dispute.[50] One finds a reference to a conventional sequestration, on the other hand, in a Neo-Babylonian promissory note, BM 78064.[51] A conflict had arisen between Ea-šuma-uṣur and Līširu regarding the status of a field that the former had sold to the latter,[52] so the two men deposited (*ipqidū*) 24 minas of silver, the price of the field, with a third party. Because the parties to the dispute initiated the bailment themselves, the arrangement constituted a

---

forme (Mesopotamia e regioni adiacenti, ca. 2500–500 a.C.), ed. Mario Liverani and Clelia Mora, Pubblicazioni del CEDANT 4 (Pavia: IUSS Press, 2008), 601–28, here 614–16.

47. For a review of literature discussing deposits as a financial tool used when a dispute prevented parties from completing a transaction, see Małgorzata Sandowicz, "Depositaries, Depositors and Courthouse in Sixth-Century B.C. Babylon," *Palamedes* 4 (2009): 15–25, here 22 n. 16.

48. See Garner, *Black's Law Dictionary*, s.v. "sequestration."

49. For this text, see Kraus, AbB 4, 160.

50. See Garner, *Black's Law Dictionary*, s.v. "sequestration."

51. This text is edited and discussed by Sandowicz, "Depositaries, Depositors and Courthouse," 15–25. A copy of the same document in fragmentary condition, BM 77602, has also survived.

52. Following the reading of Sandowicz, "Depositaries, Depositors and Courthouse," 22–23. Sandowicz rejects an alternative reading of the text, according to which both men were sellers of the field.

conventional sequestration. Years later, the deceased Ea-šuma-uṣur's son tried to reclaim the deposit but ran into resistance from the family of the also-deceased original bailee. The court therefore ordered the bailee's sons to appear before the judges; if they did not appear, they would be subject to payment of the original deposit plus interest.

These texts thus reflect special kinds of bailments—escrow, judicial sequestration, and conventional sequestration—in which property is stored for a temporary period in order to keep it safe, specifically in cases of debt or dispute.

Wartime Bailments

First Samuel 17 portrays David engaging in two kinds of bailments: When Jesse instructs his son David to visit his brothers at a military encampment, the latter leaves (ויטש) sheep with a bailee (שמר, 1 Sam 17:20) to watch while he is away. Upon arriving at the camp, David proceeds to leave (ויטש) his belongings with a second bailee (שומר הכלים, 1 Sam 17:22) before running off to find his brothers at the battlefront. Within a span of three verses, and in nearly identical language, David thus creates two bailments.[53]

As the son of the flock-owner, and a shepherd for that flock, David is responsible to arrange for the animals' care when he leaves home. Despite the fact that David is himself a shepherd, he is not a bailee; 1 Sam 17:20 is not a case of one bailee handing over the object of bailment to a second bailee. As Jesse's son, David is a family shepherd and not a commercial shepherd. In contrast to commercial shepherding arrangements, a flock-owner does not hire or contract with a family member.[54] The sons and daughters of a flock-owner may work as shepherds for their father, but the two arrangements differ. When David hands over flock animals to a bailee (שמר), he acts as a bailor representing the interests of the owner, despite not technically owning the flock himself.

First Samuel 17:20 further offers a window into the social background of bailment: a person might entrust property with a bailee while traveling. In contrast to typical herding arrangements in the ancient Near East that operated on an annual basis, 1 Sam 17 includes a scenario where the owner

---

53. Shimon Bar-Efrat (*1 Samuel: Introduction and Commentary*, 2nd ed., Miqra le-Yisra'el [Tel Aviv: Am Oved; Jerusalem: Magnes, 2008], 227) notes that the similar language of verses 20 and 22 emphasizes David's responsible behavior.

54. For family vs. commercial herding, see Morrison, "Jacob and Laban Narrative," 160; Bernard S. Jackson, *Essays on Halakhah in the New Testament*, Jewish and Christian Perspectives 16 (Leiden: Brill, 2008), 155–56. Jackson further identifies David as a family shepherd.

or his family member who typically watches the flock must travel for a temporary period—likely much shorter than a year—and so requires a short-term bailee. Although biblical law does not consider motivations for bailments, the law of herding in Exod 22:9–12 is sufficiently nonspecific that it also might encompass either of these scenarios.

Before heading from the main encampment to the battlefront where his brothers are located, David leaves his belongings (כלים) with a bailee. These belongings are referred to with the same term used by Exod 22:6 (כלים); they may include the provisions that Jesse sent with David for his brothers and likely any other possessions that he brought along for the trip.[55] Whether or not David should have been at the battlefront, his personal effects certainly did not belong there.[56] In a similar vein, during David's subsequent battles, a number of people stay at the main camp with the כלים (1 Sam 25:13; 30:10, 21–25).[57] Bailment thus constituted one task for those in the military who were not otherwise engaged in combat.[58] While Exod 22 hardly envisions a particularly military context, these narratives point to such a context as one social background for the institution of bailment: When leaving the main camp for battle, soldiers would entrust their goods to other soldiers who would be responsible to keep them safe. As a visitor to the camp, David also leaves his property with the designated bailee. The narrative leaves open whether David was entitled to this service or used it surreptitiously, pretending to belong at the battlefront when he should not have gone there. If David's visit was sanctioned, he may have been required to check in his belongings with the bailee.

Discretion and Deceit

When the prophet Elisha refuses to accept a gift from the Aramean commander Naaman (2 Kgs 5:16), his servant Gehazi decides to chase after Naaman and acquire a gift for himself, with a pretext he fabricates (2 Kgs 5:20–22a). Gehazi requests a talent of silver and two sets of clothing from Naaman, and the latter generously gives him two talents along with

---

55. Bar-Efrat (*1 Samuel*, 227) understands David's כלים as the containers that would have held the food Jesse sent. The NJPS translates "baggage."

56. While others do not seem to mind David's presence, his brother Eliab accuses him of coming down to see the war (1 Sam 17:28).

57. 1 Sam 25:13 and 30:24 use the expression ישב על הכלים to refer to the action of remaining with the belongings; neither uses the root š-m-r.

58. The invading force in Isa 10:28 also leaves (p-q-d) its כלים in Michmash as it goes on to overrun other towns. This may not have been its military base, as the invader raids one town after another; either they left behind a soldier or group of soldiers to watch their possessions, or they entrusted a person or persons from the town with this task.

the clothing (2 Kgs 5:22b–23). However, Gehazi does not want his master to know of his scheme, and so, upon returning to the citadel in Samaria, "he took [the things] … and deposited [*p-q-d*] them in the house" (2 Kgs 5:24 NJPS).

Several clues suggest that Gehazi's action in 2 Kgs 5:24 constitutes a deposit. The wide range of possible translations for the root *p-q-d* include placing or entrusting in someone's care.[59] Gehazi leaves the property in "the house" — not in his own residence, as some have translated, but in some other house, as the absence of any possessive suffix demonstrates.[60] The property that Gehazi deposits includes silver and clothing, which correspond to objects of deposits in Exod 22 (כסף, "silver," in Exod 22:6; שלמה, "garment," in Exod 22:8). In doubling the quantity of silver that Gehazi requests from one talent to two (2 Kgs 5:23), Naaman echoes the principle of double compensation from the biblical law of deposit (Exod 22:6, 8).[61] The בית ("house") where Gehazi places his property is also the place of deposit in Exod 22:6–7. Although each of these clues is of debatable significance on its own, the totality of evidence points to a casting of this narrative in light of bailment law, such that Gehazi is depicted as depositing property with a bailee.

This narrative adds a scenario to the list of social backgrounds to bailment arrangements: Gehazi stores his property with another party because

---

59. In fact, this is the same root used in the context of the Priestly laws' פקדון ("deposit") in Lev 5:21, 23. Although verbs of this meaning that take physical property as their object are frequently in the *hiphil* stem (e.g., 1 Kgs 14:27; Isa 10:28; Jer 36:20), the *qal* stem of וַיִּפְקֹד in 2 Kgs 5:24 finds parallels as well (e.g., Job 34:14). I therefore understand this verb as an act of deposit, not merely "placing."

60. For the (in my view, mistaken) understanding of the house in this verse as Gehazi's own house, see, e.g., Stuart Creason, "*PQD* Revisited," in *Studies in Semitic and Afroasiatic Linguistics Presented to Gene B. Gragg*, ed. Cynthia L. Miller, SAOC 60 (Chicago: Oriental Institute of the University of Chicago, 2007), 27–42, here 30; Jesse C. Long, *1 & 2 Kings*, College Press NIV Commentary (Joplin, MO: College Press, 2002), 329; T. R. Hobbs, *2 Kings*, WBC 13 (Waco, TX: Word, 1985), 56; Mordechai Cogan and Hayim Tadmor, *II Kings: A New Translation*, AB 11 (Garden City, NY: Doubleday, 1988), 62. Given that Gehazi leaves the property in another house, two options emerge: either Gehazi deposited his property with another person in a house near the citadel, or he hid his property in a house there, without involving any other party. The absence of another person in the verse does not mean there was no such person; in 1 Sam 6:10, for example, calves are penned in a house (בבית), surely under someone's care, although no such person is mentioned. In 2 Kgs 5:24, Gehazi's deposit of the goods occurs amid a rapid series of actions. Gehazi arrives, takes the property, deposits it, and sends away Naaman's men; then the men leave. Gehazi moves quickly (though futilely) to prevent Elisha from discovering his actions. Amid this swift progression, there is little room for extra details; thus, not even the property is mentioned. It would be perfectly reasonable, then, for 2 Kgs 5:24 to have in mind a recipient of Gehazi's deposit, despite not mentioning one.

61. This echo is ironic: Naaman is the victim of fraud, yet he effectively pays double compensation. This irony underscores the immorality of Gehazi's behavior.

he wishes to keep it a secret. Philo (*Spec.* 4.31) also describes the background of deposits as a scenario in which one party secretly deposits goods with another. In addition, this narrative alludes to a scenario that arises in the Laws of Hammurabi, but not in biblical law: the deposit of illicitly obtained goods. Gehazi obtains silver and clothing from Naaman under false pretenses. Thus, although Naaman is a willing donor, Gehazi is effectively a thief. Gehazi behaves dishonestly at every turn. He goes behind Elisha's back, lies to Naaman, and then lies to Elisha when the prophet asks where he has been. As the servant of Elisha, Gehazi further commits an act of theft by keeping the property for himself, when he should deliver it to Elisha. Gehazi's deposit is just one more example of unacceptable behavior. LH 7 addresses a similar situation amid a series of laws about theft: A person who buys or accepts property for safekeeping from a minor or slave without following the proper procedure is considered a thief and punished accordingly. Presumably, the bailee is guilty because under these suspicious circumstances, it should have been assumed that the goods were truly the property of the minor's parent or the slave's master, and the bailee should have refused to accept them. While LH 7 treats this scenario from the perspective of the bailee's liability, 2 Kgs 5 makes a different point: It is wrong to accept property under false pretenses, and it is also wrong to deposit these goods, even if the original owner gave them away willingly. 2 Kings 5:24 does not mention the bailee; it is therefore not clear whether the bailee's acceptance of deposited property from Gehazi, a servant, would be considered unlawful, as in LH 7. The narrative casts its disapproval instead on the bailor's initiation of a deposit of goods obtained through deceit. Thus, a person might create a deposit because of a need for secrecy — whether for respectable reasons or nefarious ones.

Bailment for the Performance of a Service

The biblical bailment law and its cuneiform counterparts address herding arrangements, which necessarily require the performance of services, and also treat deposits of goods, which one might assume would not involve the performance of any services beyond the safekeeping that the laws mention explicitly. In practice, however, just as herding required tasks such as feeding and breeding, the deposit of goods could involve more than simply safekeeping. An appreciation of the range of bailments in their diverse functions within Mesopotamian legal practice may enrich our view of the institution in ancient Israel, at the very least pointing to areas of practice with affinities to the classic bailments considered by Exod 22.

VAS 7 35, for example, is a contract for date cultivation:[62]

> 2 kurs of ripe dates and 1 kur of *kimru* dates (were) the yield of the orchard of PN, (in accordance with) the rental agreement of PN₂ ... which were entrusted [*paqdū*] to PN₃ for sorting.[63] At the time of the date harvest, he will deliver 2 kurs of ripe dates and 1 kur of *kimru* dates to the bearer of his sealed document.

In this contract, PN is the owner or administrator of the date orchard; PN₂ is the tenant of the orchard and presumably functions as its *šākinu*, who contracts with subordinate workers on the yield of the orchard, which he estimates and fixes; and PN₃ is a date harvester, one of these subordinates.[64] Dated to 10 Abum, the fifth month of the lunar Babylonian calendar, the contract stipulates that PN₃ will sort the dates entrusted to him into two groups (2/3 ripe dates, 1/3 *kimru* dates), and return them at the time of the date harvest.[65]

Does this text reflect a deposit? The text states that 2 kurs of ripe dates and 1 kur of *kimru* dates were given from PN₂ to PN₃. Yet the date on the contract, 10 Abum, complicates this picture. The date harvest would not have begun until over six weeks later, lasting from the seventh through the ninth months. At the time of the contract, the dates would not yet have fallen or been picked from the trees. It is implausible that these dates would have been picked so early in the season; had they been picked in Abum, they would not yet have been ripe. More likely, despite the contract's statement that 3 kurs of dates were deposited (*paqdū*) with PN₃, no actual transfer of fruit occurred at that time. While *paqādu* at times refers to nonphysical entrusting, especially when the object of the verb is an abstract noun, it is unlikely that VAS 7 35 uses the verb in this manner. With physical objects, *paqādu* typically involves physically handing over the object, and the fact that PN₃ is to return the dates places both actions squarely in the physical realm.[66]

---

62. See text in Moses Schorr, *Urkunden des altbabylonischen Zivil- und Prozessrechts*, Vorderasiatische Bibliothek 5 (Leipzig: Hinrichs, 1913), 104–5; and see Benno Landsberger, *The Date Palm and Its By-Products according to the Cuneiform Sources*, AfO Beiheft 17 (Graz: Weidner, 1967), 56; Denise Cocquerillat, "Aperçus sur la phéniciculture en Babylonie à l'époque de la Ière dynastie de Babylone," *JESHO* 10 (1967): 161–223, here 193–94.

63. For discussion of *ana kamārim* with this meaning, see Landsberger, *Date Palm*, 56; Cocquerillat, "Aperçu sur la phéniciculture en Babylonie à l'époque de la Ière dynastie de Babylone," 193–94.

64. For the *šākinu*, and the identification of PN₂ as a *šākinu*, see Landsberger, *Date Palm*, 57.

65. This was the typical ratio (2/3 ordinary dates; 1/3 better-quality *kimru* dates) that a date contractor would be responsible for delivering, for which see, e.g., TLB 1 71:8; TLB 1 72:7; and see Landsberger, *Date Palm*, 58.

66. *CAD* P, s.v. "*paqādu*." Common abstract objects of *paqādu* include *napištu* ("life") and *awatu* ("matter").

Rather than reflect a physical delivery of property on the date of its drafting, the contract records the creation of a fictional deposit based on the estimated yield of the orchard, which will become an actual deposit whenever the dates are picked and delivered to PN_3. Contracts of this kind are typically dated to the sixth month, and more rarely to the fifth month, as in the case of VAS 7 35; in either case, they always predate the date harvest.[67] These contracts thus record transactions that have not yet occurred, as if they already have.

What motivated this peculiar legal fiction?[68] Possibly, recording these transactions ahead of time was a matter of convenient bookkeeping. This practice also finds a parallel in orchard rental contracts. Rental dues owed by the tenant of a date orchard to its owner or administrator could be fixed a few weeks before the date harvest by estimating the expected yield of the orchard and charging the tenant by means of a fictional loan. An orchard rental contract might state that the owner had given a specified amount of dates to the tenant, and that the tenant will return these dates at the harvest time, when in actuality, the owner had not given anything to the tenant; the amount simply reflected the estimated yield of the orchard.[69] VAS 7 35 utilizes a similar fiction, but with the tenant (PN_2) as a bailor and the date harvester (PN_3) as a bailee charged with performing a task, namely, sorting the dates.

VAS 7 35 therefore provides an example of a deposit of a non-animal product (in this case, produce) that involved the performance of a service in addition to keeping the property until the time of its return. In addition,

---

67. Landsberger, *Date Palm*, 57.

68. I use the term *legal fiction* in its broadest sense(s), adopting a maximalist view of Lon L. Fuller's classic definition: "either (1) a statement propounded with a complete or partial consciousness of its falsity, or (2) a false statement recognised as having utility" (*Legal Fictions* [Stanford, CA: Stanford University Press, 1967], 9). Many legal commentaries speak of legal fictions in a specifically adjudicatory context, for example, of judges who pretend that the facts of the case are different from what they truly are, in order to adapt the present law to unforeseen circumstances, or to achieve justice in the face of a law they perceive as outdated or insufficient; for discussion and review of literature, see recently Karen Petroski, "Fictions of Omniscience," *Kentucky Law Review* 103 (2014–2015): 447–528, here 497–98. In contrast, I include within the scope of "legal fictions" their use as a legal instrument by citizens, for example, as a means to effect a transaction in a particular way, in service of the purposes of the parties to the transaction. For an overview of the different kinds of legal fictions that scholars have discussed, including legislative fictions, jurisprudential fictions, fictions of legal technique, fictional use of legal instruments by citizens, and fictions of adjudication, see Maksymilian Del Mar, "Legal Fictions and Legal Change in the Common Law Tradition," in *Legal Fictions in Theory and Practice*, ed. Maksymilian Del Mar and William Twining, Law and Philosophy Library 110 (Cham: Springer, 2015), 225–54, here 228.

69. See Johannes Renger, "The Role and the Place of Money and Credit in the Economy of Ancient Mesopotamia," in *New Approaches to Monetary Theory: Interdisciplinary Perspectives*, ed. Heiner Ganssmann, Routledge International Studies in Money and Banking 63 (London: Routledge, 2011), 15–36, here 32, and see references in n. 111 below.

the text sheds light on a further facet of contracts of deposit: Such contracts might be put to fictional use by recording a future deposit as if the property has already traded hands.

Another Fictional Deposit

VAS 7 35 records a deposit of dates that in reality has not yet occurred. A different element of fiction appears in TCL 1 170, a record from the sale of a slave that also includes a deposit:[70]

> 8 silver sheqels, according to the weight-stone of Shamash, (which was) the balance of 13 silver sheqels, the purchase price of the (female) slave ^{f}PN that ^{m}PN$_2$ had purchased from ^{f}PN$_2$ and ^{m}PN her son, and with their full agreement they had deposited with him before witnesses.
>
> On the day that they request it, he will give the 8 silver sheqels, according to the weight-stone of Shamash, to ^{f}PN$_2$ and ^{m}PN her son.

Although the purchase price of the slave is thirteen sheqels, the buyer pays only five sheqels to the sellers; the sellers entrust with the buyer the remaining eight sheqels for safekeeping (*ana maṣṣartim ... ipqidūšum*). The text highlights the validity of this deposit. The sellers "deposit" the eight sheqels willingly (*ina mitgurtišunu*) and, as one finds in the valid deposit of LH 122, before witnesses (*maḫar* LÚ.MEŠ *šībī*).[71] In reality, however, those eight sheqels would never have been physically deposited; functionally, the deposit of TCL 1 170 is a sale on credit. In such a transaction the property is transferred to the buyer, who will pay the seller in full at a later date; in the meantime, the buyer owes the unpaid money to the seller.

The formulation of the sale on credit as a deposit is odd on two counts: First, a deposit from the owners (the sellers) to the bailee (the buyer) never occurs in reality. Instead, the buyer will "return" to the owners silver that had never been in the buyer's possession. Second, why cast this fictive transfer of property as a deposit, rather than as a loan? A loan more closely matches the sale on credit; like the borrower, the buyer on credit *owes* money to its owner. In contrast, the bailee possesses money (etc.) for the owner's benefit; though he too will have to return property in his possession, debt does not define the arrangement.

---

70. See Edouard Cuq, "Commentaire juridique d'un jugement sous Ammi-Ditana," *RA* 7 (1910): 129–38, here 137–38; Schorr, *Urkunden des altbabylonischen Zivil- und Prozessrechts*, 72; Price, "Laws of Deposit," 252–53; and, more recently, Harris, *Ancient Sippar*, 343 n. 77.

71. Note that this occurs in the body of the transaction, and not just in a list of witnesses at the end of the contract as one frequently finds.

Edouard Cuq has suggested two advantages to the deposit form.[72] A deposit contract may allow the bailor to demand the bailed property in return at any time (*ūm irrišūšu*). This, however, is true also of loans.[73] Cuq further points to LH 124's stipulation that the bailee who falsely denies having received property for safekeeping must pay double compensation. Although one ought not assume, without corroborating evidence, that the double compensation of Hammurabi's deposit law reflected standard practice,[74] a harsh penalty in the event of wrongdoing indeed might have made the deposit a more appealing legal fiction than the loan in this case.[75]

A further feature of the fictional bailment in TCL 1 170 is that the buyer will return to the sellers the same eight sheqels that had been "deposited" with him for safekeeping. Although this is not stated explicitly, the safekeeping of this silver implies that the same silver will be returned. Regular deposits, in which exactly the same property that was deposited was returned, were the norm throughout most of ancient Near Eastern history.[76] The fictional deposit of TCL 1:170 is specifically a fictional regular deposit, so that it is standard in all ways, except for a deposit never having occurred.

Transportation Bailments

Another motivation for creating a deposit may be found in the bailment for transportation, or deposit of goods for safekeeping with a bailee responsible for delivering them to another location. This situation diverges from the paradigmatic bailment (i.e., the bailment for storage) insofar as the bailed object does not remain on the bailee's property but travels on or with their person; the bailed object does not return to the bailor but is

---

72. Cuq, "Commentaire juridique," 137–38.

73. See, e.g., YOS 5 242:9; MDP 22 22:10, of creditors.

74. For brief discussion of inconsistencies and consistencies between law collections and practice, with references, see Wells, *Law of Testimony*, 13–14.

75. Cf. the more equivocal language of Harris, *Ancient Sippar*, 343 n. 77: "A breach of trust was perhaps more severely punished than failure to pay the purchase price and, therefore, the debt is formulated in this way rather than as a loan." In favor of a penalty equivalent or similar to that depicted in LH is the absence of penalty clauses in typical records of deposit, in contrast to bailments for transportation (such as CT 8 37b, discussed above) that include an interest rate for lateness (though it does not consider fraud, the topic of LH 124).

76. See Michael Jursa, "Agricultural Management, Tax Farming and Banking: Aspects of Entrepreneurial Activity in Babylonia in the Late Achaemenid and Hellenistic Periods," in *La transition entre l'empire achéménide et les royaumes hellénistiques, vers 350–300 av. J.-C.: Actes du colloque organisé au Collège de France par la chaire d'histoire et civilisation du monde achéménide et de l'empire d'Alexandre et le Réseau international d'études et de recherches achéménides, 22–23 novembre 2004*, ed. Pierre Briant and Francis Joannès, Persika 9 (Paris: De Boccard, 2006), 137–222, here 165.

delivered to another person or place in accordance with the bailor's instructions. However, texts referring to such arrangements use the same language as that associated with bailments (e.g., *maṣṣartum, paqādu*),[77] and the basic legal premise of these arrangements is the same: property lawfully resides in the possession of a person other than its owner for a temporary period.

CT 8 37b records the agreement of Lamassi, a *nadītu* at Sippar during the Old Babylonian period, with a man instructed to deliver 8.5 minas of lead (or tin)[78] to her messenger in Eshnunna in fifteen days' time.[79] If he is late, he will be penalized with interest at the rate of 1/3 of a sheqel of lead for every ten sheqels. During this period, many affluent families from places such as Eshnunna and Babylon would send their daughters to Sippar as *nadiātu*. In addition to serving a religious function, *nadiātu* could own real estate and movable property and could serve as moneylenders for their families, thereby benefitting them financially.[80] The *nadītu* of CT 8 37b is likely a native of Eshnunna whose consigned lead will end up with her family back home, possibly as a loan.

YOS 19 101 is a Neo-Babylonian trial record that sheds light on what might happen if a transportation bailment goes awry.[81] Nergal-rēṣū᾿a recounts to the judges how his master Iddin-Marduk consigned 480 kur of dates for transportation with Amurru-natan, a boatman. When Nergal-rēṣū᾿a received the delivery of dates, he discovered that 47 kur 1 pi were missing. Amurru-natan claimed that he had not taken the dates. Upon investigating the facts of the case, using the original contractual agreement as evidence, the judges decided that Amurru-natan must repay the missing amount to Nergal-rēṣū᾿a.

---

77. See, e.g., CT 8 37b; AT 119. As we have noted, these words occur in contexts of bailments, but are not limited to bailments.

78. For the debate on the precise meaning of the word *annaku*, see Benno Landsberger, "Tin and Lead: The Adventures of Two Vocables," *JNES* 24 (1965): 285–96; P. R. S. Moorey, *Ancient Mesopotamian Materials and Industries: The Archaeological Evidence* (Oxford: Clarendon, 1994), 295–96; Benjamin J. Noonan, "There and Back Again: 'Tin' or 'Lead' in Amos 7:7–9?," *VT* 63 (2013): 299–307.

79. For an early edition of this text, see Schorr, *Urkunden des altbabylonischen Zivil- und Prozessrechts*, 103–4. I reject interpretations of this text by W. F. Leemans (*Foreign Trade in the Old Babylonian Period*, Studia et documenta ad iura Orientis antiqui pertinentia 6 [Leiden: Brill, 1960], 86–89) and Rivkah Harris ("Biographical Notes on the *nadītu* Women of Sippar," *JCS* 16 [1962]: 1–12, here 9) that suggest that Ibni-Tišpak (the bailee) would have to return the lead to the *nadītu* Lamassi in Sippar. In fact, Leemans later suggested that the text be interpreted as we understand it here; see "Old Babylonian Letters and Economic History: A Review Article with a Digression on Foreign Trade," *JESHO* 11 (1968): 171–226, here 206.

80. See Frans Van Koppen and Denis Lacambre, "Sippar and the Frontier Between Ešnunna and Babylon: New Sources for the History of Ešnunna in the Old Babylonian Period," *Jaarbericht "Ex Oriente Lux"* 41 (2008–2009): 151–77.

81. For discussion and translation of this text, see Shalom E. Holtz, *Neo-Babylonian Trial Records*, SBLWAW 35 (Atlanta: Society of Biblical Literature, 2014), 80–83.

While the Bible does not focus on the procedure for setting up deposits, the Laws of Hammurabi offer context from a neighboring society about the use of witnesses and oral contractual stipulations in the creation of such arrangements. Narrative and practice texts further address the *who* and *why* of deposits, which the law collections do not consider. A person needing to travel might require a bailee: for example, when visiting family during wartime (e.g., David in 1 Sam 17) or leaving the area for work (e.g., the shepherd of CT 4 30a). Soldiers entering a combat zone might require storage of their possessions (e.g., 1 Sam 25:13; 30:10, 21–25). The need for a bailee to store possessions might arise over the course of travel (e.g., AbB 9 117). A person might also initiate a bailment in order to hide property (e.g., 2 Kgs 5:24). The largely commercial and administrative contexts of bailments in the ancient Near East—relating to scenarios including business ventures, taxes owed, problems with creditors, sales on credit, sequestration, and bailments for transportation—find no parallel in the Bible but suggest that behind the laconic law of Exod 22 lies a rich range of possible backgrounds.

Involuntary Bailments

At the center of its laws of deposit and herding, Exodus includes an exegetically thorny verse (22:8) that refers both to goods (as in the preceding verses about deposit) and to animals (as in the following verses about herding):

על כל דבר פשע על שור על חמור על שה על שלמה על כל אבדה אשר יאמר כי
הוא זה עד האלהים יבא דבר שניהם אשר ירשיען אלהים ישלם שנים לרעהו

For any case of a willful breach—for an ox, for a donkey, for a sheep, for a garment, for any lost property—of which one says, "It is he!": The case of the two of them shall come before God. Whomsoever God declares guilty must pay double to the other.

I will return to the relationship of this verse to its context in chapter 2. At this juncture, let us focus our attention specifically on the addition of another kind of object grouped together with these goods and animals: the אבדה, or lost property.[82] As I will demonstrate in the following chapter,

---

82. Although one might argue that אבדה refers to any property that is missing, whether by theft or any other means, I understand it as referring specifically to property that one person has lost, and that another person finds. I arrive at this conclusion based on the following evidence: (1) Elsewhere (e.g., Lev 5:22–23; Deut 22:3), the noun is the object of a verb from the root *m-ṣ-ʾ*, i.e., "find"; (2) in Deut 22:1–3, a law containing numerous parallels to Exod 22:8, אבדה is used in the context of animals that stray and are found. Indeed, Deuteronomy's

Exod 22:8 in its entirety refers to willful breaches, or fraud, committed exclusively in situations that fall under the umbrella of bailments. The scenario of lost property is included alongside deposits and herding as an example of a bailment. Modern legal theorists consider lost property a paradigmatic case of involuntary bailment, where the formation of the arrangement involves neither contract nor consensus, yet the finder of property becomes a bailee with specific duties to the property's owner.[83] By listing lost property among other bailments, Exod 22 bears out this same notion: the Covenant Code considers the case of lost property as belonging to the same legal category as deposits and herding. When one person finds another person's lost property, the two individuals automatically, involuntarily, become parties to a bailment.

Although the Laws of Hammurabi treat lost property in connection with the law of deposit, the cuneiform law collection does not appear to conceive of lost property as a bailment per se in the way that biblical law does. Following the law of deposit in LH 120–125, LH 126 reads:

> If a man whose property is not lost declares, "My property is lost," and he accuses his city quarter, his city quarter shall establish against him before the god that his property is not lost; he shall restore twofold whatever he claimed and give it to his city quarter.

LH 126 contains close linguistic and thematic parallels to the preceding laws.[84] However, this law's relationship to its context requires scrutiny. Was the allegedly lost property given specifically as a deposit, as in the preceding laws, or did it go missing irrespective of any bailment arrangement? And what is the role of the city quarter?

Some have argued that LH 126 reflects a case of deposit like the previous laws, and further suggested that the accusation of the city quarter indicates that this was a deposit at the temple.[85] Yet the extant evidence does not support a connection between the city quarter and temple. The

---

clear use of Exod 22:8 in its expansion of the law of lost property in Exod 23:4 demonstrates that it understands אבדה this way in this verse (or at minimum, that it imputes to the verse this understanding).

83. See, e.g., Samuel S. Williston, *A Treatise on the Law of Contracts*, ed. Richard A. Lord, 4th ed. (Rochester, NY: Lawyers Cooperative Pub., 1990–2014), §1032.

84. As in LH 120, one party makes a declaration before the god (*maḫar ilim *burru*), and the guilty party must pay double compensation (*uštašannāma ana … inaddin*). It likewise evokes LH 125 with its reference to lost property (**mimmâ ḫalāqu*). A thematic connection further links together LH 125 with LH 126; whereas LH 125 ends by stating that the owner may (legitimately) continue to search for his property, LH 126 begins with a person who illegitimately searches for "lost" property.

85. See especially Bernard S. Jackson, "Modelling Biblical Law: The Covenant Code," *Chicago-Kent Law Review* 70 (1995): 1745–1827, here 1815 n. 166; cf. also Driver and Miles, *Babylonian Laws*, 1:245.

Old Babylonian law collections, for example, attribute to the city quarter a number of roles: notifying an owner that their ox is a gorer (LE 54; LH 251), their dog is vicious (LH 56), or their wall is buckling (LE 58); and investigating a case where a woman repudiates her husband (LH 142). Legal documents further suggest that the city quarter was a place for transactions and judgment.[86] The city quarter appears to have been an administrative body with a variety of municipal and judicial functions, but there is no reason to associate the city quarter with the temple per se.[87]

The inclusion of the city quarter in LH 126 further signifies a departure from the previous laws. Whereas LH 120–125 speak of deposit of personal property in a private person's home, LH 126 introduces the notion of a public body. Is there any connection between this public body and the law of deposit? When read on its own, without the assumption of a deposit-related context, LH 126 appears plainly to relate to a false claim of lost property. A person has not lost property but, wishing to exploit the city quarter, falsely accuses it. Although LH 126 does not elucidate the content of this accusation, other cuneiform laws offer illuminating information about the roles of public bodies in connection with lost property. The Laws of Eshnunna, for example, require a variety of governmental officials to bring lost property to the city of Eshnunna. If an official evades this responsibility and instead keeps the lost property in his house for over a month, the palace may charge him with theft.[88] According to the Hittite Laws, a person who finds a lost animal must bring it to the king's gate or to the local elders. The law allows the finder to use the animal until the owner comes for it, indicating that, when the finder brings the animal to the king's gate or elders, the finder does so in order to create a record of the lost property, but not to leave the property there. By reporting the lost property to the proper authorities, the finder prevents the possibility that the owner could successfully bring charges against the finder for theft in the future.[89]

---

86. See, e.g., BE 6.1 103:33, *RA* 25 43:5; BE 6.2 58:2; CT 2 1:24.

87. For discussion of the city quarter, including its administrative and possibly kinship-related character, see Elizabeth C. Stone, *Nippur Neighborhoods*, SAOC 44 (Chicago: Oriental Institute of the University of Chicago, 1987), 4–6. Note also examples of various officials of the city quarter in the OB period (see *CAD* B, s.v. "*babtu*"), which further support an administrative rather than temple context.

88. LE 50: "If a military governor, a governor of the canal system, or any person in a position of authority seizes a fugitive slave, fugitive slave woman, stray ox, or stray donkey belonging either to the palace or to a commoner, and does not lead it to Eshnunna but detains it in his house and allows more than one month to elapse, the palace shall bring a charge of theft against him" (translated by Roth, *Law Collections*, 66–67).

89. HL 71: "If anyone finds an ox, a horse, or a mule, he shall drive it to the king's gate. If he finds it in the country, they shall present it to the elders. The finder shall harness it (i.e., use it while it is in his custody). When its owner finds it, he shall take it in full, but he shall not have the finder arrested as a thief. But if the finder does not present it to the elders, he

LH 126 may reflect a similar background to these laws.[90] One role of the city quarter as a municipal body may have been to maintain a record of all lost property that had been found, and perhaps even to involve itself in the process of finding the owner. This capacity of the city quarter could have opened it up to accusations of misconduct, such as abusing its authority so as to misappropriate the property, neglecting to add the property to an official registry, or not doing its due diligence in locating the owner. Because such claims might be impossible to substantiate through usual means, leaving the city quarter open to exploitation, the law allows the city quarter to establish via a cultic procedure that the accuser has not truly lost any property, and requires the false accuser to pay double compensation to the accused.

Like the Covenant Code, according to this interpretation, the Laws of Hammurabi collocate a law pertaining to lost property with laws of bailment. However, whereas Exod 22 centrally embeds a reference to lost property within the law of bailment, the Laws of Hammurabi treat lost property at the very end of a series of bailment laws.[91] As noted earlier, LH

---

shall be considered a thief" (translated by Hoffner, in Roth, *Law Collections*, 227). For this law, see further David L. Baker, "Finders Keepers? Lost Property in Ancient Near Eastern and Biblical Law," *BBR* 17 (2007): 207–14, here 210. Note that HL 45 treats the finder of lost goods differently: "If anyone finds implements, [he shall bring] them back to their owner. He (the owner) will reward him. But if the finder does not give them (back), he shall be considered a thief" (translated by Hoffner, in Roth, *Law Collections*, 223). A later version of HL combines 45 and 71, eliminating the role of local authorities while adding a role for witnesses who can testify that the finder found the lost property and is maintaining custody until the owner surfaces.

90. Rabbinic literature similarly reflects the involvement of public institutions when property has been found, but in a different manner. A finder bore the responsibility of announcing that he had found the property, originally at the Temple during the Three Festivals, when all of Israel would congregate in Jerusalem; in the synagogues and academies after the destruction of the Temple; and quietly among neighbors and acquaintances once it became dangerous to do otherwise (see t. B. Meṣ. 2:6; m. B. Meṣ. 2:6; b. B. Meṣ. 28b). Officials at the institution (the Temple, synagogue, etc.) thus were not themselves apparently involved in the process related to found property, but the institution served as a setting for a public proclamation, requiring the finder to proclaim publicly what he had found. As Samuel Greengus notes (*Laws in the Bible and in Early Rabbinic Collections: The Legal Legacy of the Ancient Near East* [Eugene, OR: Cascade, 2011], 234), Tg. Pseudo-Jonathan adds a provision regarding a public proclamation to the law in Deut 22:3 about a person who finds a stray animal. However, I disagree with Greengus's translation, "you (the finder) shall have (the herald) announce it (as being found)," which introduces a public official into the mix. The Aramaic אכריז עלה most likely means "(you) announce it" (imperative) rather than "you shall have (so-and-so) announce it."

91. In fact, one finds in LH nearly the opposite of what we have described in the Covenant Code. LH 6–8 treat a number of theft scenarios, among which a reference to bailment is embedded (see LH 7: the man who accepts property *ana maṣṣarūtim* ["for safekeeping"] from a "son of a man" or a man's slave, without witnesses or contractual stipulations, is considered a thief); these laws are followed by LH 9–13, whose main interest is lost property

126 is closely bound up with the deposit law in LH 120–125 through similarities in language and theme. LH 126, however, also bears thematic connections with the law that follows it. LH 127 treats a person who causes someone to be accused but cannot bring proof, thereby linking it with 126 through the topic of unsubstantiated accusation. LH 126 thus forms a bridge between the preceding and subsequent laws, serving the dual function of bookend to the deposit laws and segue into the topic that follows.[92]

The drafters of the Laws of Hammurabi may have considered LH 126 a part of the same broader topic as LH 120–125. However, whereas a notion of lost property as bailment appears to inhere in Exod 22, the Laws of Hammurabi present challenges to reaching the same conclusion. In addition to treating lost property at the end of the deposit law rather than at its center, LH 126 considers specifically the theoretical guilt of the city quarter responsible for recording the found property (and perhaps involved in its return). LH 126 does not, however, treat the finder of the lost property, the more obvious candidate for an involuntary bailor. While in modern legal thought, a lost property scenario falls under the umbrella of bailment, and despite the drafters' collocation of lost property with a law of deposit, there is insufficient evidence to conclude that the drafters of the Laws of Hammurabi would have thought of the owner and finder of lost property as (involuntary) bailor and bailee.[93] In this regard, the Laws of Hammurabi and biblical law differ from one another.

A Failed "Involuntary Bailment"

Although biblical law legitimizes one kind of involuntary bailment, the narrative of Nabal and David in 1 Sam 25 presents another would-be involuntary bailment that it rejects as unjust. David and his crew provide protection to a group of shepherds, without arranging to do so with their employer, Nabal. When David hears that Nabal is shearing his sheep, he sends men to him to request payment for the services they rendered.

(related to LH 6–8 through issues of theft). In both the Covenant Code and LH, then, the legal topics of theft, bailment, and lost property are closely intertwined but are mapped out differently.

92. For the bridge function in ancient Near Eastern and biblical law, see Eichler, "Literary Structure in the Laws of Eshnunna," 71–84; Eichler, "Exodus 21:22–25 Revisited: Methodological Considerations," in *Birkat Shalom: Studies in the Bible, Ancient Near Eastern Literature, and Postbiblical Judaism Presented to Shalom M. Paul on the Occasion of His Seventieth Birthday,* ed. Chaim Cohen et al. (Winona Lake, IN: Eisenbrauns, 2008), 11–29.

93. On the other hand, if the city quarter functioned as an institutional lost and found, where a finder would have deposited lost property, then the city quarter effectively would have stood in as bailee. Without any evidence attributing this role to the city quarter, however, we cannot make such a determination.

Nabal laughs them off, sparking David's ire to the point where the latter nearly massacres Nabal's household. Through the intervention of Nabal's shepherds, Nabal's wife Abigail learns of David's actions and placates him in time to prevent bloodshed.

A number of scholars have compared David's actions in 1 Sam 25 to protection racketeering—providing security outside of the law, often through threats and violence, while intimidating the clients themselves into the arrangement.[94] While the comparison to protection racketeering is apt, the narrative also portrays David as attempting to bully Nabal into an involuntary bailment after-the-fact. First, David sends a delegation to Nabal to request compensation during the shearing of the flock animals (1 Sam 25:2). As demonstrated in the context of Jacob and Laban, shearing was the time during the herding cycle when contracts from the previous year expired, accounts were settled, and new contracts drawn up.[95] David inserts himself into this period of account settling as if his bailment were legitimate, like that of a shepherd with a contract. Nabal refuses to give in: "Who is David? Who is the son of Jesse? These days there are many slaves breaking away from their masters" (1 Sam 25:10). Notwithstanding the political implications of this response, Nabal's claim of "not knowing" David also underscores that the two have never contracted together; his reference to slaves and masters further insinuates that they have no professional relationship.[96] David and his men provided the following services: they did not harm the shepherds—indeed a feature of protection racketeers (1 Sam 25:7, 15).[97] The shepherds lost nothing while David's men were with them (1 Sam 25:7, 15, 21). Finally, David's crew acted like a protective wall day and night for the duration of their shepherding (1 Sam 25:7, 16). Their protection thus prevented any losses due to theft, capture, straying, or predation: no animal or person could leave or enter

---

94. See, e.g., Baruch Halpern, *David's Secret Demons: Messiah, Murderer, Traitor, King,* Bible in Its World (Grand Rapids: Eerdmans, 2001), 22; Jacob L. Wright, *David, King of Israel, and Caleb in Biblical Memory* (New York: Cambridge University Press, 2014), 204; Joel S. Baden, *The Historical David: The Real Life of an Invented Hero* (New York: HarperCollins, 2013), 12. Robert Alter hedges: "there is a certain ambiguity as to whether David was providing protection out of sheer good will or conducting a protection racket in order to get the necessary provisions for his guerilla band" (*The David Story: A Translation with Commentary of 1 and 2 Samuel* [New York: Norton, 1999], 153).

95. In fact, the David-Nabal narrative bears numerous linguistic and thematic connections to the Jacob-Laban story; see Mark E. Biddle, "Ancestral Motifs in 1 Samuel 25: Intertextuality and Characterization," *JBL* 121 (2002): 617–38.

96. For a political reading of this verse, see especially Jon D. Levenson, "1 Samuel 25 as Literature and as History," *CBQ* 40 (1978): 11–28; Jon D. Levenson and Baruch Halpern, "The Political Import of David's Marriages," *JBL* 99 (1980): 507–18, here 512–13.

97. I understand the verb הֶכְלִים* as "harm" rather than "humiliate," similar to its use in Judg 18:7, where it contrasts with security from enemies.

the premises under their watchful eye.[98] Moreover, David laments having watched Nabal's possessions for naught (1 Sam 7:21), using the same root (*š-m-r*) as Exod 22:6, 9.

Despite having forced his services upon Nabal's shepherds—as indicated by the purported virtue of having refrained from harming them—David attempts to pass off as a kind of bailee-shepherd, who comes to settle accounts at the shearing, watches over the owner's possessions, and prevents losses from the flock during the day and night. He acts as a bailee, without having ever communicated with Nabal (whom he sees as the bailor); in essence, then, David seeks to create an involuntary bailment, from which he expects to benefit. Ultimately, David receives compensation in the form of lavish gifts from Abigail. But the narrator—while hardly painting Nabal in a positive light—frowns upon David's strong-arming. Even Nabal's shepherds, when describing David's generosity toward them, do so in terror of what David and his men might do to retaliate (1 Sam 25:17). The primary goal of 1 Sam 25 does not relate to bailment, but the narrative still offers a perspective on the institution, critiquing David's unorthodox practice as flawed. Against those who might wish to force a retroactive bailment upon another person by performing the services of a bailee, 1 Sam 25 warns that this practice is corrupt and that such a "bailee" deserves no compensation. While Exod 22 places lost property under the umbrella of bailments that it considers and implicitly condones, 1 Sam 25 explores what it means for a bailment to be involuntary, and when the extent to which it is involuntary ought to render that bailment invalid.

Animal Borrowing and Rental

Following the law of herding, Exod 22:13–14 addresses a case that scholars have interpreted as pertaining to the borrowing or rental, or both the borrowing and rental, of animals:[99]

---

98. The reference to protection during the day and night echoes Jacob's reference to daytime and nighttime theft, especially in light of the many affinities between these two narratives.

99. For a reading of this law as pertaining exclusively to animal borrowing, see, e.g., Jackson, *Wisdom-Laws*, 360–62. For the view that verses 13–14 pertain to rental alone, see Martin Noth, *Exodus: A Commentary*, trans. John S. Bowden, OTL (Philadelphia: Westminster, 1962), 184–85; Westbrook, "Deposit Law," 371, referring to the "hirer" in verse 13; Rothenbusch, *Die kasuistische Rechtssammlung*, 359–61. Scholars who read the law as relating both to borrowing and rental include Cassuto, *Commentary on the Book of Exodus*, 288; Joe M. Sprinkle, *"The Book of the Covenant": A Literary Approach*, JSOTSup 174 (Sheffield: JSOT Press, 1994), 155; Cornelis Houtman, *Exodus*, 4 vols., HCOT (Kampen: Kok, 1993–2002), 3:205;

וכי ישאל איש מעם רעהו ונשבר או מת בעליו אין עמו שלם ישלם אם בעליו עמו
לא ישלם אם שכיר הוא בא בשכרו

[13]When a man borrows from another (an animal) and it is injured or dies without its owner present, he must pay. [14]If its owner is with it, he shall not pay. If it is rented, he is liable for its rental fee.

While no animal is mentioned, the options for what can go wrong—injury and death—indicate that, like the verses that immediately precede them, verses 13–14 refer to an animal.[100] As my translation indicates, I understand these verses as referring both to animal borrowing and rental,[101] reading the root *š-ʾ-l* in verse 13 with its typical meaning of "borrow" and interpreting the שכיר in verse 14 as a "rented" animal.[102] Biblical law offers almost no information about the formation of these arrangements. However, logic dictates that one would borrow or rent an animal for the purpose of labor, and indeed, cuneiform law collections and Mesopotamian legal documents attest to the widespread practice of renting animals, especially oxen, for this reason.[103]

Who might engage in animal borrowing or rental, and why?[104] While

---

David L. Baker, "Safekeeping, Borrowing, and Rental," *JSOT* 31 (2006): 27–42; Wright, *Inventing God's Law*, 276–79.

100. For *š-b-r* applied to animals, see, e.g., Ezek 34:4, 16; Zech 11:16; Dan 8:7–8; and see examples of the Akkadian cognate in *CAD* Š/2, s.v. "*šeberu*." While the root *š-b-r* could also be used with an object, its collocation with *m-w-t* ("die") indicates that, like Exod 22:9–12, verses 13–14 have animals in mind.

101. I disagree with Rothenbusch's argument (*Die kasuistische Rechtssammlung*, 360) that the usual root referring to rental (*ś-k-r*) occurs only in contexts of hiring people, to the exclusion of animals, and therefore, *š-ʾ-l* (the root used in v. 13) may refer to "borrowing" when an animal is its object. First, the root *ś-k-r* modifies an inanimate object in at least one place (Isa 7:20; cf. 1 Chr 19:6–7), indicating that its objects are not limited to people. Moreover, Zech 8:10 offers a possible reference to animal hire, albeit from a later period: "there was no wage [*ś-k-r*] for man or any wage [*ś-k-r*] for beast" (RSV). Even if one excludes this example, due to an alternate interpretation of the verse or to its relatively late date, Rothenbusch's claim remains problematic: in the absence of other references either to borrowing (*š-ʾ-l*) or renting (*ś-k-r*) animals, why should the term that normally refers to borrowing refer to rental in Exod 22:13?

102. For a thorough overview of possible interpretations of this word and of verse 14 in full, see Wright, *Inventing God's Law*, 276–78. I accept Wright's conclusions regarding the translation of this verse.

103. For an overview and sources, see especially Martha T. Roth, "The Scholastic Exercise 'Laws about Rented Oxen,'" *JCS* 32 (1980): 127–46; Baker, "Safekeeping, Borrowing, and Rental," 27–42.

104. One further possibility for understanding the nature of "animal borrowing" is that the law envisions a transaction closer to animal sharing. Such arrangements, attested in Judean exilic settlements in Babylonia during a later period (for which see Cornelia Wunsch, "Glimpses on the Lives of Deportees in Rural Babylonia," in *Arameans, Chaldeans, and Arabs in Babylonia and Palestine in the First Millennium B.C.*, ed. Angelika Berlejung and Michael P. Streck, LAOS 3 (Wiesbaden: Harrassowitz, 2013), 247–60, here 254–57; especially JWB 26,

one might assume that the law envisions specifically a poor person borrowing or renting from a wealthy animal owner,[105] a variety of reasons unrelated to socioeconomic status might cause someone to borrow or rent an animal for a temporary period: The borrower or renter might have a particularly difficult or seasonal task, for which short-term extra animal power is required; a temporary replacement might be needed while an animal heals from an injury; an owner or borrower might have lost an animal and not wish to purchase another while waiting to see if someone might find the animal and return it. Concerns of this kind underlie cattle-sharing arrangements attested in a later period at Āl-Yahūdu. As Cornelia Wunsch has demonstrated, cattle were useful only seasonally and were very expensive to maintain, so individual smallholders frequently could not afford to own even one animal. Even wealthy institutions would not always have enough cattle to fulfill their needs and needed to draw on other sources.[106] In the absence of any allusion to the socioeconomic status of the borrower or renter in Exod 22:13–14, there is no reason to assume that person's poverty.

Although the cuneiform law collections treat only animal rental and not borrowing, legal documents attest to the practice of animal borrowing in the ancient Near East.[107] The combination of rental and borrowing into a single law in the Covenant Code suggests that the law envisions these transactions as fulfilling the same function. Unlike cases of deposit and herding, in animal borrowing and rental bailees do not perform a service for the benefit of owners but use the property of an owner to serve their own needs, which likely would involve seasonal agricultural labor.

IMMP 30, IMMP 76), could involve an original owner who gives an animal to a second person for sharing. The original owner acts as silent partner, while the second person becomes the active partner who is responsible for maintaining the animal (with duties including its safekeeping). The two partners share the profits equally and are equally responsible for losses. If Exod 22:13–14 has in mind such an arrangement, it would differ from a Judean Babylonian arrangement in determining liability based on whether the owner—presumably the original owner, the silent partner—is present at the time something goes wrong. Such an interpretation would make sense of the criterion of the owner's presence: the owner might be present because the owner is a partner with a stake in the labor the animal performs. I prefer, however, to maintain a simple interpretation of "borrowing" in these verses to maintain fidelity to the usual use of Biblical Hebrew š-ʾ-l and because there are no further clues within the biblical text to elevate this interpretation from the realm of conjecture.

105. For this view, see Baker, "Safekeeping, Borrowing, and Rental," 35–39.

106. Wunsch, "Glimpses on the Lives of Deportees," 254–55.

107. Mesopotamian laws pertaining to rental of oxen include FLP 1287, YOS 1 28, Ai IV Appendix, LL 34–37, and LH 244–249, all discussed in Roth, "Scholastic Exercise," 127–46; rented animals are likely also the subject of HL 74–75. Legal documents on this topic include, e.g., KAJ 96; YOS 13 17. See also EN 9.2 360, 384, and 455 in M. A. Morrison, *The Eastern Archives of Nuzi*, SCCNH 4.1 (Winona Lake, IN: Eisenbrauns, 1993), pp. 61, 107 n. 59, 79; and see discussion on pp. 104–9; cf. Neo-Assyrian loans of animals noted by Baker, "Safekeeping, Borrowing, and Rental," 37–38 n. 29.

The Creation of Bailments

Exodus 22 groups together four bailment scenarios: the deposit of goods, herding, animal borrowing, and animal rental. Although the law itself is silent regarding who might create such arrangements, how they might go about doing so, and why they would do so in the first place, biblical narrative and documents from Mesopotamia help us reconstruct a much fuller picture of what bailments could have looked like. Bailments could occur in a number of settings: biblical and cuneiform laws refer to arrangements in the private home or homestead (בית, *bītum*) of the bailee (Exod 22:6; LH 120–121, 125). 2 Kings 5:24 also names the place of Gehazi's bailment as a בית, although the nature of this space is left vague. A number of ancient Near Eastern legal documents locate bailments in the homes of the bailees: HSS 9 108, a trial record, refers to Zigi depositing his property in the home of Ilani, and CT 6 35b records the storage of barley in the home of two bailees.[108] MVAG 35.3 330, an Old Assyrian trial record that shares the perspective of a witness to the original bailment, quotes the bailor's statement to the bailee that his sealed property "should be (kept as) a deposit in [the bailee's] house" (*ana maṣṣartim ina bītika libši*).

Biblical narrative and ancient Near Eastern texts suggest many possibilities, beyond the home, for where bailments might take place in practice. The David narrative in particular points to the role of bailments in wartime, when a person could fulfill the requirements of military service by watching the possessions of soldiers at the battlefront. Mesopotamian texts also indicate that the inn was a site for deposits, whether the bailee is the innkeeper or a traveler.[109] Moreover, transportation bailments involved the property traveling on or with the person of the bailee, rather than a deposit in a single stationary location.

Whereas the law collections do not address the *why* of bailment—why would a person give property to a bailee?—narrative and practice texts help fill this gap. Bailments served multiple functions in an agriculture-centered economy, with flock-owners hiring shepherds on an annual contractual basis, shepherds requiring bailees to watch their property during the migratory season, and owners of draft animals lending or renting them out for seasonal labor. A person might require a bailee while traveling to visit family or for work. Soldiers entering a combat zone might require storage of their possessions. The need for a bailee to store posses-

---

108. For this text, see Schorr, *Urkunden des altbabylonischen Zivil- und Prozessrechts*, 74.

109. Evidence includes LE 36's characterization of the bailee as a *napṭaru*; a reference to innkeepers (*sābû*) as bailees in CT 52 183; and AT 119, in which a bailee embezzles property that was bailed to him during the nighttime and possibly was staying at an inn as well.

sions might arise over the course of travel,[110] or when someone wished to hide property. The largely commercial and administrative contexts of deposits in the ancient Near East—relating to scenarios including business ventures, taxes owed, problems with creditors, sales on credit, sequestration, and bailments for transportation—find no parallel in the Bible, but this absence signifies nothing more than the regrettable unavailability of evidence.

In a typical situation, the bailee receiving property—for whatever reason—would meet the agreed-upon obligations and then return the property to its owner at a designated time. The law, however, is less interested in the typical than in the unexpected: What happens when something goes wrong? The next chapter explores this question.

---

110. See AbB 9 117.

2

When Bailments Go Awry

L ike many biblical and ancient Near Eastern texts, the bailment law in Exod 22 is formulated casuistically, with a sequence of conditional statements that set up a case and then explore what happens when something goes wrong.[1] The law is interested both in what might go wrong and, in some cases, in how it goes wrong. Thus, the law treats a range of mishaps—theft of deposited goods; death, injury, capture, predation, and theft of animals entrusted to a shepherd; and death and injury of borrowed and rented animals—while also considering whether some of these mishaps stemmed from fraud, negligence, or an "act of God" beyond the range of human fault. This chapter will focus on mishaps mentioned in the contexts of deposits and herding, without specifically addressing animal borrowing and rental, because of overlap between the scenarios considered in these cases and in herding.

Theft of Deposited Goods

The biblical law of bailment opens with the following case: One person (the bailor) gives money or goods to another person (the bailee) to watch, but the property is stolen from the bailee's house (Exod 22:6). When verse 6 states that the property "is stolen from the man's house" (וגנב מבית האיש), does it relay a fact or a claim? Although Bernard Jackson has pointed to this verse as an example of "[biblical] law … [formulating] a claim as a fact," Assnat Bartor has argued that the text presents objective information "from the wide perspective of the omniscient lawgiver."[2] In her view, v. 6 does not reflect a claim of one party but a statement of fact that a thief

---

1. The casuistic form is not limited to law collections but occurs in other "scientific" texts such as omen literature and medical texts. See Jean Bottéro, "Le 'Code' de Hammu-rabi," *Annali della Scola Normale Superiore di Pisa* 12 (1982): 409–44.

2. Jackson, *Wisdom-Laws*, 340 (and see n. 45 there); Assnat Bartor, "The Representation of Speech in the Casuistic Laws of the Pentateuch: The Phenomenon of Combined Discourse," *JBL* 126 (2007): 231–49, here 235, 244.

has stolen the property, which contrasts with the limited perspective of humans, who must resort to a cultic procedure in order to ascertain the truth.[3] The definite article -ה prefixed to the word גנב ("the thief") in the following verse offers further evidence of the fact of theft. Though the thief's identity may not be known (because "the thief is not found"), there is an actual thief to speak of; a theft has indeed occurred.

When a thief is identified, that thief must pay double compensation to the owner (Exod 22:6). When no thief is located, however, the bailee undergoes a cultic judicial procedure to determine אם לא שלח ידו במלאכת רעהו—if the bailee had committed a particular action, designated by the words שלח ידו (literally, "laid his hand"), with respect to the other person's property. Judicial procedures and penalties will receive further attention in chapter 3. At this juncture, I wish to focus on the nature of the transgression that the bailee might commit, which requires elucidation of the words שלח ידו in Exod 22:7 (and again in 22:10). Is the bailee suspected of having stolen the property—the premise of AT 119, a tablet from Alalakh, in which a witness testifies that a bailee stole from a container of barley entrusted to him?[4] Or is the bailee accused of having committed some other wrongdoing that renders the bailee accountable for theft by a different person? In contrast to previous interpretations, which largely understand the alleged wrongdoing of the bailee as one of theft, I will demonstrate that these words are an idiom for negligence, such that we ought to translate this part of the verse: "if he had not behaved negligently toward the other's property."[5] It makes sense, then, that the law would

---

3. Bartor, "Representation of Speech," 244.

4. For the most up-to-date reading of AT 119, see Jacob Lauinger, *Following the Man of Yamhad: Settlement and Territory at Old Babylonian Alalah*, CHANE 75 (Leiden: Brill, 2015), 97 n. 53 (translation), 348–50 (transliteration and commentary). Ignacio Márquez Rowe characterizes the text as written testimony ("Anatolia and the Levant: Alalakh," in Westbrook, *History of Ancient Near Eastern Law*, 1:693–717, here 702).

5. For previous interpretations, see Wright, *Inventing God's Law*, 242 (for v. 7), 266 (for v. 10); and cf. David Daube, "Negligence in the Early Talmudic Law of Contract (*Peshiʿah*)," in *Festschrift Fritz Schulz*, ed. H. Niedermeyer and W. Flume (Weimar: H. Böhlaus Nachfolger, 1951), 1:124–47, here 127–28. JPS translates פשע in verse 8 as "misappropriation," and various discussions of verse 7 describe the wrong envisioned there as misappropriation or theft. See, e.g., Noth, *Exodus*, 184; Brevard S. Childs, *The Book of Exodus: A Critical, Theological Commentary*, OTL (Philadelphia: Westminster, 1974), 475–77; Otto, "Die rechtshistorische Entwicklung," 152–54; Otto, *Wandel der Rechtsbegründungen in der Gesellschaftsgeschichte des antiken Israel: Eine Rechtsgeschichte des "Bundesbuches" Ex XX 22–XXIII 13*, Studia Biblica 3 (Leiden: Brill, 1988), 17; Westbrook, "Deposit Law," 363. See also Sprinkle, who does not maintain a hand idiom in translation ("trespass") but interprets similarly: "the bailee swears … that he did not 'trespass against his fellow's property', that is, he did not steal it" (*Book of the Covenant*, 150). Jackson uses the term conversion to describe the action denoted by the verbal expression שלח ידו ב-, which effectively refers to the same kind of malfeasance envisioned by the above commentaries (*Studies in the Semiotics of Biblical Law*, 95). See Garner, *Black's Law Dictionary*, s.v. "conversion": "The wrongful possession or disposition of anoth-

present the occurrence of theft as a statement of fact, rather than as the claim of a bailee who is suspected of having committed theft. At stake is not whether a theft took place, but rather whether the bailee (however wittingly) opened the door to theft.

Negligence: A New Interpretation

The expression in question, שלח ידו, occurs both in this subsection of the law regarding stolen goods and silver (in Exod 22:7) and in the following subsection regarding a case where an animal has suffered death, injury, or capture (in Exod 22:10). This verbal idiom, which here refers to the bailee's alleged transgression, occurs frequently in Biblical Hebrew. Paul Humbert has identified several nuances that the phrase encapsulates, the most common of which is an aggressive sense of grabbing or seizing something by force; it generally refers to some physical, often hostile act.[6] The idiom takes both divine and human subjects and may or may not connote violence. This section will revisit the meaning of שלח ידו, questioning whether previous interpretations of the idiom fit in the context of this law. Drawing on contextual, linguistic, and comparative evidence, I will argue that שלח ידו bears a legal valence in addition to its usual nonlegal senses.

A translation of שלח ידו that yields a coherent passage must fit with the legal contexts of both the deposit of goods and animal herding. For this reason, one cannot translate שלח ידו simply as "to touch": the duties of a bailee of goods might never require the bailee to touch those goods—and,

---

er's property as if it were one's own; an act or series of acts of willful interference, without lawful justification, with an item of property in a manner inconsistent with another's right, whereby that other person is deprived of the use and possession of the property."

Note also the language of Philo of Alexandria, who likewise identifies the alleged wrongdoing of the bailee as deliberate theft or involvement in theft but perhaps draws on שלח ידו in his depiction of the bailee who "must go of his own freewill to the court of God and with hands stretched out to heaven swear under the pain of his own perdition that he has not embezzled any part of the deposit nor abetted another in so doing nor joined at all in inventing a theft which never took place" (Philo, *Spec.* 4.34; trans. Colson LCL; cited by Greengus, *Laws in the Bible*, 188 n. 2).

6. Paul Humbert, "'Étendre la main' (Note de lexicographie hébraïque)," *VT* 12 (1962): 383–95. The idiomatic or metaphoric use of the hand, like many other body parts, is a productive phenomenon cross-linguistically. For a cognitive linguistics account of hand idioms in English—a number of which have parallels in Hebrew and other Semitic languages—see Zoltán Kövecses, *Metaphor: A Practical Introduction* (New York: Oxford University Press, 2002), 207–11. On the prevalence and nature of idioms with body parts in Semitic languages, see Edward L. Greenstein, "Trans-Semitic Idiomatic Equivalency and the Derivation of Hebrew *mlʔkh*," *UF* 11 (1979): 329–36, here 331; Greenstein also gives examples of similar hand idioms in BH and Akkadian (331).

indeed, might even forbid the bailee from doing so. The most basic tasks of the bailee of animals, however, demand physical involvement in the care of those animals.

Biblical translations normally render שלח ידו as "laid his hands" (or similar), maintaining the hand idiom of the original Biblical Hebrew.[7] David Wright's translation, "misappropriated," makes explicit the view of various scholars who maintain an idiomatic translation but go on to describe the crux of the case imagined by verse 7 as whether it was the bailee—and not some third-party thief—who stole the property.[8] That is, according to this reading, if a thief is not found, the bailee falls under suspicion of having secreted away the property and then claiming that someone else must have stolen it. While legal parlance differentiates between misappropriation and theft, scholars who describe the wrongdoing in these verses as misappropriation do so with the understanding that the bailee is suspected of stealing.[9] The choice of most scholars to preserve the idiom שלח ידו in translation (i.e., "lay/put his hand"), rather than translate "misappropriated," as Wright does, likely results from the need to translate the phrase identically in verse 7 and in verse 10, where a translation relating to theft clashes with the context. The bailee in that scenario stands accused of wrongdoing in the case of the bailed animal's death, capture, or injury, of which only capture may be construed as related to theft—and, indeed, animal theft is treated separately in Exod 22:11.[10]

Scholars have suggested a number of ways to resolve the apparent incompatibility of שלח ידו with death and injury. Horst Seebass, for example, interprets the idiom more generally (than misappropriation or theft) as doing anything—whether through ineptitude or malice—that brings about any harm to the bailed animal.[11] Joe Sprinkle similarly views שלח ידו as a broad term, which he translates as "trespass" but interprets as theft in verse 7 and as either negligence (for death or injury) or fraud (for capture) in verse 10.[12] Both Seebass and Sprinkle view שלח ידו as an idiom for committing any sort of wrongdoing, lumping together negligence with inten-

---

7. See, e.g., NJPS, NRSV, NIV, and similarly "put his hand" in KJV.

8. See Wright, *Inventing God's Law*, 242 (for v. 7), 266 (for v. 10).

9. I follow the definitions found in Garner, *Black's Law Dictionary*, s.v. "misappropriation" and "theft." Misappropriation denotes the "application of another's property or money dishonestly to one's own use," which does not necessarily entail permanently depriving the owner of his or her property, as theft does. To put it another way, misappropriation does not entail theft, but theft entails misappropriation. In a sense, then, theft is a "harsher" term than misappropriation. For the interchangeable use of these terms in discussions of these laws, see, e.g., Westbrook, "Deposit Law," 363; and see my discussion of Westbrook's interpretation of verse 10 below.

10. See, e.g., Schwienhorst-Schönberger, *Das Bundesbuch*, 196–200; Seebass, "Noch einmal zum Depositenrecht," 22–23; and see Westbrook, "Deposit Law," 370–77.

11. Seebass, "Noch einmal zum Depositenrecht," 23.

12. Sprinkle, *Book of the Covenant*, 149–50.

tional harm. While the Bible does not label its laws pertaining to negligence as such, Mesopotamian law is rife with references to negligence, and scholars have long recognized negligence as a distinct mode of transgression in biblical law.[13] Seebass's and Sprinkle's grouping together of deliberate transgression with negligence ignores this distinction inherent in biblical law.

Raymond Westbrook understands שלח ידו as a reference to deliberate breach of contract through misappropriation[14] and points to the distinction between the bailee and the hirer of animals in order to reconcile the use of this expression with death and injury.[15] The hirer pays to use the animal for personal benefit; the bailee, on the other hand, watches the animal for the benefit of the bailor. The hirer is liable for death or injury to the animal during the period of hire because such risks naturally accompany the hirer's use of the animal. The law holds the bailee, on the other hand, to a lower standard, exempting the bailee from liability for death or injury—unless the bailee has appropriated the animal for personal use, in which case the same risks that apply to the hirer apply to the bailee as well.

Westbrook's analysis of שלח ידו in verse 10 thus distinguishes between the wrong committed by the bailee (misappropriation) and the ensuing event for which the bailee is then liable (death, injury, or capture).[16] He defines the wrongdoing of the bailee reflected by שלח ידו in both verse 7 and verse 10 as misappropriation. Yet this reading is inconsistent: In verse 7, the bailee seeks to defeat a charge of misappropriating (i.e., *stealing*) the bailed item; in verse 10, the bailee seeks to defeat a charge of misappropriating (i.e., *illicitly using*) the bailed animal. In order to read שלח ידו consistently in the pericope, while resolving the contextual problems of verses 9–10 as Westbrook does, one would have to understand verse 7 as follows: The bailee seeks to be cleared of illicit use of the items bailed, which were subsequently stolen by a third-party thief who has not been found. In this reading, the crux of the law in verses 6–7 is not whether the bailee is the

---

13. On Akkadian idioms for negligence, see A. Leo Oppenheim, "Idiomatic Accadian (Lexicographical Researches)," *JAOS* 61 (1941): 251–71; on negligence in biblical law, see, e.g., F. Charles Fensham, "Liability in Case of Negligence in the Old Testament Covenant Code and Ancient Legal Traditions," in *Essays in Honour of Ben Beinart: Jura Legesque Antiquiores necnon Recentiores*, ed. Wouter De Vos, 3 vols., *Acta Juridica*, 1976–1978 (Cape Town: Juta, 1979), 1:283–94; Wright, *Inventing God's Law*, 41–42, 213–18; Barmash, *Homicide in the Biblical World*, 140. For an example of a biblical law pertaining to negligence, see Exod 21:33–34, concerning the liability of the owner or digger of a pit who fails to cover it.

14. Westbrook, "Deposit Law," 363.

15. Note that Westbrook considers the subject of verse 13 a hirer, who pays the animal's owner in order to use it, rather than a borrower. See Westbrook, "Deposit Law," 371.

16. For a similar understanding, see Rashi on verse 10; Nahmanides on verse 7; and compare their language to b. B. Qam. 105b. See also m. B. Meṣ. 3:12 and its talmudic follow-up in t. B. Meṣ 43a–b for rabbinic discussion of the term שלח ידו and the kinds of action that constitute illicit use.

thief but whether the bailee illicitly used the goods, such that the bailee becomes liable for theft regardless of whether the bailee is the thief. The difference between verse 7 and verse 6 would remain that if the thief is found, the thief pays double—and only then the bailee is exempt from payment. Otherwise, the bailee is liable for theft—even by a third party— because the bailee illicitly used the goods while under the bailee's care.

While Westbrook's interpretation, or a modification thereof (as just delineated), indeed resolves the problem of how שלח ידו fits with death and injury, it creates an unnecessary complication: one would expect the bailee's alleged wrongdoing to relate more directly to whatever mishap befell the item or animal bailed. The preceding resolution requires an additional step of the bailee becoming liable for the mishap once the obligations of the bailee have been breached by committing a wrongdoing, without that wrongdoing being the direct cause of the mishap per se; presumably, the animal's death, injury, or capture would not need to be the result of the bailee's misappropriation in order to hold the bailee liable.[17] To put this in legal terms, according to this interpretation, the bailee's action is not the proximate cause of the mishap; the death, injury, or capture of the animal was not a reasonably foreseeable consequence of the act of misappropriation. Despite the brevity of the biblical laws, we ought to prefer an explanation that requires a closer connection between the wrongdoing and what goes wrong.[18]

With the exception of those who lump together negligence with deliberate malfeasance, scholars have steered clear of interpreting the wrongdoing of the bailee in Exod 22 as a case of negligence. Based on a consideration of what the bailee's offense could be in context, negligence is a viable candidate in both verse 7 and verse 10; the bailor could suspect

---

17. Westbrook characterizes the distinction between the liability of the shepherd-bailee of verses 9–10 and the hirer (or borrower) of verse 13 as one based on whether the risks of death and injury naturally accompany the shepherd's tasks. In his view, death and injury are not risks that naturally accompany watching an animal (without using it for one's own benefit), whereas they do arise naturally from using the animal for oneself as the hirer/borrower would (371). Yet it seems that death, injury, and capture are natural risks of taking an animal out to graze in the open—something that would surely be within the scope of the bailee-shepherd's responsibilities—and that the difference in liability stems from something other than expected risk (e.g., perhaps that liability correlates to personal gain).

18. On the other hand, under Roman law, the borrower in a *commodatum* arrangement (a gratuitous loan of a material object for use) would be liable for any damage that occurred during unauthorized use of the item loaned, regardless of fault. See Andrew Borkowski and Paul du Plessis, *Textbook on Roman Law*, 3rd ed. (Oxford: Oxford University Press, 2005), 299–300. Although *commodatum* reflects a different situation from the bailment relationships in Exod 22:6–12, the law indicates that, in principle, a sizable gap could separate the illicit act from the wrong for which one can then be held liable. Without further evidence of this phenomenon in biblical or ancient Near Eastern law, however, it is preferable to pursue a more conservative interpretation.

the bailee of negligent behavior allowing for theft in verse 7, or death, injury, or capture in verse 10. Yet some have ruled out this option on linguistic grounds. Westbrook, for example, argues that "the language of the phrase [*šālaḥ yādô*] excludes negligence." Presumably, this is because throughout the Bible שלח יד represents a physical and often aggressive action, whereas negligence indicates, in Westbrook's words, "an omission on the herdsman's part."[19]

If we take a broader look at the Biblical Hebrew root *š-l-ḥ*, we find that it can refer not only to sending or extending in general but also to actions with a specifically projectile or downward orientation. For example, in both the G- and D-stems, *š-l-ḥ* is used of casting arrows[20] or fire.[21] Numerous psalms refer to God reaching down (*š-l-ḥ*) from the skies and sending down (*š-l-ḥ*) various gifts and blessings.[22] The root *š-l-ḥ* occurs in conjunction with other downwardly oriented roots, such as *m-ṭ-r* ("to rain down") and *n-p-l* ("to cause to fall") (Ps 78:23–28). Psalm 147:15–18 likewise collocates the divine actions of "sending down" (*š-l-ḥ*) God's word with various acts of precipitation; as God sends down his word to the earth, he also sends down snow, frost, and hail (cf. Job 5:10). In the D-stem, further examples of downwardly oriented actions include dropping a person down into a pit (Jer 38:6, 11).

In returning to the idiom שלח יד, let us consider that *š-l-ḥ* sometimes carries a connotation of downward or projectile motion. This suggests that, in addition to the better-known literal sense of "reaching out the hand," there may be an alternative literal translation of שלח יד as "cast down or drop the hand." This alternative literal understanding of שלח יד may allow us to identify a new idiomatic understanding of שלח יד as well, based on an Akkadian interdialectal semantic equivalent, namely, the Akkadian phrase *aḫa nadû*. The lack of other attestations of the nonliteral verbal idiom שלח יד in the pentateuchal law corpora validates a search for extrabiblical semantic evidence, despite the prevalence of the idiom in extralegal portions of the Bible.[23] Moreover, in a treatment of the relationship

---

19. Westbrook, "Deposit Law," 371. Compare Daube, who claims that the language is "unambiguous" ("Negligence," 127–28), and Jackson, *Wisdom-Laws*, 340 n. 46: "Negligence on the part of the depositee does not appear to be contemplated by the language of *shalaḥ yād* here."

20. For the G-stem, see, e.g., 2 Sam 22:15, 17 = Pss 18:15, 17; 144:6; in the D-stem, see, e.g., 1 Sam 20:20; Ezek 5:16.

21. For the G-stem, see Lam 1:13; for the D-stem, see Ezek 39:6; Hos 8:14; Amos 1:4, 7, 10, 12; 2:2, 5; for the similar phrase "cast into [*b-*] fire," see Judg 1:8; 15:5; 20:48; 2 Kgs 8:12; Ps 74:7.

22. See, e.g., Pss 57:4; 78:25; 147:15–18; cf. Job 5:10.

23. Excluding Deut 25:11, where the phrase refers quite literally to an action involving the hand (which is consequently cut off as punishment). Because the phrase there is literal, it has no bearing on its figurative idiomatic usage in the Covenant Code.

between legal and lay language, Westbrook demonstrates a semantic phenomenon in which a term develops a legal sense that subverts its usual
meaning. For example, the Akkadian term *ezēbu* ("to leave") occurs in the
context of divorce law in reference to the divorcing husband, while the
ex-wife is the party who must leave; the phrase *ul iballuṭ* (literally, "he
shall not live") could refer to the power of pardon by a ruler or the exercise
of summary justice by either a ruler or a private person.[24] According to
Westbrook,

> Where a phrase functions as a legal idiom, it takes effect within the con-
> fines of a world created by legal rules. Unless the logic of that legal world
> is taken into consideration, it may be difficult to connect the phrase with
> its context; indeed, a literal translation may produce bizarre results.[25]

An exegetical methodology that values legal logic must seriously consider negligence as a candidate for the wrongdoing of the bailee in Exod
22:7 and 10. The availability of an Akkadian linguistic parallel *aḫa nadû*,
as well as the prominence of negligence as an issue in pertinent ancient
Near Eastern laws, likewise validates consideration of this option. The
semantic phenomenon in which the legal use of a phrase diverges from
its lay sense further lends credence to the possibility that יד שלח bears a
legal meaning, "behave negligently," alongside a nearly opposite nonlegal meaning.

Akkadian *aḫa nadû* literally means "to drop the arm" but is widely
attested as an idiom for negligence or generally lax behavior.[26] It occurs
frequently in both legal and extralegal contexts (e.g., letters, wisdom literature) across various periods[27] and is often paired with *egû*, another Akkadian term for negligence.[28] While the verbal idiom *aḫa nadû* and its related
nominal idiom *nīdi aḫi* occur in various contexts, one finds numerous cases
of their collocation with verbs meaning "to guard, watch over." Consider
the following examples, the first of which pertains specifically to bailment
of grain, and all of which include directives to watch and protect without
"dropping the arm":[29]

---

24. Raymond Westbrook, "A Matter of Life and Death," *JANES* 25 (1997): 61–70.

25. Ibid., 65.

26. *CAD* N/1, s.v. "*nadû*" 6; see also Oppenheim, "Idiomatic Accadian," 269.

27. For the idiom *aḫšu iddīma* in a law collection, see LH 44, 53, 55; and see all citations
in *CAD* N/1, s.v. "*nadû*" 6.

28. See, e.g., LH xlvii 9–58—the epilogue to LH in which Hammurabi states, "I have not
been careless [*ul ēgu*] or negligent [*aḫī ul addî*] toward humankind." For this translation, see
Roth, *Law Collections*, 133.

29. Although only one of these examples is clearly identifiable as bailment, one finds
similar instructions in other contexts pertaining to bailment arrangements, which use terms
for negligence other than *aḫa nadû*. For example: "keep [*naṣāru*] that silver in your hand; do

Place into safekeeping 10 sheqels silver worth of dry bran.... Do not be negligent [*nīdi aḫi*] about safeguarding the dry bran (CT 52 183:15–16, 19–20)[30]

I don't neglect [*aḫa nadû*] to watch my body, I am very careful (ARM 10 142:9–11)[31]

[Do] not be negligent about looking after the personnel of the house / and do not be careless [*nīdi aḫi*] about guarding PN (especially) (A 3520:17, 20)[32]

[Do] not grow lax [*nīdi aḫi*] in watching over the house, the boy, and the girl (A 3530:8)[33]

Do not be careless [*nīdi aḫi*] *about* looking after the interests of the house *or about* watching over the house constantly during the night (AbB 9 117:12–16)[34]

The charge not to be negligent, with the language *aḫa nadû*, is thus well attested in contexts of watching.

At first glance, the comparison of *aḫa nadû* with שלח יד might raise doubts: the nouns יד ("hand") and *aḫa* ("arm") do not seem an exact semantic match; one might prefer a parallel between Biblical Hebrew יד and Akkadian *qātu* ("hand") or between Biblical Hebrew זרוע and Akkadian *aḫu* ("arm"). Yet the words יד ("hand") and *aḫu* ("arm") are not too far apart. While one might think of "hand" and "arm" as distinct terms, both Biblical Hebrew and Akkadian blur this distinction, and in fact, hand/arm polysemy is well documented cross-linguistically.[35] With respect to Biblical Hebrew and Akkadian in particular, Biblical Hebrew יד (usually "hand") may refer to the arm, Akkadian *aḫu* (usually "arm") may refer to the hand, and Akkadian *idu* (also usually "arm") is sometimes best translated "hand"

---

not be negligent [*egû*] in guarding [*naṣāru*] the silver" (YOS 2 11:10; translation is that of Greengus, *Laws in the Bible*, 190); "do not be negligent [*šelû*] about guarding [*maṣṣartu*] the dates" (PBS 1/2 43 no.90; translation is my own).

30. See Kraus, AbB 7 183. The translation is my own. Note that *naṣāru* occurs in the Š-stem here.

31. For this translation, see Christian W. Hess, "Oblique Core Arguments in Akkadian," in *Proceedings of the 53e Rencontre Assyriologique Internationale*, vol. 1, *Language in the Ancient Near East*, ed. L. Kogan et al., 2 vols., Babel und Bibel 4, Orientalia et classica 30 (Winona Lake, IN: Eisenbrauns, 2010), 729–49, here 735.

32. See translation in *CAD* N/2, s.v. "*naṣāru*."

33. Ibid.

34. For this translation, see Stol, *Letters from Yale*, 77.

35. See Stanley R. Witkowski and Cecil H. Brown, "Climate, Clothing, and Body-Part Nomenclature," *Ethnology* 24 (1985): 197–214; Cecil H. Brown, "Hand and Arm," in *The World Atlas of Language Structures Online*, ed. M. S. Dryer and M. Haspelmath (Leipzig: Max Planck Institute for Evolutionary Anthropology, 2013), available online at http://wals.info/chapter/129.

as well.[36] Thus, a biblical idiom could utilize the word יד where Akkadian uses *aḫu*.[37]

In addition to the commonality between nouns יד and *aḫu*, the verbs שלח and *nadû* bear numerous semantic overlaps: *š-l-ḥ* (in both the G- and D-stems) and *nadû* may refer to casting arrows or fires, or casting into fire; both are used of throwing into a pit; and both can refer to letting water flow.[38] Moreover, the equivalence of another Akkadian hand idiom, *qāta nadû* (literally, "drop/throw the hand"), with a different well-attested sense of שלח יד ("to take a hostile, destructive action") further demonstrates that שלח, particularly in the G-stem (*qal*), could correspond to *nadû* in idioms.[39] These idioms both occur in reference to the destruction of places (or, through metonymy, their inhabitants). Regardless of how Biblical Hebrew and Akkadian came to share this idiom, the comparable use of *qāta nadû* and שלח יד in close contexts indicates that they are indeed analogous and, further, that *nadû* and שלח may constitute semantic equivalents in idioms.[40]

The idioms *aḫa nadû* and שלח יד thus correspond on multiple levels. In terms of the individual components that constitute the verbal idioms, both the verbal elements *nadû* and שלח and the nominal elements *aḫu* and יד are equivalent. As for the idiom as a whole, while *aḫa nadû* occurs in varied contexts, it frequently refers to negligence in contexts of watching property. The interpretation of שלח ידו in Exod 22:7, 10 as referring to negligence allows for a coherent reading of the laws. With the correspondence of individual elements of the idiom and the contextual reading of negli-

---

36. For examples of יד referring to the arm, see P. R. Ackroyd, "יָד *yād*," *TDOT* 5:393–426, here 400; Houtman, *Exodus*, 1:24. For *aḫu* with the meaning hand, see, e.g., ABL 110 r. 8, cited in *CAD* A/1, s.v. "*aḫu*" B 1a, with the note that the "context [requires] the mng. 'hand'"—specifically "hand," and not "arm (including the hand)." For *idu* with the sense of "hand," see *CAD* I–J, s.v. "*idu*" A.

37. This is true regardless of the source of connection between the idioms. A direct calque could allow for this variation, given the blurred distinction between hand and arm in both Biblical Hebrew and Akkadian conceptions; idioms deriving from a shared ancestor could likewise result in this divergence; and idioms developing autonomously in separate places of a common culture could just as easily vary in this way.

38. With arrows as the object, see, e.g., 1 Sam 20:20; 2 Sam 22:15, 17 = Ps 18:15, 17; Ezek 5:16; for *nadû*, see HSS 13 195:5; JEN 519:7. With fire, see, e.g., Judg 1:8; 20:48; 2 Kgs 8:12; Ezek 39:6; Hos 8:14; Amos 1:4, 7, 10, 12; 2:2, 5; Ps 74:7; Lam 1:13; for *nadû* with fire, see the many citations in *CAD* N/1, s.v. "*nadû*."

39. Compare, e.g., the Akkadian line "[He] laid his hand [**qāta nadû*] to the sanctuaries of Babylonia, had destroyed Babylonia" (Asb. 178:14, cited in *CAD* N/1, s.v. "*nadû*" 6) with "So I will stretch out my hand [יד שלח*] and strike Egypt" (Exod 3:20). Akkadian *qāta nadû* should not be considered a parallel to the usage of שלח יד in the Covenant Code, though, as the action it signifies in the bailment law is not destructive per se in all cases.

40. For a summary of possible ways that Biblical Hebrew and Akkadian came to share semantically equivalent idioms, see Greenstein, "Trans-Semitic Idiomatic Equivalency," 329.

gence in the law of bailment in Exod 22:7, 10, I surmise that שׁלח ידו, like *aḫa nadû*, refers to negligent behavior.

Based on this new understanding of שׁלח ידו, I propose the following translation of the transgression of which the bailee is suspected in the first two subsections of the bailment law: "he behaved negligently toward the other's property." Verse 7 reflects the suspicion that the bailee has committed negligence and thereby allowed for theft of the bailor's goods, while verse 10 has the accused bailee swear that he did not negligently allow for the death, injury, or capture of animals in his care. This understanding of the biblical bailment law as engaging negligence also accords well with Hammurabi's laws about deposit and herding, which both explicitly treat negligent wrongdoings (125, 267).

Herding Mishaps

The understanding of שׁלח יד as a legal idiom for negligence also affects the interpretation of the law of herding. A bailee swears an oath that the bailee has not acted negligently in cases where an animal "dies, or is injured, or is captured, with no eyewitness" to clarify the circumstances of the animal's death, injury, or capture (Exod 22:9–10). Indeed, negligence constitutes a more logical suspected wrongdoing than fraud, or deliberate malfeasance, in these scenarios. After all, why would the bailor suspect the bailee of killing or injuring the animal—how would such an action benefit the bailee?[41] On the other hand, negligence fits well in this context: the animal falls victim to death, injury, or capture, and its owner, the bailor, suspects the bailee of enabling the misfortune to happen through the bailee's own negligence. A negligence reading of this verse also coheres with the Laws of Hammurabi, which cast as fraud a case of a shepherd stealing and selling the flock animals entrusted to the shepherd (265) but associate with negligence a shepherd who allows a disease *pissatum* (possibly "mange") to spread through the flock and, consequently, must pay for the losses to the flock (267).[42]

The biblical herding law groups together animal death, injury, and capture (š-b-y) in verse 9 and then separately addresses animal theft (g-n-b) in verse 11, with separate consequences for these varying scenarios. In the

---

41. For this point, see Schwienhorst-Schönberger, *Das Bundesbuch*, 199; Seebass, "Noch einmal zum Depositenrecht," 23; Westbrook, "Deposit Law," 371. Granted, this question presumes that the bailee would violate his duties only for personal gain, and not for purely malicious reasons. This assumption seems fair, as the bailor presumably would not choose as his bailee someone with some grudge against him, because of which the bailee might wish to destroy his property.

42. See translations in Roth, *Law Collections*, 130.

case of capture, as with death and injury, the accused bailee has the opportunity to achieve exoneration through an exculpatory oath by Yhwh,
whereas in cases of theft the bailee assumes automatic liability, with no
recourse for exoneration. Is there a substantive difference between animal
capture and theft, or do these verses contain contradictory laws? While
those who consider "capture" in verse 9 a later addition worthy of deletion need not find the distinction troubling,[43] others have explained the
apparent discrepancy based on the nature of the "theft." [44] According to
these views, the root *š-b-y* envisions a more forceful form of theft than
g-n-b. If an animal is captured, the accused bailee may swear to have acted
without negligence and thereby escape liability. The law considers such a
bailee as having met the expected standard of care; despite meeting this
standard, the bailee was unable to prevent capture, but for this the bailee
bears no accountability. In contrast, simple theft falls within the range of
mishaps that the bailee is reasonably expected to prevent under any circumstances.

The herding law also distinguishes between cases of animal injury
(*š-b-r*), for which an oath by Yhwh may provide exculpation, and a case of
predation (*ṭ-r-p*), for which the bailee may achieve exoneration by producing physical evidence in the form of animal remains.[45] These roots repre-
sent distinct scenarios: an animal designated by the root *ṭ-r-p* is dead, and
verbs from the same root with a wild animal as their subject always entail
the death of the animal. The animal is no longer a living creature but a
carcass—food for the predator.[46] Hammurabi's law on predation (266)
likewise groups together the *lipit ilim* ("epidemic," literally, "act of a god")
with a case where "a lion make[s] a kill," indicating that the bailed animal
has ended up dead.[47] Scholars have long associated Amos 3:12, which

---

43. For this emendation, see, e.g., Jackson, *Wisdom-Laws*, 354–55; however, Jackson does
distinguish between the meaning of the two terms; see Jackson, *Theft in Early Jewish Law*
(Oxford: Clarendon, 1972), 39.

44. See, e.g., Houtman (*Exodus*, 3:203), distinguishing between "theft by a gang of rob-
bers" and "theft by a single individual"; Jackson (*Theft in Early Jewish Law*, 39), distinguishing
between "brigandage" and "theft"; Wright (*Inventing God's Law*, 267), differentiating between
theft through "extreme force" and simple theft; and Sprinkle (*Book of the Covenant*, 150–51),
arguing that capture is a case of *force majeure*, as opposed to simple theft.

45. For other interpretations, which distinguish between these scenarios on the basis of
the circumstances rather than the meaning of the roots of the verbs themselves, see Cassuto,
Commentary on the Book of Exodus, 287; Jackson, *Wisdom-Laws*, 346–49; Wright, *Inventing God's
Law*, 274.

46. See, e.g., Exod 22:30; Num 23:24 (where טרף is parallel to חללים); Nah 2:13.

47. See translation in Roth, *Law Collections*, 130: "If, in the enclosure, an epidemic
should break out or a lion make a kill, the shepherd shall clear himself before the god, and
the owner of the enclosure shall accept responsibility for the loss sustained in the enclosure."
In contrast, HL 75 distinguishes between a case where a wolf devours an animal and where
the animal dies at the hand of a god, allowing for exoneration only in the latter case.

describes the scanty remains of an animal savaged by a lion, with the animal parts the shepherd of Exod 22:12 may salvage as evidence. The verse also calls to mind Gen 37:31–33, in which Joseph's brothers present his blood-soaked garment to their father as false evidence that he has suffered predation.[48] The case of predation envisions not merely a brutal injury at the hands of an animal but specifically mauling to death.

Unlike *ṭ-r-p*, *š-b-r* does not entail death. Thus, Ezekiel and Zechariah speak of healing the wounded animal (נשברת), which certainly would not be an option if the animal were dead (Ezek 34:4; Zech 11:16). Although contexts in which the root *š-b-r* collocates with animals offer little clarifying information as to the type of wound involved, inner-biblical and cognate evidence, as well as the basic meaning of the root, suggest a broken bone or limb.[49] With reference to humans, Biblical Hebrew *š-b-r* takes objects such as the bone, tooth, neck, and arm.[50] The Akkadian cognate *šebēru* takes similar objects, belonging to both animals and humans.[51] While *šebēru* may occur in hendiadys with *mâtu*, meaning "injure to death," when it stands on its own, it refers to the breaking of a body part that may heal.[52]

The distinction between injury and predation in the biblical herding law rests on the nature of the injury or attack. Injury suggests a physical wound such as the breaking of a limb or bone that does not kill the animal;[53] predation signifies that a wild beast has mauled the animal to death. If this is true, then the question worth asking is not why the law differs with regard to injury and predation, but why it diverges in its treatment of predation and death. Umberto Cassuto's distinction between death of the animal's own accord and at the hand of a beast is apt: Although the root *m-w-t* (Exod 22:9) covers a wide range of forms of death, it certainly includes nonviolent death and death at the hand of God;[54] *ṭ-r-p*, on the other hand, is specific to death by another animal (Exod 22:12).[55] Natural

---

48. Cf. David Daube, *Studies in Biblical Law* (Cambridge: Cambridge University Press, 1969), 4–5.

49. An exception to this is Dan 8:7–8, which speaks of an animal's broken horns.

50. For bones, see Prov 25:15; Exod 12:46; Num 9:12; Isa 38:13; Ps 34:21; Lam 3:4; for tooth, see Ps 3:8; Job 29:17; for neck, see 1 Sam 4:18; for arm, see Jer 48:25; Ezek 30:21–25.

51. See examples in *CAD* Š/2, s.v. "*šebēru*."

52. On this hendiadys and its possible parallel in Exod 22:13, see E. A. Speiser, "Notes to Recently Published Nuzi Texts," *JAOS* 55 (1935): 432–43, here 440. Note that the grammatical subject of the verbs in this hendiadys changes from the perpetrator who effects the injury (*šebēru* in the causative Š-stem) to the animal that dies (*mâtu* in the G-stem).

53. For this understanding, see also F. Charles Fensham, "The Mišpāṭîm in the Covenant Code" (PhD diss., John Hopkins University, 1958), 103–4, who describes נשבר as an animal "so badly injured that its bones are broken."

54. *Gesenius' Hebrew and Chaldee Lexicon to the Old Testament*, trans. Samuel P. Tregelles (Grand Rapids: Eerdmans, 1949), s.v. "מות."

55. See Cassuto, *Commentary on the Book of Exodus*, 287.

death would leave an animal's corpse without a clear indication of what transpired, so that without eyewitness testimony, the bailee could only prove innocence through a cultic procedure. In contrast, mauling would leave obvious evidence of predation, bypassing the need for recourse to religious ritual.

Although in Exod 22:9–10 the law specifically considers cases of death, injury, and capture that stem from the bailee's negligence, the preceding verse (22:8) also covers any case of fraud through its use of the term פשע. This word, also associated with political rebellion and rebellion against God, refers to what Westbrook has called a "fundamental willful breach," that is, a deliberate wrongdoing, or fraud.[56] Exodus 22:8 collapses the goods from both the preceding verses (in this verse, "a garment") and the animals from the following verses into a single statement about fraud and functions as a bridge.[57] Whereas verses 6–7 and 9–10 introduce the border-line case of negligence and stipulate how to respond in these cases, verse 8 attends to the relatively obvious case of fraud and makes the point that, whether the bailee acted negligently or fraudulently, whether with respect to goods or in a case involving animals, whether for voluntary bailments as in the surrounding verses or in involuntary bailments (as in the case of lost property, introduced in v. 8)—the penalty is the same. I will return to this point later in this chapter, in the discussion of false accusations.

The range of herding mishaps that might occur broadens if one looks also to biblical narrative and prophecy. In Gen 31:36–42, when Jacob defends his conduct as a shepherd to his father-in-law (as well as uncle and employer) Laban, he cites a number of cases with parallels to Exod 22's herding law. These most explicitly include predation and theft (Gen 31:39a, c). Jacob also mentions the consumption of rams (Gen 31:38c), an example of fraudulent activity that a shepherd might undertake and which is more specific than the general statement in Exod 22:8 against פשע, with which it accounts for any case of fraud.[58] In addition, Jacob uses the enigmatic phrase אנכי אחטנה (Gen 31:39b), which may be understood as referring to animal "injury."[59] Beyond these cases—predation, injury,

---

56. Westbrook, "Deposit Law," 367. For discussion of פשע, see further Rolf Knierim, *Die Hauptbegriffe für Sünde im Alten Testament* (Gütersloh: Gütersloher Verlagshaus Gerd Mohn, 1965), 143–44, 163.

57. In arguing that Exod 22:8 functions as a bridge in this law—one that is integral to it—I disagree with scholars who view the verse necessarily as a later addition to the peri-cope, due to its divergence from the typical casuistic form of the Covenant Code's laws and to its generalizing style. For such views, see citations in Jackson, *Wisdom-Laws*, 342 n. 55; Assnat Bartor, *Reading Law as Narrative: A Study in the Casuistic Laws of the Pentateuch*, AIL 5 (Atlanta: Society of Biblical Literature, 2010), 95 n. 21.

58. In fact, a malfeasant shepherd would be more likely to consume rams, which are male, than female flock animals, as Morrison demonstrates based on debt statements from Nuzi ("Jacob and Laban Narrative," 157–58).

59. See Yael Landman, "Herding in Haran: A Note on Jacob's Claim in Genesis 31:39,"

and theft, which all have clear parallels in the biblical herding law; and consuming rams, which loosely corresponds to Exod 22's mention of fraud—Jacob also speaks of another mishap that might occur, which Exodus does not consider, specifically, the possibility that a female flock animal might miscarry (Gen 31:38b).

The prophets also consider acts of fraud and negligence that derelict shepherds—who stand in for leaders of Israel—might commit, in contrast to the ideal shepherd, namely, God. Ezekiel 34 includes one such famous prophecy (see also Jer 23 and Zech 11). Like Gen 31, Ezek 34 refers to specific examples of fraud relating to the consumption of flock animals: "eating the fat [*חלב]" and "slaughtering the fat female flock animal [בריאה*]" (34:3).[60] The sheep's fat was considered a delicacy; for the shepherds to eat it thus constitutes a display of audacity.[61] In Ezek 34:3, the חלב stands in for the sheep in its entirety, functioning synecdochically while highlighting the flagrance of these shepherds' violation. Not only did they misappropriate animals from their flock for consumption; they even ate their fat. The slaughter of the בריאה—the fat, female flock animal (e.g., a ewe)—constitutes a separate, also egregious offense. As noted in the context of Jacob's speech, normally, a shepherd misappropriating sheep for consumption would likely have eaten a male sheep (i.e., a ram) rather than a female one (i.e., a ewe) in order to minimize the potential penalty. In Ezek 34:3, the choice of the verb "slaughter" for the female sheep, as opposed to "eat" used of the animal's fat, emphasizes the particularly destructive aspect of this action: In killing the ewe, the shepherds cut off her future offspring as well. The word בריאה ("fat [one]"), which is used to designate the slaughtered animal, instead of a word such as צאן ("sheep, flock animal") or רחל ("ewe"), further underscores the ewe's birthing potential. Studies of fertility in ewes have demonstrated a correlation between a

---

ZABR 25 (2019): 173–80, arguing against the usual translation "I myself made good the loss" or similar.

60. Some scholars reject the MT's vocalization of חלב as *ḥēleb* ("fat, choice part") in favor of the vocalization reflected in the LXX and the Vulgate, *ḥālāb* ("milk"), for reasons including the often-cultic context of the word חֵלֶב, which would be out of place in this prophecy; the co-occurrence of "milk" with "wool" (which also occurs in Ezek 34:3) with regard to a shepherd in the New Testament and the Mishnah (see 1 Cor 9:7; m. B. Qam. 10:9); and the alleged redundancy with "slaughtering the בריאה" in the same verse (see, e.g., Moshe Greenberg, *Ezekiel 21–37: A New Translation with Introduction and Commentary*, AB 22A [New York: Doubleday, 1997], 696–97). However, Ezek 39:19 also speaks of the consumption of חלב in its noncultic sense, and, as I will demonstrate shortly, the point of "slaughtering the בריאה" is distinctly different from "consuming the fat."

61. Edward L. Ochsenschlager notes that, among modern Marsh Arabs living in conditions similar to those of ancient Sumerians of millennia past, the fat of sheep is considered one of its most valuable by-products (*Iraq's Marsh Arabs in the Garden of Eden* [Philadelphia: University of Pennsylvania Museum of Archaeology and Anthropology, 2004], 213). However, fat is never explicated as a by-product of sheep that ancient Near Eastern shepherds may have received.

ewe's weight at time of breeding and her likelihood to conceive.[62] These studies corroborate the natural phenomenon that anyone familiar with herding would have recognized, of fat ewes conceiving more than thin ewes. Thus, in addition to eating the sheep's fat, which stands in synecdochically for the rams consumed, the shepherds slaughter the fat, fertile ewes, recklessly disregarding the far-reaching effects of their loss.

Along with consuming the fat and slaughtering the fat ewe, Ezekiel mentions a third specific example of a shepherd's deliberate malfeasance: wearing the sheep's wool. On its face, this action appears legitimate; in the ancient Near East, wool was one of the most common by-products of sheep that shepherds received as part of their compensation. Yet this was not always the case. At the Eanna in the Neo-Babylonian period, for example, contractual agreements ensured that, in practice, the temple that owned the flocks would keep all of the wool shorn from its sheep.[63] The Neo-Babylonian background of the book of Ezekiel[64] supports the possi-

62. See C. T. Gaskins et al., "Influence of Body Weight, Age, and Weight Gain on Fertility and Prolificacy in Four Breeds of Ewe Lambs," *Journal of Animal Science* 83 (2005): 1680–89, here 1683, indicating a positive relationship between weight at breeding and probability of pregnancy among three out of four different breeds of ewe lambs tested; G. K. Hight and G. E. Jury, "Hill Country Sheep Production," *New Zealand Journal of Agricultural Research* 16 (1973): 447–56, demonstrating increased barrenness among lower-weight ewes; and R. A. Corner-Thomas et al., "Ewe Lamb Live Weight and Body Condition Scores Affect Reproductive Rates in Commercial Flocks," *New Zealand Journal of Agricultural Research* 58 (2015): 26–34, finding that as ewe lamb breeding live weight increased from < 32.5 to 47.5–52.4 kg, the percentage of ewes identified as pregnant increased, while above 52.4 kg there was no substantial difference in fertility.

63. Kozuh, *Sacrificial Economy*, 131–40. While these agreements were between the temple and its herdsmen, who in turn managed the shepherds directly caring for the flocks, the principle is the same: agreements were subject to variation, especially in different periods, and the owner of the flocks could determine the likelihood of the owner's contractor receiving wool. Although these contracts did not technically prevent herdsmen from receiving wool, the terms had the effect of making this nearly impossible, so that perhaps one or two lucky herdsmen could have received wool in an unusually bountiful year.

64. See Ezek 1:1–3 for the book's first identification of its setting. Recent scholarship affirming the Neo-Babylonian background of Ezekiel includes Tova Ganzel and Shalom E. Holtz, "Ezekiel's Temple in Babylonian Context," *VT* 64 (2014): 211–26; Abraham Winitzer, "Assyriology and Jewish Studies in Tel Aviv: Ezekiel among the Babylonian *literati*," in *Encounters by the Rivers of Babylon: Scholarly Conversations between Jews, Iranians and Babylonians in Antiquity*, ed. Uri Gabbay and Shai Secunda, TSAJ 160 (Tübingen: Mohr Siebeck, 2014), 163–216; Jonathan Stökl, "'A Youth without Blemish, Handsome, Proficient in All Wisdom, Knowledgeable and Intelligent': Ezekiel's Access to Babylonian Culture," in *Exile and Return: The Babylonian Context*, ed. Jonathan Stökl and Caroline Waerzeggers, BZAW 478 (Berlin: de Gruyter, 2015), 223–52; and, in the same volume, Madhavi Nevader, "Picking up the Pieces of the Little Prince: Refractions of Neo-Babylonian Kingship Ideology in Ezekiel 40–48?," 268–91.

bility that its author(s) could have been familiar with this kind of arrangement.[65]

Although Ezek 34 is a prophetic text, with sheep representing the humans of Israel, it is well grounded in herding practices from the ancient Near East and specifically from the Neo-Babylonian period. Ezekiel 34:3 lists three actions the shepherds undertook that were not within their rights and would not have been their right even if they had performed their duties flawlessly.[66] In conjunction with Jacob's claim that he has not eaten Laban's rams, the shepherds' consumption of sheep fat and fat, fertile ewes suggests that, in the Bible as well as in the ancient Near East, eating flock animals constituted a form of misappropriation for shepherds. Indeed, because this specific wrongdoing appears in two different herding-related literary sources from different periods, it was likely considered fraudulent behavior for shepherds throughout the history of ancient Israel. However, the accusation that the shepherds have worn the sheep's wool finds a parallel specifically in a practice known from the Eanna, and not elsewhere or during other periods. Therefore, while this accusation is grounded in Neo-Babylonian reality, it does not necessarily reflect a shepherd's rights in herding arrangements during other periods and, in fact, may not reflect an ancient Israelite or Judahite reality at all—in contrast to the prohibition against consuming flock animals, which seems to reflect a conservative, more broadly practiced custom. It would be wrong to assume that the Pentateuch's blanket injunction against fraud in bailments would have imagined wearing a sheep's wool as a specific

---

65. The book of Ezekiel refers to the Khabur River, which is mentioned in the name of the Khabur River Village (Āl nār Kabara) in tablets from towns inhabited by Judean deportees in Babylonia; see Francis Joannès and André Lemaire, "Contrats babyloniens d'époque achéménide du Bît-Abî-Râm avec une épigraphe araméenne," *RA* 90 (1996): 41–60, here 50 (text 7 line 5′). Similarities between other agricultural work in the Judean exile settlements and at the Eanna in Uruk further highlight the plausibility of affinities between herding practices at both places, with which the author(s) of Ezekiel could have been familiar, despite the institutional, urban context of the Eanna arrangements. See Laurie E. Pearce, "Cuneiform Sources for Judeans in Babylonia in the Neo-Babylonian and Achaemenid Periods: An Overview," *Religion Compass* 10 (2016): 230–43, here 236; and see Wunsch, "Glimpses on the Lives of Deportees," 254, regarding cultivation of grain. Note that, although the requirement to return all wool at the Eanna may have been related to its economic interests, namely, its involvement in the textile industry, the similarities in grain cultivation in Judean communities and at the Eanna also fit better with an institution and its various functions, in contrast to cultivation practices of private individuals in contemporaneous communities. Therefore, there is a possibility that practices involving wool returns known from the Eanna would have been in effect also among the Judean exiles, despite the incongruity of institution-like practices among a community of private individuals with varying economic interests.

66. Contra Greenberg, who considers the consumption of milk (following LXX, etc.) and wool "a recognized perquisite" of the shepherd (*Ezekiel 21–37*, 697).

example of fraud, although it is safe to make this assumption in the case of eating rams.

In the continuation of Ezek 34, the prophet also addresses a case of predation (34:5). But, in contrast to the blanket absolution from liability for predation that one finds in Exodus and in Mesopotamian law, Ezekiel introduces a case of predation for which a shepherd would indeed be liable. If the shepherd is so negligent as to allow the flock to scatter without any supervision or care, thereby enabling an attack by wild beasts, that shepherd surely would be held accountable. The shepherd's absence constitutes evidence of such negligence. Whereas Exodus does not consider the possibility that a shepherd would allow a flock to roam completely unsupervised in this fashion, Ezek 34 highlights a fundamental expectation of the shepherd in any herding arrangement; at the very least, the shepherd must be present. If the shepherd does not fulfill this most basic, obvious duty of shepherds, then the shepherd certainly bears fault for whatever goes wrong. In this case, prophecy complicates the law of the Pentateuch by introducing an exception into what would appear to constitute an absolute: sometimes even "acts of God" can be prevented with baseline care.

Ezekiel 34 is an example of a prophetic text bearing points of contact with pentateuchal law, biblical narrative, and Mesopotamian legal documents. When examined together with these other sources, this text clarifies examples of fraud that the law itself does not elucidate but that, in some cases, the law might have had in mind. It also suggests an exception to the predation rule in Exod 22:12, which it is reasonable to imagine would have been observed in practice, despite the pentateuchal law not acknowledging this possibility. Lastly, Ezek 34 also contains an example of a practice that we can identify as realistic based on Neo-Babylonian evidence. Because it is possible to isolate this practice to a particular, atypical setting, it would not figure into a reconstruction of herding practices for the majority of ancient Israel and Judah's history.

The False Accuser

Between the laws of deposit and herding in Exod 22 is a verse that functions as a bridge (22:8):

עַל כָּל דְּבַר פֶּשַׁע עַל שׁוֹר עַל חֲמוֹר עַל שֶׂה עַל שַׂלְמָה עַל כָּל אֲבֵדָה אֲשֶׁר יֹאמַר כִּי
הוּא זֶה עַד הָאֱלֹהִים יָבֹא דְּבַר שְׁנֵיהֶם אֲשֶׁר יַרְשִׁיעֻן אֱלֹהִים יְשַׁלֵּם שְׁנַיִם לְרֵעֵהוּ

For any case of a willful breach—for an ox, for a donkey, for a sheep, for a garment, for any lost property—of which one says, "It is he!": The case of the two of them shall come before God. Whomsoever God declares guilty must pay double to the other.

The form and content of this verse have long occupied scholars interested in the laws of Exodus, leading many to conclude that the verse in question must be an addition to the law.[67] Formally, Exod 22:8 deviates from the casuistic style typical of the Covenant Code, and its language is notably general (e.g., with repetition of the word כל, "any"). The content of the verse also raises questions; it appears to cut short the preceding verse, without completing an apodosis, and to introduce unexpected information with exegetically thorny language. In fact, the difficulties in verse 8 have led to so many different suggestions for interpretation that Rolf Knierim once compiled a table of no fewer than sixteen such possibilities.[68] Among the exegetical issues at stake is the question of whether this verse pertains exclusively to bailment or more generally to other areas of law.[69]

A new understanding of שלח ידו as referring to negligence in the verses surrounding Exod 22:8 affects the interpretation of this verse as well. The introduction of פשע—a willful breach, or fraud—at the beginning of this verse sets up a contrast between the flanking cases of negligence and this transitional verse, which relates to deliberate malfeasance, specifically in a situation of bailment. In the apodosis of the verse, Exod 22:8 uses the formulation, אשר ירשיען אלהים ("whomsoever God declares guilty"), implying that either of the two parties (the bailee, or the bailor who entrusted property to the bailee) might be a candidate for guilt. As Westbrook has argued, the law considers the possibility of a counter-charge of false accusation:[70] the bailor accuses the bailee of deliberate malfeasance, but the bailee accuses the bailor of lying. With no evidence to prove one person's word true over the other's, the law resorts to a cultic procedure: God will adjudicate and declare either the bailee guilty of a willful breach, or the bailor guilty of false accusation. Whichever party is guilty must pay double compensation to the other. The law protects the bailor, who is vulnerable to the bailee in possession of the bailor's property, by warning the bailee that if the bailor's property is stolen, the bailee risks losing property as well. At the same time, the law discourages the bailor from exploiting this possibility of

---

67. See, e.g., Schwienhorst-Schönberger, *Das Bundesbuch*, 194; Otto, "Die rechtshistorische Entwicklung," 154–58; Seebass, "Noch einmal zum Depositenrecht," 24–25; Jackson, *Wisdom-Laws*, 342 n. 55; Bartor, *Reading Law as Narrative*, 95 n. 21. For discussions of verse 8 that read the law from a synchronic perspective, see Westbrook, "Deposit Law," 363; Sprinkle, *Book of the Covenant*, 148–50; Wright, *Inventing God's Law*, 252, and 183–84, 251.

68. Knierim, *Die Hauptbegriffe für Sünde*, 162.

69. Dale Patrick, for example, views verse 8 as a formulation in general language of the principles emerging from the surrounding laws (*Old Testament Law* [Atlanta: John Knox, 1985], 81), while Otto ("Die rechtshistorische Entwicklung," 139–63) and Bartor (*Reading Law as Narrative*, 95–98) understand verse 8 as an expansion of verse 7, extending the cases requiring cultic decision beyond bailment to all cases of disputed theft. For further citations, see also Houtman, *Exodus*, 3:199 n. 167.

70. Westbrook, "Deposit Law," 370.

double compensation by holding the bailor equally liable for falsely accusing the bailee.

In a study of principles of composition in the Laws of Eshnunna, Barry
Eichler has identified in the cuneiform law collection a literary principle of
juxtaposing individual legal cases in order to create a particular legal
statement. The same principle emerges also in the laws of Exodus.[71] A
vertical relationship emerges between legal cases that often is more
important than the details of the individual cases themselves. This is especially prominent in cases where the apodosis appears incomplete in relation to its protasis. For example, amid a section of laws relating to betrothal
and marriage (LE 25–28), LE 28 (which Eichler blocks off into sections [a]
and [b]) introduces a case of adultery:

> (28a) If [a man] set forth the nuptial feast and stipulations with her father
> and mother and then took her, she is a wife. (b) On the day she is seized
> in the lap of a(nother) man, she shall die—she shall not live.[72]

As Eichler points out, 28b appears to contain an incomplete apodosis,
relaying only the consequences for the adulterous wife but neglecting to
stipulate a punishment for her illicit lover. Moreover, in stark contrast to
other cuneiform law collections, LE 28b does not discuss the cuckolded
husband's right to pardon his wife.[73] These omissions, Eichler argues, call
for attention to the vertical interplay between LE 28a and 28b. Rather than
understanding LE 28 as a law that is purely "about" adultery, we ought to
read it instead as a law that highlights the definition of a "legal wife"
through its juxtaposition of sections (a) and (b). This status is defined by
whether the discovery that the woman in question has committed adultery leads to the death penalty. The law therefore focuses not on adjudi-
cating the case of adultery but on establishing a husband's exclusive right
over his legal wife.[74]

This understanding of LE 28 further illuminates its relationship to LE
27:

> If a man took a man's daughter without asking her father and mother,
> and did not set forth the nuptial feast and stipulations with her father
> and mother—should she remain in his house for an entire year, she is
> not a wife.[75]

---

71. Eichler, "Literary Structure in the Laws of Eshnunna," 72; Eichler, "Exodus 21:22–
25 Revisited," 11–29.

72. Translated by Eichler, "Exodus 21:22–25 Revisited," 16; cf. Eichler, "Literary Structure in the Laws of Eshnunna," 73.

73. These include the Laws of Hammurabi (136), the Middle Assyrian Laws (A15), and
the Hittite Laws (198).

74. Eichler, "Literary Structure in the Laws of Eshnunna," 73–74.

75. Ibid., 74.

The juxtaposition of LE 27 and 28 points to the requirement for formal marriage arrangements with parental consent in order to change the legal status of a daughter to her husband's legal wife. LE 27 stipulates the formal steps; LE 28 establishes the test for whether the parties involved have met these requirements. Together, these paragraphs generate a legal statement about what is necessary to effect a change in the personal status of a woman so that her husband gains exclusive rights over her. By noting what is missing and examining the vertical interplay between juxtaposed laws, we achieve a better understanding of how the law is structured to communicate its primary points.

Eichler's model offers a fruitful means of unpacking the bailment law as well. Exodus 22:7 stipulates that, if a thief is not found, the owner of the house shall approach God to undergo a cultic procedure, but the verse does not mention any penalty or further information. This absence is especially striking in comparison with the similarly worded Exod 22:10, which continues past the point where verse 7 ends with a stipulation regarding the bailee's exemption from payment.[76] However, if one views verse 7 and verse 8 in juxtaposition, the focus shifts: Exod 22:7 establishes liability for the bailee in a "borderline" case of negligence—the case in which the bailee's liability might not be assumed, since the bailee has not acted maliciously, nor has the bailee committed theft personally. Exodus 22:8 refers to the "obvious" case, that of deliberate malfeasance, which of course renders the bailee liable, and establishes that the falsely accusing bailor receives the same penalty that the bailor would have had imposed on the bailee, that is, double compensation. Together, verses 7–8 set forth the following:

1. The bailee is held to a high standard of liability, considered liable for anything from negligent behavior allowing for theft to an outright willful breach, for example, the commission of theft.
2. When the bailor accuses the bailee of wrongdoing—whether of negligence or of outright theft—the bailee may achieve exoneration through a cultic procedure.
3. If the bailor has falsely accused the bailee, then the bailor is liable. The bailor must pay double compensation, just as the bailee would have had to do had the bailor's accusation proven true.

Exodus 22:8 serves as a bridge between verses 6–7 and verses 9–12. Flanked by borderline cases of negligence leading to theft of goods or death, injury, or capture of animals, verse 8 states in the context of the obvious case of deliberate malfeasance with regard both to goods and animals that the

---

76. This absence partly motivates Westbrook's reimagining of verse 7 as the entire protasis with verse 8 continuing as its apodosis ("Deposit Law," 362–63; see also Jackson, *Wisdom-Laws*, 338).

accusing bailor risks suffering the same fate as the accused bailee. Thus, the law complements its high standard of liability for the bailee with a corresponding level of protection from a bailor who might wish fraudulently to exploit the opportunity for double compensation, despite not having been wronged.

Although other law collections from the ancient Near East do not address a case of false accusation among their laws of deposit, precisely this issue is at stake in HSS 9 108, a trial record from Nuzi.[77] Zigi had deposited sealed containers of barley in Ilanu's house. He then initiates a lawsuit, accusing Ilanu of refusing to return to him the entirety of his deposit. Ilanu in turn claims that Zigi had already taken back all of his barley and produces witnesses who verify his statement. Ultimately, the judges find Zigi guilty and fine him an unspecified quantity. While Exod 22:8 suggests that a false accuser might face a penalty equally harsh as that imposed upon a guilty bailee, HSS 9 108 does not provide sufficient information to determine whether Zigi's fine equaled the amount he wished to extract from Ilanu. Despite this suit's not indicating the type of penalty that one might incur for fraud, it points to the verisimilitude of Exod 22:8's scenario of false accusation.

When Bailments Go Awry

Pentateuchal law enumerates a range of possible mishaps that might occur in a bailment. A deposit might be stolen or an animal might suffer death, injury, capture, predation, or theft. In some cases, the bailee might do nothing wrong but might face the false accusation of a malfeasant bailor. Narrative and prophetic texts offer further examples of what might go wrong, especially in cases of herding: a female flock animal might miscarry, leading to an overall smaller yield at the end of the herding arrangement; the shepherd might consume (typically male) flock animals, perhaps even brazenly feasting on their fat, or slaughter a ewe and thereby extinguish her birthing potential. The malfeasant bailee or shepherd might deliberately commit fraud, for example, stealing flock animals or slaughtering them for personal consumption, or might negligently allow for calamity to strike. At times, however, an "act of God" might occur through no fault of the bailee.

This chapter examined the manners in which a bailment might not proceed as expected. In the next chapter, we will look at what happens next, including the establishment of the facts of the case and, when appropriate, the means of righting the wrong that has transpired.

---

77. A translation of this text appears in Westbrook and Wells, *Everyday Law in Biblical Israel*, 48.

3

Establishing Facts, Establishing Justice

When a bailment goes awry, the wronged party has the opportunity to seek justice and make things right. This process includes a number of possible steps. First, the court may employ one of a number of fact-finding methods to determine exactly what transpired. These methods include standard forensic measures, such as examination of physical evidence or hearing eyewitness testimony, as well as cultic judicial procedures, such as allowing the accused to swear an exculpatory oath by Yhwh.[1] Second, the court may determine and declare which party, if any, is liable, as well as the degree of compensation for which the liable party shall be responsible. In some cases, the accused will escape liability altogether. At times, the court may reach an incorrect verdict based on the false oath of one party, but the person who swears falsely may eventually face grave repercussions.

Establishing the Facts of the Case

When a plaintiff (here, the owner of property or bailor) accuses a defendant (here, the bailee) of some form of malfeasance, the court must

---

1. For the labels "cultic" and "forensic" (with cultic procedures including an exculpatory oath, ordeal, and oracle; and forensic procedures including use of eyewitness testimony or physical evidence), see Bruce Wells, "The Cultic versus the Forensic: Judahite and Mesopotamian Judicial Procedures in the First Millennium B.C.E.," *JAOS* 128 (2008): 205–32, here 205–6, 208. Wells's terms are to be preferred over the traditional differentiation between "suprarational" and "rational" procedures, which anachronistically superimposes modern notions of "rationality" onto the ancient mindset. Laura E. Culbertson has further argued that any such dichotomy, regardless of taxonomy, implies that only forensic procedures can engage empirical reality and infallibly establish facts, when in truth cultic and forensic procedures were considered equally capable of establishing facts and equally prone to inaccuracy ("Dispute Resolution in the Provincial Courts of the Third Dynasty of Ur" [PhD diss., University of Michigan, 2009], 84–85; and cf. Małgorzata Sandowicz, *Oaths and Curses: A Study in Neo- and Late Babylonian Legal Formulary* [Münster: Ugarit-Verlag, 2012], 1). While Culbertson highlights areas of overlap between the cultic and forensic, these terms remain useful as accurate descriptions of the different judicial proceedings they denote; therefore, I will continue to use them.

ascertain the facts of the case: What happened? In cases of stolen deposits, the cuneiform law collections—though not the Covenant Code—entertain the possibility that the house in which the property was stored might bear physical markers of a break-in (e.g., on the doorjambs or a window of the home).[2] Although Exodus does not consider these factors, it circuitously acknowledges that the court might establish facts based on eyewitness testimony, by addressing what might happen in the absence of such testimony. Thus, in the case of an animal's death, injury, or capture, Exod 22:9–10 calls for recourse to a cultic procedure—specifically, the oath by Yhwh—when no eyewitness surfaces. The "oath by Yhwh" is an exculpatory oath that the court imposes on a litigant whose version of events is believed because of that litigant's willingness to impose a self-imprecation should the litigant be lying. In the case of a stolen deposit, when a thief is not found (presumably through standard forensic procedures), the bailee also may achieve exoneration by undertaking a cultic procedure. In contrast to Exod 22:9–10, however, the deposit law does not explicate whether the cultic procedure envisioned is an oath by Yhwh or some other method (Exod 22:7). Exodus 22:8, which treats any case of fraud or lost property relating to bailments of both animals and goods, likewise mentions recourse to a cultic procedure without clarifying its character.

Scholars debate whether Exod 22:7–8 envisions an "oath by Yhwh" as in verse 10; whether both verse 7 and verse 8 refer to an oracle, unlike verse 10; or whether verse 7 refers to an oath while verse 8 alludes to an oracle. In the following section, I will examine evidence adduced in favor of and against the oath and oracle in both verses, including linguistic claims and arguments based on the character of each procedure. This section will also investigate the biblical judicial oath more broadly, in an attempt to isolate its features and identify the extent of its comparability to the ancient Near Eastern judicial oath. Ultimately, and perhaps frustratingly, I will demonstrate the indeterminacy of the evidence: the language of verse 7 and verse 8 allows for an oath or oracle in either case, and assumptions about the character of the biblical judicial oath have relied too heavily on comparative data. Given this indeterminacy, I will argue that the procedure in both verses is most likely an oath, and that the law allows the accused party the opportunity to avoid liability by swearing an oath of innocence.[3]

---

2. See LE 36; cf. LH 125, which does not go into specific details but mentions a "breach" (*pilšim*) as one method of burglary.

3. Contra Westbrook, who suggests ("Deposit Law," 361–77) that, if one were to read verse 7 as referring to an oath, then the person swearing would be the accuser (the bailor)—a problem because the oath requires that a person swear to facts within his or her personal knowledge, but the bailor could not know with certainty that the bailee had committed the crime of which he is accused. Cf. also William H. C. Propp, *Exodus 19–40: A New Translation with Introduction and Commentary*, AB 2A (New York: Doubleday, 2006), 246–48. The diffi-

Exodus 22:7–8: Oath(s) or Oracle(s)?

Exodus 22:7 is oddly elliptical, obfuscating precisely what the accused does upon approaching God,[4] as well as what the verdict should be (presumably, that the accused is exonerated).[5] Despite the verse's cryptic formulation, however, scholars have tended to adopt definitive positions regarding whether it refers to an oath by Yhwh, as in verse 10, or to an oracular procedure involving consultation with the deity. Those who interpret the procedure as an oath normally cite versional evidence as well as the parallel to verse 10;[6] those who identify it as an oracle primarily point to the use of the root *q-r-b* found elsewhere in oracular procedures.[7]

---

culty with this view is that the person who swears is "the owner of the house," that is, the bailee in whose "house" the theft occurred in verse 6.

4. There is no compelling evidence to bear out the traditional understanding of "Elohim" as judges (for which see Tg. Onqelos, Palestinian Tg., Peshiṭta, Rashi, Ibn Ezra; cf. KJV, NIV). For the debunking of this view, see especially Cyrus Gordon, "אלהים in Its Reputed Meaning of Rulers, Judges," *JBL* 54 (1935): 139–44. Gordon proposed a parallel to Nuzi household deities (*ilāni*) in both this context and Exod 21:6, which was adapted further by Anne Draffkorn and has found acceptance among some scholars (see Draffkorn, "Ilāni/Elohim," *JBL* 76 [1957]: 216–24; Anthony Phillips, *Essays on Biblical Law*, JSOTSup 344 [London: Sheffield Academic, 2002], 119; Houtman, *Exodus*, 3:197; Karel van der Toorn, *Family Religion in Babylonia, Syria, and Israel: Continuity and Change in the Forms of Religious Life*, SHCANE 7 [Leiden: Brill, 1996], 233–34). This view translates אלהים as "gods." Most scholars, however, understand the word in its usual sense as referring to the God of Israel, so that when this verse states that the owner of the house (i.e., the accused bailee) will approach Elohim, it means that he will go to Elohim's locale, that is, the sanctuary; cf. the similar language in LE 37, which states that "the owner of the house [*bēl bītim*] shall swear an oath … at the gate of (the temple of) the god Tishpak [*ina bāb Tišpak*]." See further Noth, *Exodus*, 184–85; Wright, *Inventing God's Law*, 255; Levinson, *Deuteronomy and the Hermeneutics of Legal Innovation*, 112 n. 37; Wells, "Cultic versus the Forensic," 226.

5. Westbrook's attempt to resolve this second problem by reading all of verse 7 as the protasis of verse 8 has not been received favorably; see Eckart Otto, "Diachronie und Synchronie im Depositenrecht des 'Bundesbuches': Zur jüngsten literatur- und rechtshistorischen Diskussion von Exodus 22:6–14," *ZABR* 2 (1996): 76–85, here 79; Rothenbusch, *Die kasuistische Rechtssammlung*, 357 n. 546.

6. For versional evidence, see LXX, Vulg.; cf. Tg. Pseudo-Jonathan; Philo, *Spec.* 4.34; Josephus, *Ant.* 4.287; Mekhilta on this verse. For the view that the procedure in verse 7 is an oath, see citations in Jackson, *Theft in Early Jewish Law*, 237 n. 1; and see Cassuto, *Commentary on the Book of Exodus*, 286; Childs, *Book of Exodus*, 475–77; Noth, *Exodus*, 184–85; Otto, "Die rechtshistorische Entwicklung," 139–63; Sprinkle, *Book of the Covenant*, 146–48; Levinson, *Deuteronomy and the Hermeneutics of Legal Innovation*, 115–16; Rothenbusch, *Die kasuistische Rechtssammlung*, 357; Wright, *Inventing God's Law*, 254–57; Bartor, *Reading Law as Narrative*, 110–11 n. 61; Baker, "Safekeeping, Borrowing, and Rental," 32; Greengus, *Laws in the Bible*, 188.

7. For the view that the procedure in verse 7 is an oracle, see citations in Jackson, *Theft in Early Jewish Law*, 237 n. 1; and, more recently, Jackson, *Wisdom-Laws*, 344; Schwienhorst-Schönberger, *Das Bundesbuch*, 202–3; Westbrook, "Deposit Law," 363–65; Houtman, *Exodus*, 3:198; Wells, *Law of Testimony*, 142 (and see n. 30 there).

In addition to noting the root *q-r-b* in verse 7, some have assumed that verse 8 refers to the same procedure as the preceding verse and therefore adduce evidence of an oracle from verse 8, including the option for either of two parties to receive a guilty verdict and the words יבא and דבר.[8] However, in the absence of a consensus regarding the relationship between verse 7 and verse 8, including debate as to the originality of verse 8 vis-à-vis its context, any consideration of the procedure in verse 7 must not rely on evidence from verse 8. Therefore, the procedure in each verse should be considered separately.

When one omits verse 8 from discussion of verse 7's procedure, a single positive evidentiary criterion remains in favor of an oracle: the use of the root *q-r-b* in verse 7. Indeed, this root occurs in a number of contexts that appear to include an oracular decision.[9] Yet the same root occurs in various legal contexts that do not relate to an oracle per se, but more generally pertain to parties approaching or being brought near in a legal dispute or inquiry.[10] The use of the root *q-r-b* in Exod 22:7 does not necessarily reflect an oracular proceeding. Although verse 7 and verse 10 (which refers to an oath explicitly) utilize different formulations, the general reference to "approaching God" in verse 7 renders it semantically compatible with the specific mention of the oath in verse 10. There is no definitive evidence against an oath-taking procedure in verse. 7.

---

8. See especially Westbrook, "Deposit Law," 364–65. Westbrook's inclusion of evidence from both verse 7 and verse 8 is consistent with his view that the two verses constitute the protasis and apodosis of the same law. However, others who do not consider verse 8 to be the apodosis of verse 7 per se still consider verse 8 as referring to the same procedure as verse 7, whether that procedure is an oath or an oracle; see, e.g., Knierim, *Die Hauptbegriffe für Sünde*, 143–84; Otto, *Wandel der Rechtsbegründungen*, 15; Schwienhorst-Schönberger, *Das Bundesbuch*, 201; Seebass, "Noch einmal zum Depositenrecht," 25; Houtman, *Exodus*, 3:199; Sprinkle, *Book of the Covenant*, 149–50. For the allegedly oracular language of verse 8, see Jackson, *Wisdom-Laws*, 344.

9. See Num 9:6; 27:1, 5; 36:1; Josh 7:14–18; 1 Sam 10:20–21; 14:36. For a discussion of *q-r-b*, see especially Jackson, *Wisdom-Laws*, 338; and Jackson, *Theft in Early Jewish Law*, 233–44.

10. See citations in Yair Hoffman, "The Root *QRB* as a Legal Term," *JNSL* 10 (1983): 67–73. For a nonoracular use of *q-r-b* that explicitly involves a cultic judicial proceeding, see Num 5:16 (and cf. v. 25), according to which the priest is to bring forth or place before Yhwh (*q-r-b*, hiphil) the suspected Sotah for a procedure that Michael A. Fishbane refers to as an "oath-ordeal" ("Accusations of Adultery: A Study of Law and Scribal Practice in Numbers 5:11–31," in *Women in the Hebrew Bible: A Reader*, ed. Alice Bach [New York: Routledge, 1999], 487–502). Although Fishbane's view of Num 5:11–31 as a unity is subject to debate, some scholars who identify two compositional layers within this law also view the oath and ordeal as components present in each layer; see, e.g., Sarah Shectman, "Bearing Guilt in Numbers 5:12–31," in *Gazing on the Deep: Ancient Near Eastern and Other Studies in Honor of Tzvi Abusch*, ed. Jeffrey Stackert, Barbara Nevling Porter, and David P. Wright (Bethesda, MD: CDL, 2010), 479–93, contra Jaeyoung Jeon, "Two Laws in the Sotah Passage (Num. v 11–31)," *VT* 57 (2007): 181–207. For the view that Num 5:11–31 does not involve an ordeal at all but refers to a formal oath ritual, see Anne Marie Kitz, "Effective Simile and Effective Act: Psalm 109, Numbers 5, and *KUB* 26," *CBQ* 69 (2007): 440–56.

Interpretations of the procedure in verse 8 have fallen along lines similar to the exegetical divide surrounding verse 7. Some scholars identify the verse as an oath like the procedure in verse 10 and, in their view, also in verse 7;[11] others cite as evidence of an oracle the words יבא and דבר and the concept of a procedure that might result in one of two parties' guilt.[12] Yet arguments based on linguistic evidence remain unconvincing. Although a number of verses pertaining to oracular procedures attest the word דָּבָר,[13] דבר also occurs more broadly in various legal contexts referring to a "case," "charge," or "verdict," and it may be translated along these lines both in cases resulting in oracles and in those that do not.[14] In fact, Exod 18:22 uses language very similar to Exod 22:8 (the root *b-w-ʾ* + דבר) with respect to indisputably nonoracular judicial proceedings, in Jethro's recommendation to Moses to appoint judges: "Have them bring [יביאו] every major dispute [הדבר] to you, but let them decide every minor dispute [הדבר] themselves" (NJPS).[15] The terms *b-w-ʾ* and דבר also collocate in other legal contexts with respect to nonoracular and even noncultic procedures.[16] Moreover, verbs from the root *b-w-ʾ* co-occur with nouns from

---

11. See, e.g., Sprinkle, *Book of the Covenant*, 149–50; Levinson, *Deuteronomy and the Hermeneutics of Legal Innovation*, 113–16; Levinson, *"The Right Chorale": Studies in Biblical Law and Interpretation*, FAT 54 (Tübingen: Mohr Siebeck, 2008), 73; and see further citations above.

12. See, e.g., Westbrook, "Deposit Law," 365; Jackson, *Wisdom-Laws*, 344. For another option see Cassuto, who distinguishes between an oath in verse 7 and "Divine judgement, passed by the judges in God's name" in verse 8 (*Commentary on the Book of Exodus*, 286); cf. Childs, who maintains the targumic and Jewish medieval understanding of אלהים as "judges," viewing verse 7 as referring to an oath before judges and verse 8 as referring to adjudication (*Commentary on the Book of Exodus*, 286). For the understanding of verse 8 as referring to an ordeal (though with the acknowledgment that it is difficult to prove), see Fensham, "Mišpāṭîm in the Covenant Code," 102–3. According to Henri Cazelles, verse 8 is deliberately vague, leaving it to the judge to decide which procedure to employ (*Études sur le code de l'alliance* [Paris: Letouzey et Ané, 1946], 66–69).

13. See references in Jackson, *Wisdom-Laws*, 344 n. 69; and Jackson, *Theft in Early Jewish Law*, 241–42.

14. For further discussion of the legal senses of דבר, see Werner Schmidt, דבר "dabhar," *TDOT* 3:84–125; Pietro Bovati, *Re-establishing Justice: Legal Terms, Concepts and Procedures in the Hebrew Bible*, trans. Michael J. Smith, JSOTSup 105 (Sheffield: JSOT Press, 1994), 212–13.

15. Regarding Exod 18:22, Jackson argues that "[although] the term is used of judicial determination, this seems to be a late usage, reflecting the demise of the oracle, which the ancient sources themselves attest" (*Theft in Early Jewish Law*, 242). However, the laws of Exodus hardly exclude forensic criteria. Even within the law of bailment one finds reference to physical evidence, which is sufficient to exonerate the shepherd-bailee in cases of predation (22:12), and to an eyewitness, the absence of which creates a need for recourse to an exculpatory divine oath (22:9–10). Exodus 23:1–3, 6–8 relate to false testimony and just court proceedings, prime concerns in a forensic context involving witnesses and human judgment. In light of the many nonoracular, legal usages of the term דבר and the presence of both cultic and forensic methods in Exodus's laws, I question Jackson's view that דבר in reference to "judicial determination" in Exod 18:22 reflects a later usage.

16. See, e.g., Deut 17:8–13. While Jackson understands this passage as involving an

the same semantic realm as דבר (such as ריב, "legal contention") in phrases referring to judicial procedures that do not involve the deity,[17] and they even occur in the context of at least one judicial oath.[18] Thus, the use of neither *b-w-ʾ* nor דבר (nor the combination of the two) is helpful for clarifying the nature of the procedure in Exod 22:8.

Unlike others who have relied on linguistic evidence to interpret the procedure in Exod 22:8 as an oracle, Westbrook has offered evidence based on the character of judicial proceedings in the ancient Near East. According to him, throughout most of ancient Near Eastern history, an exculpatory oath would transpire in a situation where one party was accused of guilt. The court would impose the oath upon one party, generally the defendant, but also possibly the plaintiff or either party's witnesses. A defendant who swore would win the case, but one who refused to swear would automatically lose.[19] In Westbrook's words, "[The] true judgment of the court has been in deciding which party is to take the oath."[20] Because the continuation of Exod 22:8 refers to the pronouncement of a verdict and resultant compensation, thereby indicating that further judgment follows the cultic proceeding, Westbrook argues that the procedure cannot be an oath and, therefore, must be an oracle.[21]

In determining whether the procedure in Exod 22:8 is an oath or an oracle, we ought to consider the biblical exculpatory oath on its own terms before drawing conclusions based on oaths in other settings. Previous scholarship on the biblical exculpatory oath has tended to focus on comparative evidence due to the scarcity of information in the Bible about the nature and function of this procedure. Still, the Bible attests to a small number of exculpatory oaths that merit attention.[22] One of these occurs in the herding law of Exod 22:9–10:

---

oracle, Wells ("Cultic versus the Forensic," 226–27) has argued that the law contains an exclusively forensic procedure.

17. For *b-w-ʾ* + ריב, see, e.g., Isa 1:23; 2 Chr 19:10. On this meaning of ריב, see Michael De Roche, "Yahweh's Rîb against Israel: A Reassessment of the So-Called 'Prophetic Lawsuit' in the Preexilic Prophets," *JBL* 102 (1983): 563–74. Another similar expression, *b-w-ʾ* + למשפט ("approach … for judgment"), where the grammatical subject of the verb "approaches" is not "the case" (as in Exod 22:8) but a party to the dispute, also suggests human disputants and judges (see 2 Sam 15:2, 6).

18. See 1 Kgs 8:31, which I will discuss shortly. The verb *b-w-ʾ* also occurs in the context of oaths that are not judicial but covenantal; see, e.g., Ezek 7:13; Neh 10:30; and compare 1 Sam 20:8; Ezek 16:8; Jer 34:10; 2 Chr 15:12.

19. See Westbrook, "Deposit Law," 363–64; Bruce Wells, Cornelia Wunsch, and F. Rachel Magdalene, "The Assertory Oath in Neo-Babylonian and Persian Administrative Texts," *Revue Internationale des droits de l'Antiquité* 57 (2010): 13–29, here 14–15.

20. Westbrook, "Deposit Law," 365.

21. Ibid., 363–64.

22. I include among these Exod 22:9–10, Lev 5:20–26, Num 5:11–31, Deut 21:1–9, and 1 Kgs 8:31–32, following Sophie Lafont, "La procédure par serment au Proche-Orient ancien," in *Jurer et maudire: Pratiques politiques et usages juridiques du serment dans le Proche-*

⁹When a man gives to another a donkey, or an ox, or a sheep, or any animal to watch, but it dies, or is injured, or is captured, with no eyewitness, ¹⁰there shall be an oath by Yhwh between the two of them (to determine) if he has not behaved negligently toward the other's property; the owner shall accept (the verdict), and he shall not pay.

Although these verses are brief, we can glean the following about this oath: It is taken in the absence of forensic means of adjudication; there is no witness to testify to the bailee's innocence or guilt. It is sworn in the name of Yhwh. Finally, immediately following the oath, the owner shall accept [ולקח בעליו] an unspecified object, which I have translated here parenthetically as "the verdict," based on this usage of *l-q-ḥ* and its Akkadian cognate *leqû*.²³ The phrase may alternatively refer to acceptance of the oath.²⁴ Either of these translations suggests that the oath in Exod 22:10 is not dispositive. The judicial proceedings do not end automatically as soon as the accused swears; instead, the owner, whose accusation proves unfounded, must *accept*.

Another oath appears in the law of the adulterous woman in Num 5:11–31, a passage that has spurred ample debate about whether it constitutes a unity or contains two layers of composition.²⁵ Here I focus on the

---

Orient ancien, ed. Sophie Lafont (Paris: L'Harmattan, 1996), 185–98, here 193–97; Wells, "Cultic versus the Forensic," 207. Only Wells includes Exod 22:9–10. I exclude here passages that utilize oath language for rhetorical purposes, which may be more useful as a window into the formulation of oaths.

23. See, e.g., Isa 40:2; and see Stephen A. Geller, "A Poetic Analysis of Isaiah 40:1–2," *HTR* 77 (1984): 413–20, here 418–19 n. 17 regarding the legal valence of this verse. For *leqû* referring to the acceptance of a verdict (e.g., *dīnu, amatu*) or to the acceptance of a divine decision (*têrtu*), see, e.g., PBS 7 7; CT 29 42. PBS 7 7 recounts a trial in which a defendant swore a divine exculpatory oath (*nīš ilim*), but the plaintiff still would not accept the verdict (*dīnam šuāti ul leqi*): precisely the sense of ולקח בעליו in Exod 22:10, in which the oath by Yhwh allows for judicial determination, and the plaintiff accepts the resulting verdict. For text and translation of PBS 7 7, see Stol, *Letters from Yale*, 4–7; the pertinent language is in lines 20–23.

24. For accepting the oath, see, e.g., Schwienhorst-Schönberger, *Das Bundesbuch*, 203–4; Baker, "Safekeeping, Borrowing, and Rental," 33 n. 18. I do not accept the proposed understanding of ולקח בעליו as "he shall take (the animal)" (for which see Cassuto, *Commentary on the Book of Exodus*, 287; Sprinkle, *Book of the Covenant*, 145 n. 1), on the grounds that this interpretation poses a difficulty for the scenario of animal capture, in which case the animal is absent. Both Westbrook ("Deposit Law," 372) and Jackson (*Wisdom-Laws*, 350), who approach the text from the perspective that this oath must be dispositive, offer interpretations that sacrifice economy; Westbrook considers ולקח בעליו a reference to an allegation that an owner has recaptured his own animal, such that verse 10 lumps together possible wrongdoings of the bailee and bailor, as well as their respective exculpatory oaths; while Jackson understands בעליו—the person who "takes"—as the bailee watching the sheep who swore his innocence, rather than the owner. In his reading, the innocent shepherd may keep the animal he was accused of doing wrong by; however, this interpretation of בעליו strays from the standard meaning of the word ("owner").

25. Shectman divides the passage into two layers, which she calls Layer A and Layer B ("Bearing Guilt," 479–93). In this division, Layer A includes verses 12–13, 15, 18, 21–24a,

final verse in the pericope, 5:31, which caps off either one compositional layer of the law or, if the verses are viewed as a compositional unity, the entire passage. Following a complex oath rite that includes both an oath and a drinking or water ritual, verse 31 states that the woman shall "bear her punishment."[26] Tikva Frymer-Kensky understands this phrase as referring to punishment that God—and not the human court—will mete out; therefore, she argues that the procedure itself would have ended the trial of the accused.[27] On the other hand, Sophie Lafont interprets the same verse as a reference to further judgment. In her view, verse 31 alludes to a judicial sentence; the woman must bear the penalty pronounced by a judge or possibly by her husband.[28] In Lafont's account, the oath in itself does not put an end to the proceedings, despite indicating whether the accused is innocent or guilty. Depending on how one interprets this verse, then, it is possible that the oath and accompanying ritual in the law of the suspected adulteress are to be construed as nondispositive.

First Kings 8:31–32 comprises a section of Solomon's prayer at the dedication of the Temple:

> (31) If someone sins against a neighbor and is given an oath to swear, and comes and swears [ובא אלה] before your altar in this house, (32) then hear in heaven, and act, and judge [$*š$-p-$ṭ$] your servants, condemning the guilty [להרשיע רשע] by bringing their conduct on their own head, and vindicating the righteous [ולהצדיק צדיק] by rewarding them according to their righteousness. (NRSV)[29]

In this portion of his prayer, Solomon addresses a case where one person wrongs another and one party swears an oath at the altar. The king asks God to judge between the two parties, finding one guilty and one inno-

---

25–26a, 27aβ–b, 29, 31, while Layer B includes verses 14, 16–17, 19–20, 24b, 27aα, 28, 30. Various views have emerged regarding the division of Num 5:11–31 into two primary layers; for overviews, see Jeon, "Two Laws in the Sotah Passage," 182–83; Dalit Rom-Shiloni, "'How can you say, "I am not defiled …?"' (Jeremiah 2:20–25): Allusions to Priestly Legal Traditions in the Poetry of Jeremiah," *JBL* 133 (2014): 757–75, here 773–74.

26. For the nature of this ritual (which I do not consider an ordeal per se but part of a single complex oath rite), see Tikva Frymer-Kensky, "The Strange Case of the Suspected Sotah (Numbers V 11–31)," *VT* 34 (1984): 11–26, here 24–25; Kitz, "Effective Simile and Effective Act," 440–56.

27. Frymer-Kensky, "Strange Case of the Suspected Sotah," 22. Frymer-Kensky cites the view that the Priestly use of the phrase "bear punishment" (נשא עון) refers to divine punishment, for which see further Walther Zimmerli, "Die Eigenart der prophetischen Rede des Ezechiel: Ein Beitrag zum Problem an Hand von Ez 14:1–11," *ZAW* 66 (1954): 1–26, here 8–11.

28. Lafont, "La procédure par serment," 196–97.

29. Textual and exegetical difficulties have led to a wide range of interpretations of these verses; for an extensive review of scholarship, see Martin J. Mulder, *1 Kings*, trans. John Vriend, HCOT 7 (Leuven: Peeters: 1998), 421–26.

cent.[30] Although Lafont argues here (unlike in the case of Num 5:31!) that this verse merely requests that God mete out justice in time,[31] 1 Kgs 8:31 is commonly understood to refer to some unspecified ritual through which the parties would learn God's decision, on the basis of which compensation would be determined.[32] Indeed, 1 Kgs 8:32 heavily evokes the language of Deut 25:1: "Suppose two persons have a dispute and enter into litigation, and the judges decide [*$\check{s}$-p-t] between them, declaring one to be in the right [והצדיקו את־הצדיק] and the other to be in the wrong [והרשיעו את־הרשע]." The linguistic affinities between the actions of God in 1 Kgs 8:32 and the actions of judges in court in Deut 25:1 indicate that the former context also involves adjudication, although it leaves unclear the extent to which that adjudication resembles that of a human court. At minimum, 1 Kgs 8:32 appears to suggest some form of additional judgment following the swearing of an oath. As such, the oath in this prayer is not dispositive.

These three sources, in Exodus, Numbers, and 1 Kings, include references to oaths that may not have been dispositive. Of the two other biblical passages that have been understood as referring to exculpatory oaths, one offers no information about whether the oath was dispositive or not (Lev 5:20–26), and one aims to stem expiation of bloodguilt already in force, rather than to prevent a penalty (Deut 21:1–9), so that "further judgment" is irrelevant.[33]

Biblical references to exculpatory oaths are few and far between. Due to the paucity of references, their eclectic sources, and the range of variation between them, no clear picture of the biblical exculpatory oath emerges. Yet even these few sources cast doubt upon a wholesale equation

---

30. Contra Simon J. De Vries, who has both parties swearing contradictory oaths (*1 Kings*, WBC 12 [Waco, TX: Word, 1985], 126); and Volkmar Fritz, who has neither party swearing an exculpatory oath, instead understanding the passage as referring to a person who is cursed unjustly and may choose to undergo a trial by ordeal to acquit himself (*1 & 2 Kings*, trans. Anselm Hagedorn, Continental Commentary [Minneapolis: Fortress, 2003], 98).

31. Lafont, "La procédure par serment," 193–94.

32. See Mordechai Cogan, *1 Kings: A New Translation with Introduction and Commentary*, AB 10 (New York: Doubleday, 2001), 284–85; Mulder, *1 Kings*, 425; Eep Talstra, *Solomon's Prayer: Synchrony and Diachrony in the Composition of 1 Kings 8, 14–61*, CBET 3 (Kampen: Kok, 1993), 112.

33. Unless the oath served a purpose separate from that of the elimination rite; see, e.g., Lafont, who argues that the oath took place as part of a trial, where the victim's dependents served as plaintiffs, and the oath would have served to prohibit vengeance or sanctions against any resident of the city ("La procédure par serment," 195–96). This view relies heavily on reconstructing information absent from the biblical text. For the view that this text does not involve an exculpatory oath at all, but rather a declaration of innocence, see Jeffrey H. Tigay, *Deuteronomy* דברים: *The Traditional Hebrew Text with the New JPS Translation*, JPS Torah Commentary (Philadelphia: Jewish Publication Society of America, 1996), 474–75.

between biblical and ancient Near Eastern exculpatory oaths. One may choose to construe the oaths in Exod 22:9–10, Num 5:11–31, and 1 Kgs 8:31–32 as dispositive or not, but one ought to decide between these interpretations based on an understanding of each text in its own right, rather than assuming that they resemble their ancient Near Eastern counterparts.

Scholars who interpret the judicial procedure in Exod 22:8 as an oracle rather than an oath have argued that the formulation "whomsoever Elohim declares guilty"—indicating that either one of the two parties to the dispute might be found guilty—comports better with an oracle than with an oath, and that the inclusion of "further judgment" in verse 8 contradicts the dispositive nature of oaths. Yet 1 Kgs 8:31–32 also makes reference to the deity declaring one party guilty and even explicates that the other party is declared innocent. This pronouncement of judgment indicates that, like Exod 22:8, 1 Kgs 8:31–32 envisions a scenario involving two options for who may be found guilty. The notion of judgment between two parties present in Exod 22:8 thus does not clash with how a biblical exculpatory oath might function. The "nondispositive" character of the procedure in Exod 22:8 likewise does not preclude the possibility that the verse refers to an oath, because biblical exculpatory oaths may not have been dispositive.

Scholarship remains divided regarding whether the procedures in Exod 22:7–8 reflect an oath or an oracle. Examination of arguments in favor of an oracle, based on linguistic criteria and the incompatibility of the procedure(s) in these verses with an oath, has demonstrated that there is no compelling evidence favoring an oracle over an oath, or excluding an oath altogether. Unlike Exod 22:10, which explicitly mentions an "oath by Yhwh," the formulation of verse 7 and verse 8 simply leaves vague the nature of the procedure(s) they envision.

Although these verses remain open to interpretation, in the absence of convincing evidence to the contrary, I prefer to view the procedure in both as an oath. As Eckart Otto has argued, the shared language of verse 7 and verse 10 highlights the parallel between them; and versional evidence and ancient interpretations point to an oath as well. Without any evidence excluding an oath or favoring an oracle in verse 8, I prefer to read it as sharing the same procedure as its context, rather than assume that it diverges from it.[34] Based on this reading, Exod 22 calls for recourse to a cultic judicial procedure—specifically, an oath—in a number of cases. These include the following scenarios:

---

34. In light of the further ritual activities accompanying other biblical exculpatory oaths, such as the water or drinking ritual in Num 5 and the elimination rite in Deut 21, it is possible that the oaths of Exod 22:7, 8, and 10 would have shared elements with other cultic procedures beyond the pronouncement of the oath itself, including perhaps some means of elucidating divine judgment. The scarcity of evidence bars definite conclusions.

1. A bailee of goods is accused of negligently allowing for theft to occur, and no thief has been found who can assume culpability and compensate the owner.
2. One party accuses the other of fraud—whether it is the bailor accusing the bailee of fraud in a deposit or case of herding, an owner of lost property accusing the finder of misappropriating the property, or an accused bailee who counter-accuses the bailor of bringing false charges against the bailee.
3. Animals in the care of a shepherd suffer death, injury, or capture, with no witness to testify to the facts of the case.

The mention of no witness in Exod 22:9 in particular suggests that recourse to an oath emerges in cases where standard forensic methods fail. There is at least one case, however, where the presence of physical evidence eliminates a need for cultic procedures. This is the case of predation, to which we turn presently.

Predation and the Production of Physical Evidence

Exodus 22:12 introduces an exceptional case of animal death that does not have the accused swear by Yhwh in order to achieve exoneration. If a wild beast mutilates an animal, thereby killing it, the shepherd must produce evidence in the form of the carcass—or what little remains of it—to automatically escape liability.[35] The physical evidence of predation obviates the need for recourse to a cultic ritual, which the lack of eyewitness testimony might have otherwise necessitated in other cases of animal death. Similar to Exod 22:12, biblical narratives refer to one party bringing evidence of an animal attack to the mutilated sheep's owner (Gen 31:39) or to the human victim's father (Gen 37:31–33).[36]

The shepherd's delivery of animal remains also finds a parallel in the ancient Near Eastern practice of recording deficits in the flock, which the Laws of Hammurabi address (266) and to which legal documents from different periods and sites widely attest. Herding arrangements followed a yearly cycle, at the end of which accounts were adjusted to reflect losses and additions. Although shepherds and other herders typically bore

---

35. Commentaries going as far back as the Mekhilta have pointed in this context to Amos 3:12, which draws on the image of a shepherd saving "[two] shank bones or the tip of an ear" (NJPS) from the mouth of a lion (see Mekhilta de-Rabbi Ishmael Mishpatim 16). For an argument that Amos 3:12 deliberately invokes the law of Exod 22:12 for rhetorical purposes, see Yuichi Osumi, *Die Kompositionsgeschichte des Bundesbuches Exodus 20, 22b–23, 33*, OBO 105 (Freiburg, Switzerland: Universitätsverlag; Göttingen: Vandenhoeck & Ruprecht, 1991), 169.

36. See discussion in Jackson, *Wisdom-Laws*, 348–49 n. 89.

responsibility for losses, contracts exempted them from liability for *miqittu*, animals that died of natural causes, such as disease or mutilation by wild beasts.[37] In cases of *miqittu*, the herder had to produce whatever remained of the animal, usually its skin (and sometimes, perhaps, its tendons) — also termed *miqittu* — in exchange for a receipt recording the loss and confirming the herder's exemption from liability.[38] For example, a Middle Assyrian document records the number of skins deducted from the number of losses for which a donkey-herd bore liability:

> After 3 skins of adult female donkeys, 1 skin of a 2-year old female donkey, 1 skin of a weaned female donkey, 1 skin of a 4-year-old male donkey, 2 skins of weaned male donkeys, a total of 8 skins of his have been deducted from his liability, his accounts are finalized. His birth(-rate) is at 40. PN, donkey-herd.[39]

As this statement demonstrates, a herder settling accounts at the end of a herding period could produce animal skins and thereby reduce the losses for which the owner could hold the herder accountable. The production of animal remains to which Exod 22:12 refers reflects a practice that was widespread and well documented in the ancient Near East.

---

37. See *CAD* M/2, s.v. *"miqittu"*; A. Leo Oppenheim, *Catalogue of the Cuneiform Tablets of the Wilberforce Eames Babylonian Collection in the New York Public Library*, AOS 32 (New Haven: American Oriental Society, 1948), 62; F. R. Kraus, *Ein Edikt des Königs Ammi-Ṣaduqa von Babylon*, Studia et documenta ad iura Orientis antiqui pertinentia 5 (Leiden: Brill, 1958), 113–14; Kraus, *Staatliche Viehhaltung im altbabylonischen Lande Larsa*, 14; Finkelstein, "Old Babylonian Herding Contract," 35; J. N. Postgate, "Some Old Babylonian Shepherds and Their Flocks," *JSS* 20 (1975): 1–18, here 6; Morrison, "Evidence for Herdsmen," 271, 279.

38. Some contracts explicitly identify remains as *miqittu* (or RI.RI.GA); others do not. Although *miqittu* frequently follows KUŠ (*mašku*), "skin," when not preceded by KUŠ it need not be understood as skin per se. On this point, see Kraus, *Staatliche Viehhaltung im altbabylonischen Lande Larsa*, 14. For tendons (SA), see Oppenheim, *Catalogue of the Cuneiform Tablets*, 80–81. SA has alternatively been understood as "intestines," on which see Kilian Butz, "Ur in altbabylonischer Zeit als Wirtschaftsfaktor," in *State and Temple Economy in the Ancient Near East: Proceedings of the International Conference organized by the Katholieke Universiteit Leuven from the 10th to the 14th of April 1978*, ed. Edward Lipiński, 2 vols., OLA 5–6 (Leuven: Departement Oriëntalistiek, 1979), 1:258–409, here 349–50; see also Postgate, *Early Mesopotamia*, 160 and 316 n. 246.

For the association between Exod 22:12 and the delivery of animal skins, see the opinion of R. Josiah, cited in Mekhilta de-Rabbi Ishmael Mishpatim 16, that עד יבאהו refers to producing the עדר, apparently referring to "skin" (perhaps a scribal error for עור). In fact, Arnold B. Ehrlich suggested emending verse 12's עד יבאהו to יביא העור, "he shall bring the skin" (*Randglossen zur hebräischen Bibel: Textkritisches, sprachliches und sachliches*, 7 vols. [Leipzig: Hinrichs, 1908–1914], 1:353–54).

39. Wolfgang Röllig, *Land- und Viehwirtschaft am Unteren Habur in mittelassyrischer Zeit*, BATSHDK 9 (Wiesbaden: Harrassowitz, 2008), text no. 40:9–19; this translation is adapted from Postgate, *Bronze Age Bureaucracy*, 308.

The practice of delivering *miqittu* served two purposes: to prove that the animal had died through no fault of the shepherd, and to provide the owner with the animal's parts, which were valuable in their own right.[40] In his commentary on Exod 22:12, Cassuto suggests that "[the] word עֵד *ʿēdh* … contains a play on, and a reference to, עַד *ʿadh*, which means *prey*."[41] Despite the "legal" genre of Exod 22, the presence of a literary device of this kind would not be surprising; the laws of Exodus contains numerous examples of wordplay, double entendre, stylistic variation, irony, and chiasmus.[42] The collocation of the root *ṭ-r-p* with עַד ("prey") in Gen 49:27 lends further support to the possibility that Exod 22:12 has in mind the uncommon Biblical Hebrew word עַד.[43] The word עֵד in verse 12 may thus allude to the dual function of *miqittu*, providing the owner both with (a) evidence of predation (עֵד) and (b) value in the form of salvaged parts (עַד).

A. Leo Oppenheim has collected numerous examples of Ur III legal documents that record shepherds taking oaths to clear themselves of liability upon delivery of *miqittu* from animals that, in his view, had "probably been killed by wild beasts."[44] Although Exod 22:9–10 calls for an oath in other cases of animal death without witnesses, in cases of death by predation the production of remains appears to satisfy the law for the purposes of exculpating the shepherd. On the other hand, Exod 22 does not address the possibility of death by predation where the shepherd cannot salvage any remains. In the absence of evidence, would the death fall under the purview of Exod 22:9–10's animal death, allowing the shepherd to take an exculpatory oath? Liability statements from Durkatlimmu in the Middle Assyrian period demonstrate that, under special circumstances, shepherds who were unable to skin the cadaver for evidence could exonerate themselves instead through an oath.[45] Although these records indicate the plausibility of an oath replacing the production of an animal's remains, there is no way to determine whether the same would hold true in the biblical scheme.

---

40. Regarding the purposes of *miqittu* delivery, see Postgate, "Some Old Babylonian Shepherds," 6; Postgate, *Bronze Age Bureaucracy*, 308.

41. Cassuto, *Commentary on the Book of Exodus*, 287.

42. See examples in Gary A. Rendsburg, "Repetition with Variation in Legal-Cultic Texts of the Torah," in *Marbeh Ḥokmah: Studies in the Bible and the Ancient Near East in Loving Memory of Victor Avigdor Hurowitz*, ed. S. Yona et al. (Winona Lake, IN: Eisenbrauns, 2015), 435–63; Sprinkle, *Book of the Covenant*, 141, 173–74, 184–85, 192, 206; Chaya T. Halberstam, "The Art of Biblical Law," *Prooftexts* 27 (2007): 345–64; Bartor, *Reading Law as Narrative*.

43. Gen 49:27: "Benjamin is a ravenous [*ṭ-r-p*] wolf, / in the morning devouring the prey [עַד], / and at evening dividing the spoil" (NRSV). For other occurrences of עַד with this meaning, see Isa 33:23 and Zeph 3:3; Ibn Ezra further cites Isa 64:5.

44. Oppenheim, *Catalogue of the Cuneiform Tablets*, 62; see also Postgate, *Early Mesopotamia*, 160.

45. Röllig, *Land- und Viehwirtschaft am Unteren Habur*, especially nos. 43, 48.

No Way Out

When a shepherd accepts flock animals for herding but something goes wrong, the situation may call for the use of various means of fact-finding: an eyewitness might recount the details of an animal's death, injury, or capture. When there is no witness, the accused has the opportunity to swear by Yhwh that no negligence caused the situation. In cases of predation, shepherds may produce physical evidence in the form of animal remains to prove that they bear no fault, and thereby avoid liability.

Exodus 22:11 introduces an exception to these scenarios. If an animal is stolen—apparently in a manner less forceful than capture—then the shepherd automatically assumes culpability and must compensate the owner. In cases of animal theft, the shepherd lacks any means of exoneration, a premise echoed in Jacob's claim of accepting liability of all animals stolen, whether during the day or at night (Gen 31:39). Exodus 22 differs in its treatment of goods or silver and its treatment of animals in two regards. When deposited goods or silver are stolen, the accused has the opportunity to undergo a cultic procedure whereby innocence can be proven. The shepherd has no such option. Moreover, unlike the law of deposits, which first notes that if the thief is found, that thief is liable (Exod 22:6), the law of herding does not address whether the bailee still must compensate the owner if the thief is located.

Does the difference between the bailee's liability in cases of deposit-theft versus animal-theft pose a contradiction?[46] Although some have accepted a rabbinic distinction between a gratuitous bailee (who watches property free of charge) and non-gratuitous bailee (who receives compensation for watching property) in their interpretations of these verses,[47] the simplest reading of Exod 22's first two laws of bailment does not distinguish between them on this basis. The basis of the distinction between these laws should instead be located in the usual mode of watching goods versus watching animals. Because shepherds must take the animals out into the open, their tasks naturally require a higher degree of vigilance.[48] If the shepherd were to protect the animals in the manner expected, theft would be impossible; therefore, that shepherd is liable. Bailees of goods, on the other hand, simply store the items alongside their own property, in their own home. Because the nature of their duties is less hands-on, the

---

46. Schwienhorst-Schönberger does not attribute the discrepancy to different compositional levels but considers verse 7 defectively formulated and imports details from verse 11 into the former (*Das Bundesbuch*, 207–8).

47. Cassuto, *Commentary on the Book of Exodus*, 287; Westbrook, "Deposit Law," 371 n. 36; Rothenbusch, *Die kasuistische Rechtssammlung*, 358.

48. Cf. Rashbam, ad loc.; Sprinkle, *Book of the Covenant*, 151 (distinguishing between inanimate and animate bailments and corresponding degrees of expected supervision).

law expects of these bailees a lower degree of vigilance. Thus, while in cases of deposits the bailee should do whatever possible to prevent theft, the law acknowledges that theft could reasonably occur anyway, notwithstanding the provision of satisfactory care.

The Owner's Presence

Immediately following the law of herding, the law of animal borrowing and rental in Exod 22:13–14 addresses scenarios that overlap with those of the herding law—including animal death and injury. However, instead of suggesting that the accused swear by Yhwh, the law introduces an unprecedentedly specific fact-finding method, which to the best of my knowledge is attested nowhere else in the Bible or in all of cuneiform literature:

יג) וכי ישאל איש מעם רעהו ונשבר או מת בעליו אין עמו שלם ישלם

יד) אם בעליו עמו לא ישלם אם שכיר הוא בא בשכרו[13]

When a man borrows from another (an animal) and it is injured or dies without its owner present, he must pay. [14]If its owner is with it, he shall not pay. If it is rented, he is liable for its rental fee.

According to these verses, the borrower's liability hinges on whether the "owner is with it"—that is, with the animal.[49] This criterion is strikingly odd. Why would an animal's owner be present? And, perhaps more important, why would this exonerate the borrower?[50]

Numerous commentaries have explained the exculpatory power of the owner's presence as follows: If the owner is present, then the owner shared responsibility for the animal's well-being and so remains personally accountable for it despite the involvement of a borrower.[51] Others have understood this criterion as signifying that the owner has witnessed that the death or injury lay outside the control of the borrower.[52] The law's

---

49. Rothenbusch argues that the owner's presence signifies that he is with "it"—the animal—rather than with "him"—the borrower/renter (*Die kasuistische Rechtssammlung*, 360).

50. See this question, acutely formulated, in Jackson, *Wisdom-Laws*, 360. I reject Jackson's solution that the word בעל* refers not to the "owner" (as it is typically understood) but to the borrower himself. This reading is unsupported by internal biblical evidence, and I disagree with Jackson's understanding of Hittite Laws 76 as relating to borrowing. For further critique of this view, see Wright, *Inventing God's Law*, 471 n. 56.

51. See, e.g., Cassuto, *Commentary on the Book of Exodus*, 288; Noth, *Exodus*, 185; Houtman, *Exodus*, 3:205; Sprinkle, *Book of the Covenant*, 155.

52. See, e.g., Childs, *Book of Exodus*, 475–77; cf. Wright, *Inventing God's Law*, 282: "The owner would act as a deterrent to the misuse of his animal and also as a witness." A third view (found in Saul Levmore, "Rethinking Comparative Law: Variety and Uniformity in Ancient and Modern Tort Law," *Tulane Law Review* 61 [1986]: 235–87, here 274 n. 109)

emphasis on means of establishing facts—with methods including exculpatory oaths, use of eyewitness testimony, and the production of physical
evidence—weighs in favor of the second view. The owner's presence can
exonerate the borrower because of the owner's role as witness. Although
in a case of herding, presumably any person who would typically qualify
as a witness could testify about an animal's death, injury, or capture, the
law of animal borrowing restricts its set of eligible witnesses to a single
person: the animal's owner. The evidentiary function of the owner's presence further demonstrates that, although the law does not spell out this
point, the borrower escapes liability only if the owner actually witnesses
the borrower's innocence. If the owner witnesses any action or inaction
that puts the borrower at fault, then the mere presence of the owner at the
scene of the crime does not exempt the borrower from payment. Like the
laws of deposit and herding before it, which ignore the possibility that the
bailee might refuse to undergo a cultic procedure because the bailee might
in fact be guilty, Exod 22:14a ("If its owner is with it, he shall not pay")
speaks from a point of view that assumes the suspect's innocence.

In addition to limiting drastically the pool of eligible witnesses, Exod
22's law of animal borrowing and rental also deviates both from its own
laws of deposit and herding and from cuneiform law collections insofar as
it does not allow the accused the opportunity to avoid liability by swearing an exculpatory oath. Law of Hammurabi 249 caps off a unit of six laws
(244–249) treating an animal renter's liability when the animal suffers various forms of injury or death:

> If a man rents an ox, and the god strikes it and it dies, the man who rented
> the ox shall swear an oath by the god and he shall be exempt.

In contrast to LH 244, which treats a case of predation where the animal's
remains allow the renter to avoid liability, LH 249 involves another form
of *force majeure* ending with the animal's death. In such cases, the renter
may swear an exculpatory oath. Similarly, according to Hittite Law 75,

> If anyone hitches up an ox, a horse, a mule or an ass, and it dies, [or] a
> wolf devours [it], or it gets lost, he shall give it in full. But if he says: "It
> died by the hand of a god," he shall take an oath to that effect.[53]

---

interprets the criterion as follows: Liability depends on whether the owner is present at the
time the bailment is created (as opposed to a scenario where a person borrows an already-
borrowed animal, in which case the owner would not be present). This interpretation does
not cohere with the plain sense of the text, which mentions the absence or presence of the
owner only after laying out what might befall the animal after it has been borrowed.

53. Translated by Hoffner, in Roth, *Law Collections*, 227.

In a case of death or predation, HL 75's default position is that the renter is liable.[54] However, the renter has the opportunity to claim *force majeure* and swear an exculpatory oath. HL is similar to Exodus insofar as neither allows an automatic exemption for predation in cases of animal rental (in contrast to cases of herding in Exod 22:12). Unlike Exodus, however, both HL and LH afford the renter the opportunity to attribute the animal's death to a god and achieve exoneration through an oath. The biblical law thus dramatically restricts the renter's and borrower's opportunities for exoneration, in comparison both with other sections of the biblical bailment law and with laws from Mesopotamia and Hatti.

The criterion of the owner's presence applies in cases of both animal borrowing and rental. In the case of rental, the law adds a final clause, אם שכיר הוא בא בשכרו, which I translate as follows: "If it [i.e., the animal] is rented, he [i.e., the renter] is liable for its rental fee."[55] Exodus 22:13–14a establishes that a borrower is liable in all cases of animal death or injury, except when the owner is present to witness the truly accidental nature of the mishap. Exodus 22:14b then extends the law to the case where the animal is not borrowed, but rented, and adds that in cases of animal rental, the loss of the animal (whether or not the owner is present) does not excuse the renter from paying the rental fee. Rather, in all cases of animal rental—even when the renter is not liable to pay for the loss of the animal—the renter "is liable for its (i.e., the animal's) rental fee."

Although some have argued that the owner's presence at the scene of the animal's death or injury is highly implausible,[56] the law may have in mind a number of possible scenarios. The owner's presence might be limited to the time of the animal's delivery and return; or the owner might work or live in proximity to where the borrower uses the animal, perhaps

---

54. Although LH 244 mentions predation by a lion and HL 75's animal of prey is a wolf, the difference between these animals appears to be of no legal import (in contrast to Greengus, *Laws in the Bible*, 206, arguing that a wolf was thought to pose a less serious threat than a lion). A review of cuneiform law collections suggests that HL and LH each chose a paradigmatic wild predator, which for HL was the wolf and for LH was the lion. LH's choice of a lion coheres with the standard choice among ancient Near Eastern collections from Mesopotamia; none of the Mesopotamian collections refers to a wolf (see, e.g., LOx 7, 8; SLEx 9; SLHF vi 16–22, vi 32–36; LH 244, 266). HL, on the other hand, never refers to a lion, but in two other laws mentions a wolf. HL 80 portrays the wolf as a predator from whom a brave shepherd might save sheep; and HL 37 curiously has people say to the man who abducts a woman he intends to marry, which resulted in a number of deaths, that he has "become a wolf."

55. Following Wright, *Inventing God's Law*, 276–77. Wright summarizes and reasonably rejects other possible interpretations, including those that understand the שכיר as a "hired person" instead of as a "rented animal," and those that read the subject of the participle בא as "it" (i.e., the loss) or as "he" referring to the hired person, instead of "he" (i.e., renter).

56. See, e.g., Jackson, *Wisdom-Laws*, 360.

even working together with the borrower.[57] The plausibility of the scenario, however, may not be as crucial as its very unusualness as a criterion in fact-finding, both in the immediate context of the Covenant Code's bailment law and in the broader corpus of biblical and cuneiform law collections, as well as within the wide-ranging hodge-podge of legal documents available to us from Mesopotamia. In contrast to nearly every other detail in Exod 22:6–14, which more or less fits with what we can reconstruct in broad strokes about bailment in ancient Israel based on other sources, the owner's presence is an odd condition for establishing facts that has no analog.

Compensation and Consequences

Exodus 22 assigns different levels of compensation to the liable party depending on the case. When deposited goods or silver are stolen, the thief is required to pay *duplum*, or double compensation (Exod 22:6). When no thief is found, the bailee assumes the same level of liability that the thief would have borne, whether the bailee is suspected of negligently allowing for theft to occur (22:7) or of defrauding the owner by stealing the property (22:8). Exodus 22:8 extends this penalty of *duplum* also to cases of fraud involving animals or lost property, and to an owner who falsely accuses the bailee in an effort to extort double compensation. Although Exod 22:9–10 does not specify the penalty of a shepherd who is liable for negligently allowing an animal to suffer death, injury, or capture, the inclusion of animals in verse 8, which serves as a bridge between two borderline cases of negligence (pertaining to deposits and to herding), suggests that the penalty of *duplum* applies in these cases as well.

The equal penalty of double compensation in Exod 22 for cases of negligence, fraud, and false accusations in deposits and herding differs from compensation standards in comparable paragraphs from the Laws of Hammurabi and from what one finds in Mesopotamian legal documents from a range of milieux. LH 124 requires double compensation for cases of fraud with respect to deposits. In cases of negligence, however, the Laws of Hammurabi typically assign single compensation, including when a bailee of goods negligently allows for theft to occur (LH 125), when a herdsman negligently causes losses in the flock (LH 263), and when a shepherd negligently allows a disease to spread among the flock animals

---

57. For which, see especially, Rothenbusch, *Die kasuistische Rechtssammlung*, 360. Rothenbusch cites other laws pertaining to renting an animal along with its driver (LE 3, 10; LH 271) and further compares m. B. Meṣ. 8:1, which interprets verses 13–14 along these lines.

(LH 267). Although it is not clear whether ancient Near Eastern legal practice matched LH 124's requirement of double compensation for fraud, legal documents bear out the standard of *simplum* one finds for cases of negligence in the Laws of Hammurabi.[58]

Exodus 22:11 establishes liability for the shepherd in cases of theft but does not specify whether the shepherd must remunerate the owner with single or double compensation. Typically, however, the statement that a liable person "must pay," without further clarification, refers to *simplum*, or single compensation.[59] The law of animal borrowing and rental similarly establishes a *simplum* standard for the liable party (Exod 22:13–14).

Exodus 22:12 generates an automatic exemption from liability for any shepherd who can produce remains as evidence of predation. LH 266 similarly exonerates a shepherd from liability for death to the flock caused by an "affliction of a god" or a lion. Ancient Near Eastern legal documents suggest, however, that this blanket statement did not reflect herding practices with complete accuracy. Although predation indeed constituted grounds for escaping liability, the shepherd typically received in advance a maximum allowance for such deficits. Losses in excess of the set percentage incurred liability. Thus, for example, at Larsa in the Old Babylonian period, the shepherd was liable for losses to the flock caused by predation in excess of 15 percent, and at Durkatlimmu in the Middle Assyrian period, only a 7-percent loss was excusable.[60] Although the dearth of evidence leaves us in the realm of conjecture, one can imagine that the same discrepancy that one finds here between a cuneiform law collection and documents reflecting legal practice may also have been true of biblical law and Israelite herding practices.[61]

---

58. See, e.g., JEN 335, a trial record from Nuzi where the accused is required to pay a (single) cow for a cow; and BM 76038, a Neo-Babylonian trial record in which the accused is sentenced to pay the quantity (but not double the quantity) of silver and jewelry missing from a box entrusted to her. For an edition and discussion of JEN 335, see Edward Chiera and Ephraim A. Speiser, "Selected 'Kirkuk' Documents," *JAOS* 47 (1927): 36–60, here 50; for BM 76038, see Sandowicz, *Oaths and Curses*, 395–97 (O. 265).

59. For the view that verse 11 requires single compensation, see, e.g., Noth, *Exodus*, 184–85; Rothenbusch, *Die kasuistische Rechtssammlung*, 358. Although one might posit that the twofold compensation mentioned in verse 6 and verse 8 applies throughout the bailment law, the exceptional character of verse 11 (as a case in which there is no option for the accused to undertake a cultic procedure in order to escape liability) bars this conclusion.

60. For Larsa, see Postgate, "Some Old Babylonian Shepherds," 6; for Durkatlimmu, see Postgate, *Bronze Age Bureaucracy*, 309. For losses at Nuzi, see Morrison, "Evidence for Herdsmen," 257–96.

61. Discrepancies of this kind are unsurprising, nor do they truly constitute contradictions, given the brevity of biblical and cuneiform law and the choices of their drafters to emphasize certain points at the expense of others.

Between Narrative and Law: 1 Kings 20

A biblical narrative relating to deposit suggests a penalty for malfeasance that far exceeds the *duplum* standard of the deposit law. 1 Kings 20 recounts the story of a prophet who approaches the king of Israel to judge his case and then reveals that the case is a parable for the king himself wrongfully setting free his enemy, the king of Aram:[62]

> [39]As the king passed by, [the prophet] cried out to the king and said, "Your servant went out into the thick of the battle. Suddenly a man came over and brought a man to me, saying, 'Guard [שמר] this man! If he is missing [הפקד יפקד], it will be your life for his, or you will have to pay a talent of silver." [40]While your servant was busy here and there, [the man] got away." The king of Israel responded, "You have your verdict; you pronounced it yourself." [41]Quickly he removed the cloth from his eyes, and the king recognized him as one of the prophets. [42]He said to him, "Thus said Yhwh: Because you have set free [שלחת ... מיד] the man whom I doomed, your life shall be forfeit for his life and your people for his people."

This narrative is a juridical parable in which the prophet attempts to open the king's eyes to his own unjust behavior.[63] Whereas the king was prepared to send a man from Israel to his death per the terms of his contract, without considering leniency, he had no difficulty setting free the enemy king whom Yhwh wished dead.

The narrative is laden with legal language, and scholars have long noted its relevance to bailment in particular.[64] In the prophet's story, he has been tasked with guarding a prisoner of war, and is liable for the prisoner's loss. The narrative uses the roots *š-m-r* and *p-q-d* (1 Kgs 20:39), which feature in the Pentateuch's bailment-related laws (Exod 22:6, 9; Lev 5:21, 23),[65] as well as an expression involving the words "send" and "hand"

---

62. For a discussion of 1 Kings 20, see Jeremy Schipper, *Parables and Conflict in the Hebrew Bible* (New York: Cambridge University Press, 2009), 74–92.

63. But not, as Halberstam includes in the definition of a juridical parable (*Law and Truth*, 162), "to act accordingly." See Schipper (*Parables and Conflict*, 91): "As with other parables in the Hebrew Bible, the prophet does not use this parable to convince his addressee to change his ways. Rather, the prophet exposes Ahab's interpretative inadequacies and condemns his handling of a larger conflict in the surrounding narrative." On the other hand, the audience of the narrative, and not the audience in the narrative (i.e., the king), might be expected to act accordingly. Note further that Schipper (144 n. 13) disputes the existence of a "juridical parable," instead casting this narrative as a "petitionary narrative."

64. See, e.g., Daube, *Studies in Biblical Law*, 14–15; Tikva Frymer-Kensky, "Israel," in Westbrook, *History of Ancient Near Eastern Law*, 2:1026.

65. Although this narrative uses the root *p-q-d* differently from Lev 5, its presence in this narrative, given the narrative's content and connections with the theme of bailment, is noteworthy. It should be mentioned that the object of "bailment" here is a human being, and,

(1 Kgs 20:42), which evokes שלח ידו, the idiom for negligence in Exod 22:7, 10.[66] Despite these thematic and linguistic connections, the narrative diverges sharply from the biblical bailment law when it comes to setting a penalty. In the parable, the bailee agrees to a penalty of "a life for a life," with the possibility of paying an exorbitant ransom instead (1 Kgs 20:39). This penalty appears excessively severe in comparison with the penta-teuchal law's standard of double compensation. The disparity further stands out in light of the king's response to the parable: "You have your verdict; you pronounced it yourself" (1 Kgs 20:40). The king's statement that the oral agreement is binding suggests that, in the view of this narra-tive, a penalty could be set by the parties who arranged the bailment themselves, irrespective of whether it adhered to the standard set out in biblical law.

First Kings 20 sets a penalty for negligence in bailment that far exceeds the double compensation of biblical law (and even more so, the *simplum* standard of the Laws of Hammurabi and cuneiform legal documents): a life for a life, or an exorbitant monetary ransom. Is this the stuff of fantasy, a hyperbolized punishment serving a literary purpose, or might it bear some basis in reality, especially considering that the object of bailment in this case is human rather than an inanimate object or animal?[67] After all, despite the perceived extremity of this punishment, the narrative makes clear that it results directly from the contractual stipulations of the bailee and bailor who created the arrangement. In ancient Israel, could the bailor and bailee determine their own penalties, or did those penalties have to accord with an external standard—either that found in Exod 22 or some

---

indeed, labeling this story as a case of bailment would be imprecise. The story, however, remains relevant to bailment as it uses bailment language and involves one person agreeing to watch something (in this case, someone) for another person, with a penalty attached for failure to do so properly.

66. The expression שלחת ... מיד in 1 Kgs 20:42 is best translated in context as "you set him free." The formulation, however, is peculiar. Elsewhere in Biblical Hebrew, מיד is con-structed to a suffix or another noun; here it occurs in the absolute form. In fact, some of the versions append a possessive suffix to מיד-, which further highlights the linguistic oddity of its form in the MT. The strangeness of this formulation is mitigated, however, if one views it as intertextually connected to the bailment law of Exod 22, with 1 Kgs 20 drawing directly on the very language that the Covenant Code uses for the wrongdoing of the bailee (although 1 Kgs 20 uses the D-stem instead of the G-stem). This intertextual understanding of שלחת ... מיד in 1 Kgs 20:42 eliminates an apparent mismatch between the prophet's parable (in which the accused has accidentally lost track of his captive) and his message (in which the king has set free the enemy). In choosing these words, the writer not only draws on bailment vocabulary but also preserves the idiom's association with negligence, which accords better with the parable. Like the prophet who did not deliberately allow, but negligently allowed for the captive to escape, the king has negligently failed to live up to his divinely mandated standard of care.

67. For discussion of unrealistic use of law in literature, see Magdalene, *Scales of Righ-teousness*, 51.

other non-extant (oral or written) authoritative source? Moreover, if the Covenant Code's penalty of double compensation had any basis in reality, is one to understand it as the required penalty, a typical penalty, a maximum penalty, or a minimum penalty? We might also consider the possibility that Exod 22's equal penalty of double compensation for negligence, fraud, and false accusations alike serves a function unrelated to realistic legal practice per se, such as promoting honesty and diligence among parties in a bailment, or more broadly demonstrating the compassion, equity, and high moral standards of Yhwh. In the absence of more data from ancient Israel we are left with more questions than answers on this front.

When Fact-Finding Fails

When a person swears an exculpatory oath by Yhwh, the very willingness to swear would be seen as a sign of that person's innocence. But what if someone swore falsely? Despite the fact that the bailment law does not address explicitly the possibility that its fact-finding methods might fail, the Covenant Code demonstrates its concern with the effects of a corrupt court or false eyewitness in Exod 23:1–3, 6–8. Moreover, the Priestly laws take up precisely this problem of a false oath in the context of bailments (and in other circumstances) in Lev 5:20–26:

> [20]The Lord spoke to Moses, saying: [21]When a person sins and commits a trespass against the Lord by dealing deceitfully with his fellow in the matter of a deposit [פקדון] or a pledge, or through robbery, or by defrauding his fellow, [22]or by finding something lost and lying about it; if he swears falsely regarding any one of the various things that one may do and sin thereby—[23]when one has thus sinned and, realizing his guilt [ואשם], would restore that which he got through robbery or fraud, or the deposit that was entrusted to him, or the lost thing that he found, [24]or anything else about which he swore falsely, he shall repay the principal amount and add a fifth part to it. He shall pay it to its owner when he realizes his guilt. [25]Then he shall bring to the priest, as his penalty to the Lord, a ram without blemish from the flock, or the equivalent, as a guilt offering. [26]The priest shall make expiation on his behalf before the Lord, and he shall be forgiven for whatever he may have done to draw blame thereby. (NJPS)

This pericope treats scenarios involving a person who swears falsely regarding any one of a number of offenses, including the פקדון, generally translated as "deposit" and understood as property that one person gives to another for temporary safekeeping.[68] After swearing falsely and "real-

---

68. Although the root *p-q-d* has a wide semantic range, including meanings unrelated to deposits, the noun פקדון occurs in only one other place (Gen 41:36) referring to property

izing his guilt" (ואשם, Lev 5:23), the offender must restore the property from the initial dispute along with an additional 20-percent fine and must also bring an אשם offering.

The bailment law of Exodus requires double compensation for malfeasance, while Lev 5:20–26 requires that a false swearer pay single compensation (restoring the stolen property) plus an additional 20 percent. Scholars have resolved this discrepancy in a number of ways, attributing it to factors relating to the Priestly laws' cultic interests or to historical developments in attitudes toward the oath.[69] Most commentaries, however, harmonize the conflicting texts by restricting the subject matter of Lev 5:20–26 to the false swearer who voluntarily confesses. In this view, voluntary confession constitutes a mitigating factor in favor of the offender, whose penalty is reduced from *duplum* (double compensation) to *simplum* (single compensation) plus one-fifth.[70]

What is the experience of the false swearer who voluntarily owns up to deceitfulness? In a commentary on Lev 5:20–26, Jacob Milgrom has proposed understanding ואשם in verse 23 as "he *feels* guilt" (as opposed to, e.g., "he becomes guilty" through sinning).[71] The false swearer voluntarily admits, out of contrition, to the action, and the law rewards the psychological state and subsequent admission of guilt with a reduction in penalty. Milgrom further argues that the ancients viewed emotional and physical suffering as a single phenomenon. Whether physical or psychological, "unexplainable suffering is held to be the result of sin, and the sufferer's efforts are therefore directed toward the discovery of the specific offense that gave rise to his plight."[72] In this case, the false swearer's pangs of guilt lead to the admission of falsehood and compensation for the victim (at a reduced rate). Bruce Wells, in contrast, cautions that a psychological interpretation is anachronistic. Instead, he offers a narrower understanding of the suffering that the swearer experiences, explaining ואשם as referring to the "onset of adverse circumstances, designed to prompt a person to seek

---

(specifically grain) that is stored for a temporary period (if not quite in a bailment scenario); Akkadian similarly attests a noun *puquddû* or *puqdû* referring to entrusted property, for which see *CAD* P, s.v. "*puquddû*"). Verbs from this root may refer to entrusting property with another person (e.g., 1 Kgs 14:27; 2 Kgs 5:24; Isa 10:28; Jer 36:20). It is possible that in Lev 5, the noun פקדון envisions a wider range of meanings than just "deposit" — including possibly a pledge entrusted to a creditor (as one finds in the Dead Sea Scrolls, e.g., 4Q418 [4QInstr^d] 8, 3–5; 4Q424 [Instruction-like Composition B] 1, 6).

69. For factors relating to cultic interests, see, e.g., Otto, "Die rechtshistorische Entwicklung," 161–63; cf. Lafont, "Procédure par serment, " 194–95. For a historical approach comparing the Priestly laws' attitude toward oaths to Neo-Babylonian texts, see Wells, *Law of Testimony*, 140.

70. For extensive bibliography, see Jackson, *Theft in Early Jewish Law*, 176 n. 6.

71. See especially Jacob Milgrom, *Leviticus 1–16: A New Translation with Introduction and Commentary*, AB 3 (New York: Doubleday, 1991), 365–78.

72. Ibid., 343.

atonement for sin."[73] The one who swore falsely experiences physical suffering that causes that person to come forward and make amends. Faced with misfortune, the perpetrator seeks to reverse circumstances by righting the wrong; presumably, once the perpetrator has atoned, the misfortune will cease.

The nature of this misfortune may offer a key to understanding not only the experience of the false swearer but also the reason for the reduced penalty. The perpetrator in question has not only committed a property offense with respect to the owner's deposit, but has also committed perjury, averring innocence through an oath in the name of Yhwh. Although the law of bailment in Exod 22 does not cite the language of an oath that the accused party would swear, biblical and comparative evidence suggests a conditional formulation: "If I committed such and such, (may such and such befall me)" — with the punishment in the parenthetical apodosis either given explicitly or, more commonly, left unstated.[74] We may therefore push Wells's interpretation one step further. The term אשׁם in Lev 5:23 likely refers not only to any misfortune that a false swearer experiences but specifically to the effects of the false oath. By deceptively swearing an exculpatory oath, the perpetrator accepts the dire consequences of the oath's apodosis, whether or not the offender knows in advance the nature of those consequences. When the false swearer later experiences the "onset of adverse circumstances," the adversities are interpreted not merely as the consequence of the wrongdoing but as the fruition of the apodosis of the oath that the offender falsely swore.

The majority of biblical and ancient Near Eastern oath formulas omit an explicit apodosis, presumably out of fear that merely expressing the consequences of the oath could inadvertently cause those consequences to take effect.[75] A number of oaths, however, include such an apodosis, and these examples illuminate the range of consequences that the false swearer might expect. The only fully formulated biblical judicial oath reflects a bodily consequence: the adulterous woman's belly will swell and thigh

---

73. Wells, *Law of Testimony*, 140; cf. his discussion on 67–68.

74. Blane Conklin characterizes this section of the oath, which may explicate consequences for keeping or not keeping it, as an "authenticating element" (*Oath Formulas in Biblical Hebrew*, Linguistic Studies in Ancient West Semitic 5 [Winona Lake, IN: Eisenbrauns, 2011], 5).

Another way to translate oaths beginning with a conditional particle "if" but lacking an apodosis is as a declarative statement: not "If I committed such and such ..." but "I did not commit such and such." This type of translation, however, ignores the attestations of oaths that in fact include an apodosis, suggesting that all oaths beginning with conditional particles are in fact conditional. On these two options, see, e.g., Wells, Wunsch, and Magdalene, "Assertory Oath," 21. Sandowicz favors a declarative translation in the interests of more consistent translations of different kinds of oaths, and for other reasons listed there, despite acknowledging the suppressed apodosis of the assertory oath (*Oaths and Curses*, 6, 22–23).

75. See, e.g., Sandowicz, *Oaths and Curses*, 22, and the references in n. 125.

will fall (Num 5:21–22).[76] In extralegal sections of the Bible, especially in the Psalms, apodoses of oath formulas delineate punishments such as agricultural failure, property damages, loss of one's wife, bodily harm, and death.[77] Consequences of Mesopotamian oaths include rejection by deities;[78] death at the hand of the deities;[79] death of one's family members and personal illness;[80] and skin disease, poverty, and childlessness.[81]

Persons who swear regarding a property offense might pronounce a specific consequence for the wrongdoing of which they seek to clear themselves, or they might utter a more general formula. The term ואשם in Lev 5:23 refers to the offender's experience of suffering that the offender understands as a false oath coming to fruition. David Lambert has argued that "[to] be *ashem* is to be condemned; sacrifices are brought in anticipation of the affliction that is thought to follow from a state of guilt."[82] In this case, the offender believes that the offender is condemned and has already begun to experience affliction as a consequence. The offender therefore admits to dual wrongdoing, in order to curb the effects of the false oath and prevent any further affliction.

This understanding of ואשם requires a reconsideration of the relationship between the contradictory penalties in Exod 22 and Lev 5. Guiding previous discussions of the relationship between these two laws is the premise that, in Lev 5, the offending bailee faces a lighter penalty than that bailee's counterpart in Exod 22.[83] What is missing from these discussions is a sense of the incomparability of the situations to which the two laws respond. The offender in Exod 22 has committed a property offense, for which double compensation must be paid. The offender in Lev 5, on the other hand, has committed both a property offense and perjury and has

---

76. Whether or not this reflects an oath's apodosis depends on an interpretation of this part of the rite as intrinsic to the oath procedure or part of a separate ritual.

77. Sheldon H. Blank, "The Curse, Blasphemy, the Spell, and the Oath," *HUCA* 23 (1950–1951): 73–95, here 91–92, citing Pss 7:4–6; 137:5–6; Job 31:5–8, 9–10, 19–22, 38–40.

78. See, e.g., BIN 6 39:18–19; BIN 6 97:20–22, cited by Małgorzata Sandowicz, "'Fear the Oath!' Stepping Back from Oath Taking in First Millennium B.C. Babylonia," *Palamedes* 6 (2011): 17–36, here 18 n. 5.

79. See, e.g., M. 5719 IV: 11–15, quoted in Dominique Charpin, *Reading and Writing in Babylon*, trans. Jane Marie Todd (Cambridge: Harvard University Press, 2010), 163. Cf. EA 209, lines 13–16: "… may the gods who are with you strike my head" (cited by Conklin, *Oath Formulas in Biblical Hebrew*, 87).

80. UET 4 171, for which see Sandowicz, *Oaths and Curses*, 400–401.

81. For the final three, see, e.g., UET 6 402, cited by Sandowicz, "Fear the Oath," 18.

82. David A. Lambert, *How Repentance Became Biblical: Judaism, Christianity, and the Interpretation of Scripture* (New York: Oxford University Press, 2016), 61.

83. An exception is Jackson, who views the penalty in Lev 5 as harsher than that of Exod 22 (*Theft in Early Jewish Law*, 175–76). According to his interpretation, Lev 5 requires the bailee who falsely swears to pay 220 percent of the item's original value, rather than Exod 22's 200 percent (i.e., *duplum*).

also already begun to suffer the effects of the self-imprecation that was part of the false oath. In addition to motivating a process of atonement, this suffering constitutes punishment in and of itself. Although the false oath causes the misfortune signaled by ונאשם, that misfortune serves as a punishment for the original offense (and not for the oath), in accordance with the oath the bailee swore. In contrast to Exod 22, Lev 5 establishes the penalty for an offender who has already experienced some form of a personally decreed, cosmically executed punishment for wrongdoing. The scope of this punishment and its relationship to compensating the wronged party is unknowable. Perhaps the law assesses the "value" of this punishment at 80 percent of the property stolen, therefore reducing compensation from double to single plus 20 percent; more likely, the reduction in penalty reflects not an actual estimation but a general sense that the offender has already paid in part.

Understood this way, the Priestly laws' reference to bailment in Lev 5 does not contradict the law of Exod 22 but complements it by addressing a further, related scenario. If a malfeasant bailee dares to undertake a false exculpatory oath, thereby committing a cultic offense in addition to one involving property and, as a result, begins to suffer the effects of that oath, spurring the bailee to seek atonement, then the penalty will be lower than that of a bailee declared guilty from the get-go, in order to account for the punishment that the suffering bailee has already experienced. This is not because the voluntary confession mitigates the severity of the punishment, but because the law acknowledges that the false swearer has already "served time," so to speak, by beginning to suffer the effects of the false oath. In explicitly acknowledging the possibility that the accused might swear falsely, Lev 5 corroborates the premise underlying Exod 22's introduction of its final method of fact-finding, the personal testimony of the wronged party. The need for this high degree of certainty rests on the fear that other fact-finding methods, including even the exculpatory oath by Yhwh, are capable of failure—precisely because of people such as the Priestly laws' false swearer (or the "malicious witness" of Exod 23:1).

In Lev 5, the law focuses on the offender and on making right the offense against Yhwh. The offender experiences the effects of self-imprecation for as long as the offender refuses to atone for the cultic wrongdoing. But, even as the offender is punished, the wronged party of the original property offense remains a victim who initially receives no compensation for loss and ultimately, when the offender comes clean, receives only a percentage of what the wronged party would have received, had the offender been declared guilty in the first place. In contrast to Lev 5, Exod 22 places the perspective of the victim of a property offense—understood as the person who experiences a property loss of some kind—at its center, even as it requires the victim to live in most cases with a small degree of uncertainty as to the innocence of the accused. The contrast between the respective interests of the Priestly laws and the Covenant Code in the accused versus the accuser highlights one defining concern of Exod 22's bailment law: How can one know whether the accused is guilty?

Establishing Justice

As a biblical text, Exod 22:6–14 serves more than just one function. The functions it serves emerge most starkly when one views the pericope in comparison with related laws, including Lev 5:20–26, the analysis of which helps to underscore the victim-centered epistemological question at stake in Exod 22. The functions of Exod 22:6–14 are further elucidated when the text is viewed in comparison with cuneiform parallels from neighboring societies, to which we now turn.

Exodus 22 and Cuneiform Law: A "Law of Bailment"

First and foremost, Exod 22:6–14 is a law about thematically and linguistically related scenarios that are aptly captured by the legal term *bailment*. Couched among other laws treating related topics such as watching animals and negligence (Exod 21:28–36), theft of animals (Exod 21:37–22:3), and damage to another's property (Exod 22:4–5), Exod 22:6–14 forms a distinctive, delimited unit about property belonging to one person that lawfully and temporarily resides in another person's possession. Although this point may appear obvious, it is important to state it explicitly because no other law collection from the ancient Near Eastern world groups together its laws pertaining to bailments in the manner of the Covenant Code. The Laws of Hammurabi, which include the largest number of parallels to the biblical laws about bailment, offer a clear example of this contrast.

LH 120–126, regarding deposits and lost property, follow a series of laws that also treat scenarios where one person's property resides in another's possession, lawfully or unlawfully: LH 111 relates to a loan; the subject of 112 is a man engaged in a trading expedition who gives property to another person under consignment for transportation; and 113–119 treat cases of distraint arising from an unpaid loan. In fact, a definition of the term *bailment* not bound by Exod 22:6–14 might consider all of LH 111–126 a series of bailment-related laws.

LH's animal rental laws occur within a series of laws about oxen. LH 241 treats distraint of an ox; 242–243 introduce the topic of ox rental, which

244–249 then take up; and 250–252 treat the case of the goring ox.[84] The context of Hammurabi's animal rental laws is not one of bailment, as in Exodus; rather, these laws have the ox as a common theme.

Finally, LH 261–267, regarding herding arrangements, occur within the larger unit of 253–277, which relates to themes of hire for labor: hired workers (a man hired to care for a field, an agricultural laborer, an ox driver, a craftsman, etc.) and hired animals or vessels (oxen, donkeys, goats, wagons, boats, etc.). These range from laws about a malfeasant laborer's penalty to laws establishing hire rates. Within this unit, LH 259–260 might appear to form an exception, treating theft of agricultural tools; however, these laws likely have in mind a hired laborer as the typical culprit.[85]

The organization of laws about deposits, herding, and animal borrowing and rental into a single unit about bailment in Exod 22 signifies a departure from Near Eastern law. There is indeed a "biblical law of bailment" to speak of, based on the organization of law inherent in the Pentateuch itself,[86] and not only from the perspective of a modern legal scholar culling thematically connected but sequentially disconnected topics from a larger body of law. While the biblical law of bailment's subsections bear numerous cuneiform parallels, the unit as a discrete whole stands alone.

---

84. As noted earlier, LH 244 also mentions a donkey, although 245–249 and the surrounding laws mention only an ox. This is likely because an ox represented the typical draft animal, although 269 and 270 also mention rental of a donkey or goat.

85. For an alternate characterization of 253–265 as laws relating to theft and loss, see Wright, *Inventing God's Law*, 42–43.

86. A long history of scholarship supports the deliberate associative and conceptual organization of both the biblical and cuneiform corpora. See, notably, Herbert Petschow, "Zur Systematik und Gesetzestechnik im Codex Hammurabi," *Zeitschrift für Assyriologie und Vorderasiatische Archäologie* 57 (1965): 146–72; Petschow, "Zur 'Systematik' in den Gesetzen von Eschnunna," in *Symbolae Iuridicae et Historicae Martino David Dedicatae*, ed. J. A. Ankum et al. (Leiden: Brill, 1968), 2:131–43; Eichler, "Literary Structure in the Laws of Eshnunna," 71–84; Eckart Otto, *Rechtsgeschichte der Redaktionen im Kodex Ešnunna und im "Bundesbuch": Eine redaktionsgeschichtliche und rechtsvergleichende Studie zu altbabylonischen und altisraeliti-schen Rechtsüberlieferungen*, OBO 85 (Freiburg, Switzerland: Universitätsverlag; Göttingen: Vandenhoeck & Ruprecht, 1989). For further bibliography, see Wright, *Inventing God's Law*, 366 n. 18. The associative organization of the laws is further supported by three late Old Babylonian manuscripts of LH that include subject headings scattered throughout the laws, such as "legal decisions concerning soldier and fisherman" (before LH 26) and "legal decisions concerning storage" (before LH 120). Regarding these headings, see Roth, *Law Collections*, 75–76.

Exodus 22 and Cuneiform Law:
Not Just a "Law of Bailment"

A comparison of the Covenant Code's law of bailment with cuneiform parallels also offers the opportunity to consider what the biblical law chooses to discuss and which concerns go unaddressed. For example, the Laws of Eshnunna (36–37) and the Laws of Hammurabi (125) both mention physical evidence of a home invasion as one sign that a deposit has been stolen by someone other than the bailee. Both laws also cite joint loss of the bailee and bailor's property as evidence of an outside thief. The biblical law, on the other hand, adopts the voice of an omniscient lawgiver in stating succinctly that a theft has occurred (Exod 22:6), without elaborating on how the court might arrive at such a conclusion; and that the bailee is innocent of negligence allowing for theft (Exod 22:7), without explaining on what grounds the bailee has escaped suspicion of having stolen the property. Instead, the law focuses on how the bailee establishes innocence of the wrongdoing that the bailor suspects; the bailee undergoes a cultic procedure averring that negligent behavior has not occurred. The biblical law of bailment does not spend time addressing how to determine that a theft by an unknown party has occurred (e.g., through physical evidence such as a broken window or joint loss), perhaps considering this uninteresting or irrelevant; instead, it focuses on the methods of fact-finding that might be engaged when it is otherwise impossible to discern whether the accused is truly at fault.

Hammurabi's robust deposit law further highlights features absent from Exod 22. While monetary loans and distraint concern the Covenant Code (Exod 22:24–26), it does not consider these topics a part of its bailment law, but rather germane to its theme of compassion for the weaker elements of society (22:20–23). Exodus 22 does not depict its shepherd in verses 9–12 as a laborer or professional any differently from its other bailees (all are referred to simply as רעהו), though this shepherd is likely an individual hired for compensation. The biblical law, unlike the Laws of Hammurabi, includes the topic of animal rental (as well as borrowing) as part of the bailment pericope, rather than linking it with the goring oxen laws that one finds earlier in the Covenant Code (Exod 21:28–32, 35–36). These choices may not reflect deliberate departures from the Laws of Hammurabi, but the accumulated contrasts highlight a number of roads not taken in favor of promoting other priorities.

One distinguishing feature of the bailment law in Exod 22 lies in its assignment of double compensation for cases of negligence, fraud, and false accusation alike. This differs from what one finds both in corresponding sections of the Laws of Hammurabi and in legal documents from Mesopotamia from various periods. These latter texts bear out that, in

Mesopotamia, the standard penalty for wrongdoings of negligence was single compensation. The insistence of the biblical law upon an equally harsh penalty for fraud, negligence, and false accusation may lie in its interest in the vulnerable, a concern that emerges in various ways throughout the Covenant Code (e.g., in laws focusing on poor or marginalized members of society).[87] Bailments create scenarios that require a high degree of trust and leave both the bailee and bailor open to exploitation. The law demands a relatively harsh penalty for negligence, despite the lower level of fault involved, thereby encouraging bailees to execute their safekeeping duties with diligence, and requires the same harsh penalty in order to discourage false accusations by a bailor who might scheme to extort double compensation from an innocent bailee. Whether or not these standards of compensation reflect operative law, they convey the law's interest in limiting the means by which someone vulnerable to loss of property might be exploited.

Perhaps most prominently, Exod 22 does not share the Laws of Hammurabi's interest in the correct procedure for creating bailments, limiting its treatment of this topic to its protases: "when a man gives to another ... to watch" and "when a man borrows." In contrast, the Laws of Hammurabi devote a number of sections to how one might establish a valid bailment; LH 122–124 in particular highlight the requirement to set up deposits before witnesses and under a contractual agreement. Without these elements, the delivery of property to the would-be bailee is legally meaningless, such that the owner of the property has no legal recourse if that person denies the deposit. The Laws of Hammurabi also address storage and rental rates and compensation of professionals, whether at a set rate or in accordance with contractual stipulations. All of these features demonstrate the cuneiform law's interest in how one sets up a legally binding bailment, none of which concerns the Covenant Code.

Exodus 22's lack of interest in matters of procedure with respect to setting up a valid bailment arrangement, and also in the various gradations of injuries and penalties that one finds in the Laws of Hammurabi, stands in direct contrast to its preoccupation with methods of fact-finding. The Laws of Hammurabi pertaining to bailments also address fact-finding methods: the owner of the grain establishes the grain that is owned through an oath (120); the renter of an animal struck dead by a deity, and the shepherd whose herd has suffered a plague or lion attack, may clear themselves through an oath (249, 266). These details differ from those of

---

87. It is worth noting, however, that the position of the Covenant Code is not always to act to the benefit of the poor, specifically; Exod 23:3 warns against favoring the poor in judgment, and indeed it is plausible that Exod 22:9–12 and 13–14 envision scenarios in which the owner is typically in a better economic position than the shepherd or animal borrower or renter. The law treads a balance between multiple values.

the Covenant Code in a few points. In cases of suspicion of negligence or deliberate malfeasance in a deposit of goods, the Covenant Code—similar to the Laws of Eshnunna—allows the accused to swear to innocence, rather than requiring an oath of the accuser. Moreover, the accuser's oath in LH 120 testifies not to innocence or guilt; instead, the accuser "establishes his grain," testifying to the amount of grain in the original bailment.[88] LH 120 does not envision an exculpatory oath at all, but an oath that will assist in determining the basis for double compensation. LH 266 also calls for a shepherd to swear an oath in a case where it is possible to produce remains of predation, unlike Exod 22:12, which considers the production of animal remains sufficient (without requiring an oath as well). Exodus 22:13–14 does not afford the animal renter the opportunity to swear under any circumstances, in contrast to LH 249. This final difference further highlights the narrow parameters that Exod 22:13–14 establishes for fact-finding in cases of animal borrowing and rental, allowing only the personal testimony of the animal's owner to exonerate the borrower or renter, and nothing else.

Beyond these comparisons of details within individual laws, larger distinctions emerge. The Laws of Hammurabi mention methods of fact-finding with regard to a number of different cases. These methods include determining the outcome of a case based on proof that an accuser brings, or fails to bring, against the accused;[89] examining the case, in some instances listening to witness testimony;[90] requiring the suspect to undergo an ordeal;[91] and having a party swear an oath.[92] Of these, swearing an oath is the most common method throughout the law collection in general, and also the most common method specifically within laws relating to bailment. LH 125 also mentions joint loss as evidence of a thief other than the bailee. Yet, viewed in context, Hammurabi's bailment laws do not emphasize fact-finding in any meaningful way; they merely include methods of fact-finding in relevant cases just as they do throughout the law collection,

---

88. According to LH 120, the owner of the grain, whose innocence the law assumes, establishes his grain through a cultic procedure denoted by the language *maḫar ilim šeʾašu ubârma*. This formulation is similar to LH 23, which stipulates that a person who has been robbed "shall establish the extent of his lost property before the god" (*mimmâšu ḫalqam maḫar ilim ubârma*; for this translation, see Roth, *Law Collections*, 85). The victim should quantify the loss, declaring what has been stolen.

89. E.g., LH 1, 2, 106–107, 127. An example of such proof might be having caught the suspect in the act, for which see, e.g., LH 130.

90. E.g., LH 9–11, 18, 142, 168, 177. Note that, while this method of fact-finding is absent from the Covenant Code, the Deuteronomic laws offer a parallel; see, e.g., Deut 13:15; 17:4; 19:18.

91. E.g., LH 2, 132.

92. E.g., LH 20, 23, 103, 120, 126, 206, 207, 227, 249, 266.

while also treating modes of effecting valid bailments and penalties when a bailment goes wrong.

The Covenant Code, on the other hand, does not frequently broach the subject of fact-finding, but, within this unit of nine verses, it cites four different methods: an oath, an eyewitness, physical evidence, and personal testimony of the animal's owner. The concentration and variety of methods within this brief pericope emerge starkly in contrast to the Laws of Hammurabi, where fact-finding methods are relevant but not central. The comparison with these laws strengthens the premise that Exod 22:6–14 is not just a law of bailment, concerned with protecting the vulnerable, but also a law about fact-finding, which contends with the question: How does one restore justice when things do not go as planned? To this question, with which the law itself is concerned, I add one of the questions motivating this study: What is the relationship between the law that the Covenant Code sets forth here and operative law in ancient Israel? With regard to predation, strong parallels with cuneiform law, biblical prophecy, and Mesopotamian legal documents allow us to make a case for the fidelity of the Covenant Code to actual herding practices. Thus, according to the Covenant Code, the production of physical evidence in the form of remains—an empirically observed method of fact-finding—satisfies a need for justice in cases of predation. The text, in this case, draws on operative law to make a statement about the establishment of justice. On the other hand, the incomparability of the criterion of the owner's presence in the law of animal borrowing and rental leaves us incapable of connecting the dots between biblical law and legal practice in the same way. Does the plausibility of the remainder of the bailment law suggest that this detail also finds its basis in legal practice? This question lingers. Yet, while the connection between "the law" of Exod 22 and legal practice occupies the scholar of biblical law, it does not appear to motivate the biblical law itself. Instead, the desire to establish justice through appropriate fact-finding methods and standards of compensation emerges as a driving concern in Exod 22:6–14.

4

Legal Writing, Legal Thinking

The laws of the Pentateuch and the cuneiform law collections do not comprise "law codes" in the modern sense of the word, nor should they be used in isolation to reconstruct operative law in the societies from which they emerged. Specifically, when examined in conjunction with the pictures that materialize based on biblical narrative and prophetic texts and Mesopotamian legal documents, these ancient law corpora increase in reliability as a source for the practice of law in ancient Israel. Beyond providing a partial, if potentially distorted, window into ancient legal practice, pentateuchal and cuneiform law collections also offer an important point of entry into the legal thinking that shaped them. What do these texts say about how people in the biblical and ancient Near Eastern world thought about law?

In considering this question, we may find a useful starting point in scholarship that examines the relationship between law and culture. Legal scholar Naomi Mezey has defined "culture" as "any set of shared, signifying practices—practices by which meaning is produced, performed, contested, or transformed."[1] According to Mezey, "law is one of the most potent signifying practices.... [The] relationship between culture and law ... is always dynamic, interactive, and dialectical—law is both a producer of culture and an object of culture."[2] An inquiry into how people thought about law directly informs an understanding of how people thought more generally. As an aspect of culture, law is not just a system involving rules and legal statements; it can also provide information about how the society from which it stems makes sense of reality and constructs meaning.[3] Because law is inherently meaning making, the study of law may have

---

1. Naomi Mezey, "Law as Culture," *Yale Journal of Law and the Humanities* 13 (2001): 35–68, here 42; see 38–42 regarding the history of debate surrounding the definition of "culture."

2. Ibid., 45–46.

3. Regarding this phenomenon cross-culturally and historically, see Lawrence Rosen, *Law as Culture: An Invitation* (Princeton: Princeton University Press, 2006); and see Mezey, "Law as Culture," 35–68.

far-reaching implications for understanding the society in which it formed.[4]

In the case of Exod 22:6–14, this framework for understanding law in connection with culture is particularly apt, for two reasons. First, our analysis of the biblical bailment law suggests that, while the text may reflect operative law more or less accurately, its primary purpose is neither to prescribe nor to describe legal practice; instead, the law's purpose is to set forth a standard of divine justice that both promotes the God who established it and demands that it be emulated. Mezey's definition of culture squares well with my view of what the biblical bailment law does. The very formulation of this law and its inclusion within the pentateuchal text constitute "signifying practices," where the text uses its contents (the topic of bailment refracted through a focus on methods of fact-finding) to negotiate meaning, specifically about the establishment of justice. Indeed, although all law makes meaning, in the bailment law, meaning making itself appears to constitute the Covenant Code's primary purpose, instead of supplementing a different primary function such as legislating practice and penalties.

Second, the biblical bailment law is also a law of fact-finding that probes the possibilities and limitations of a range of judicial procedures under varying circumstances. Legal anthropologist Lawrence Rosen has argued that "fact-finding is partly about seeking truth, partly about defusing conflict, partly about maintaining a workable sense of one's experience of the world—and all about stitching together law and culture so that each informs and supports the other."[5] Methods of fact-finding illuminate and may even shape how members of a society conceive of, acquire, and settle on the boundaries of knowledge, and thus are a critical site for the production and negotiation of meaning—a paradigmatic meeting ground for law and culture.

Of course, the study of any society's law—whether holistically, in reference to laws of fact-finding, or with respect to another specific topic—is one of many possible ways to understand how people create meaning and engage with knowledge. In the case of the ancient Near Eastern world, though, law was less distinct from other bodies of knowledge than one might imagine. Thus, for example, scribes utilized the same conditional list-based style of writing (with a protasis and apodosis: "if A, then B") to record texts about topics ranging from law to medicine to divination, so

---

4. Regarding the "meaning-making" power of law, see Austin Sarat and Thomas R. Kearns, "The Cultural Lives of Law," in *Law in the Domains of Culture*, ed. Austin Sarat and Thomas R. Kearns, Amherst Series in Law, Jurisprudence, and Social Thought (Ann Arbor: University of Michigan Press, 1998), 1–20, here 10.

5. Rosen, *Law as Culture*, 93.

that an omen list might appear indistinguishable in genre from a law collection.[6] This uniformity in form suggests some level of commonality also in how these topics were thought about and strengthens the premise that law's functions exceed the legal.

When speaking about how particular topics were "thought about," we have to consider *whose* thinking the texts in questions reflect. Ancient legal thinking—as with medicine, divination, and other areas of knowledge—would have fallen within the province of an elite scholastic circle, across a chasm of indiscernible depth from the everyday experience of people such as shepherds and laborers. Of course, the textual data through which we can access these "common" people's experiences are mostly mediated by the literate, complicating efforts to narrow down with precision the identity or character of those to whom our reconstructions of legal practice apply. Ultimately, every reconstruction requires squinting through the kaleidoscope of fragmented evidence that the vicissitudes of production and transmission have shaped, so that we may cautiously frame our conclusions as approximations. Bearing in mind these caveats, this chapter complements the question of how (some) people practiced law with a focus on how (some, perhaps other) people thought about the law during the biblical period, an inquiry that illuminates also how people thought about concepts such as truth and fault.

How are we to go about thinking about legal thinking? While exegetical analysis is useful for uncovering salient features of an ancient text—for example, the biblical bailment law's interest in methods of fact-finding and protecting the vulnerable from exploitation—modern legal analysis offers a sophisticated means of harnessing that data and exploring the ways in which the law addresses a range of issues. Bernard Jackson has cautioned against anachronistically misapplying modern thought to ancient texts:

> [We] may run the risk of applying a modern (some would say modernist) Western post-Enlightenment mode of thought to a quite different culture. This may prove just as hazardous as the application to the biblical texts of modern, Western models of law.[7]

Yet the benefits of drawing on modern legal analysis may outweigh the risks of anachronism, so long as one remains conscious of these risks. In this vein, Aryeh Amihay has cogently defended the application of modern

---

6. See discussion and bibliography in Amar Annus, "On the Beginnings and Continuities of Omen Sciences in the Ancient World," in *Divination and Interpretation of Signs in the Ancient World*, ed. Amar Annus, University of Chicago Oriental Institute Seminars 6 (Chicago: Oriental Institute of the University of Chicago, 2010), 1–18.

7. Jackson, *Studies in the Semiotics of Biblical Law*, 171.

legal theory to Essene texts, contending that "precision and accurate terminology are crucial in the humanities" even while "[it] is imperative that the introduction of legal theory into the study of ancient law recognize its limits."[8] The modern legal discourse surrounding bailments facilitates an understanding of the full range of conceptual problems that a bailment may create in its distinction between possession and ownership, and assists in unpacking the jurisprudential undercurrents of biblical and cuneiform law. The following sections utilize legal analysis to examine the ways that the biblical and cuneiform bailment laws treat methods of fact-finding and gradations of fault and liability, and consider whether ancient bailments may be categorized using the modern categories of contract, tort, and property. Throughout, I will also reflect on the ways in which modern legal thought may enhance an understanding of biblical law, as well as its limitations.

Methods of Fact-Finding

Exodus 22:6–14 introduces four scenarios (deposits of goods, herding, animal borrowing, and animal rental) with three distinct standards for fact-finding methods. In cases of deposit, the accused has the greatest opportunity to achieve exoneration, including when a theft has occurred. In the herding scenario, in contrast, the law denies the accused the opportunity for exoneration in cases of theft, limiting cases where the accused has such an opportunity to instances of animal death, injury, capture, and predation. The animal borrower and renter face an even more restrictive standard, allowing an opportunity for exoneration only under the limited circumstances wherein the animal's owner is present at the time when the animal suffers death or injury. The bailee (depositee, shepherd, borrower, or renter) has the greatest chance of defeating liability in a deposit scenario, and the smallest chance of doing so in a case of animal borrowing or rental; the shepherd falls somewhere in between. In other words, out of the bailees that Exod 22 introduces, the accused animal borrower or renter faces the greatest burden of proof, whereas the depositee faces the lowest burden of proof.

From a legal perspective, we can characterize these varying standards as follows. Burdens of proof and fact-finding methods may reflect a substantive basis of liability. The bailee is similar to the modern category of the fiduciary, who holds the assets of another party and owes that party both a duty of care and a duty of loyalty.[9] The fiduciary has a relatively

---

8. Amihay, *Theory and Practice in Essene Law*, 187–88.

9. For laws pertaining to fiduciaries of trusts in modern-day American law, see the

high burden of acting in the interests of the owner; for example, the considerable obligations incumbent upon a fiduciary extend beyond the reactive to the prophylactic. In trusts, the more discretion a fiduciary has with respect to the entrusted property, the greater the burden of accounting for the property. One can interpret the biblical bailment law through this lens as well. A bailee of goods has the least discretion with respect to the bailed property, because that property essentially remains in safekeeping for the duration of the bailment. A shepherd has more discretion, as the shepherd's responsibilities may include taking an animal out to pasture and feeding it, among other duties. Therefore, a shepherd has a greater responsibility to account for bailed property than the bailee of goods, a difference that manifests in cases of theft: the shepherd is always liable, without recourse to defeating liability, whereas the depositee has the opportunity to swear an exculpatory oath. A borrower or renter has the most discretion to use the bailed property, as they not only care for the animals in their temporary possession but also use them for labor. Correspondingly, they bear the greatest burden to account for that property, which they must do unless an owner is present.

This legal interpretation of the biblical bailment law also sheds light on its organization. We have already observed a possible connection between deposits and herding as arrangements that might co-occur in practice, based on a record of deposit by a shepherd about to embark on the migratory phase of the herding cycle, and therefore in need of a bailee for his personal possessions. Beyond this connection, however, Exod 22:6–14 follows an order of increasing discretion among its bailees to use the property bailed to them and a corresponding increase in the burden of proof that the law places upon them in order to defeat liability (or: a corresponding decrease in methods of fact-finding of which the accused may avail themselves). This kind of graded structure emerges in biblical and ancient Near Eastern law in other ways; Barry Eichler, for example, has argued that Exod 21:12–17 is organized in descending order with respect to severity of physical violence, and Martha Roth has demonstrated that LH 245–249 list injuries to oxen in the order of decreasing payment of damages.[10] Exodus 22:6–14 similarly utilizes an editorial structure of gradation, only with respect to discretion and burden rather than regarding compensation.

The law clearly envisions a direct relationship between discretion and accountability, or, put differently, an inverse relationship between discretion and opportunities to exercise methods of fact-finding. Though this kind of relationship may be intuitive, the choice literarily to map the law

---

Uniform Trust Code (last revised or amended in 2010), available online at http://www .uniformlaws.org.

10. Eichler, "Exodus 21:22–25 Revisited," 21–22; Roth, "Scholastic Exercise," 132.

along these axes speaks to its cultural underpinnings, both with respect to concerns that shape the law and with respect to the stylistic tradition of gradation in which the law partakes for navigating and expressing these concerns.

Law and Truth

The legal discourse of truth provides another lens through which to characterize the varying standards facing bailees in different scenarios, particularly through the stream of discussion centered on fact-finding.[11] At the crux of this discourse is the question, Does the legal finding of fact accord with "substantive truth"—that is, the actual truth—or with "formal legal truth" (also called "procedural truth")—that is, the result that a court reaches based on correct procedure, irrespective of whether it corresponds with substantive truth?[12] Although ideally formal legal truth and substantive truth will correspond, numerous factors may contribute toward a divergence between the two. In modern legal systems, these factors include various exclusionary rules of evidence, such as legal professional privilege, spousal privilege, a right against self-incrimination, omission of confessions elicited under duress, and a ban on evidence procured through an illegal or late search.[13] These exclusionary rules serve to satisfy various social functions, such as the protection of individual

---

11. The legal discourse of truth has taken the form of three different streams of discussion. The two that we will not engage here are the following: (1) Must the law reflect data and beliefs about the way things are in fact, or does the act of legislation in itself create a "truth" to be accepted irrespective of the law's coherence with fact? For this discourse, see, e.g., Jack M. Balkin, "The Proliferation of Legal Truth," *Harvard Journal of Law and Public Policy* 26 (2003): 5–16. (2) A second discourse finds expression in the monism vs. pluralism debate. In hard cases, is there a single, true, "right answer" that the court either succeeds or fails to uncover, or are there multiple possible outcomes that are equally valid and true? For the one law principle, see especially Ronald Dworkin, *Law's Empire* (Cambridge: Belknap Press of Harvard University Press, 1986), 239, 264–65: an ideal judge, whom Dworkin names Hercules, can come up with a single right answer to every hard case. For a critique of this view, see Michel Rosenfeld, "Dworkin and the One Law Principle: A Pluralist Critique," *Revue internationale de philosophie* 3 (2005): 363–92.

12. For these categories, see especially Robert S. Summers, "Formal Legal Truth and Substantive Truth in Judicial Fact-Finding – Their Justified Divergence in Some Particular Cases," *Law and Philosophy* 18 (1999): 497–511, here 498–99.

13. Mirjan R. Damaška, "Truth in Adjudication," *Hastings Law Journal* 49 (1998): 298–308, here 301; Jenny McEwan, "Ritual, Fairness and Truth: The Adversarial and Inquisitorial Models of Criminal Trial," in *The Trial on Trial: Truth and Due Process*, ed. Antony Duff et al. (Oxford, UK, and Portland, OR: Hart, 2004), 51–70, here 66; Joseph M. Fernandez, "An Exploration of the Meaning of Truth in Philosophy and Law," *University of Notre Dame Australia Law Review* 11 (2009): 53–83, here 74.

privacy and preventing coercion.[14] Available evidence and testimony may thus be rendered unusable and excluded from judicial proceedings, despite their ability to demonstrate to the court what has occurred with greater clarity. As a result, in the courtroom, substantive truth may or may not accord with formal legal truth, which is limited by rules governing the fact-finding process and the production of evidence.[15] A legal system may accept this sacrifice of substantive truth when it views "truth" and "justice" as distinct, and prioritizes justice (however it may be defined within a given system) over truth.[16]

On its face, the biblical bailment law might appear to place a premium upon the recovery of substantive truth: Within the span of a few verses, various methods of fact-finding are invoked to establish what has happened in reality, and to assign liability based on the results of the inquiry. Yet as the bailee's discretion increases with respect to the property bailed, the law increasingly creates exclusionary rules with regard to which methods of fact-finding it permits, with the animal borrower and renter facing extraordinarily limiting rules for how they might defeat liability. Correlated with the biblical law's structure of increasing discretion and an increasing burden of proof is an increase in exclusionary rules, and a potentially increasing gap between substantive truth and formal legal truth. In a case of deposit, therefore, the results of fact-finding are most likely to align with substantive truth. But in a case of animal borrowing or renting, the exclusion of most possible means of establishing facts—gathering physical evidence, hearing eyewitness testimony, permitting an exculpatory oath—means that in many cases, the results of fact-finding simply will not correspond to what happened in fact.

If one accepts the premise that the law seeks to establish justice in all situations, it appears that, for biblical law as for other legal systems, truth and justice are not identical. Figuring out what truly happened is not always the best way to achieve a just result. In the case of bailments, the greater discretion that the bailee has vis-à-vis the bailed property, the greater the chance that the owner—irrespective of socioeconomic status and how it compares to that of the bailee—may experience property loss or damage of some kind. In this regard, the law deems the property-owner the more vulnerable party to the arrangement, and accordingly adds protections in the form of exclusionary rules of fact-finding, commensurate with the vulnerability of the property owner. From the perspective of biblical law, these gradations effect justice, even if they do not always establish substantive truth.

---

14. Summers, "Formal Legal Truth," 499–500.

15. Thomas Weigend, "Is the Criminal Process about Truth?: A German Perspective," *Harvard Journal of Law & Public Policy* 26 (2003): 157–74, here 170.

16. Fernandez, "Exploration of the Meaning of Truth," 67.

Chaya Halberstam has argued that "in legal texts, the Hebrew Bible exhibits confidence in human decision making, allowing the appeal to divine omniscience for help with implementing perfectly proportional justice in alignment with absolute, substantive truth."[17] She points for example to Deut 17:8–9:

> [8]If a case is too baffling for you to decide, be it a controversy over homicide, civil law, or assault—matters of dispute in your courts—you shall promptly repair to the place that the Lord your God will have chosen, [9]and appear before the levitical priests, or the magistrate in charge at the time, and present your problem. [They shall announce] to you the verdict in the case. (NJPS, adapted)

For Halberstam,

> [C]ertainty is virtually guaranteed by the provision in Deuteronomy.... Besides providing an avenue through which a clear decision may be reached, this stipulation also reinforces the idea that most matters are not too difficult to judge, that the truth may be known and understood in most cases. Only in specific, and one would assume rare, instances will the truth not become apparent. And in such cases, certitude is nonetheless provided by the agents of the divine cult.[18]

Halberstam contrasts this biblical rhetoric of certainty—which amounts to the coincidence of substantive truth with formal legal truth—with a "rabbinic posture of uncertainty" in Tannaitic literature.[19] Christine Hayes has further argued that the rabbis divorce divine law from truth in a number of ways, including in judicial contexts. As Hayes demonstrates, the rabbis place a higher value on "peace" (defined as "settling a dispute through a compromise that forgoes determining actual liability or guilt") than on "truth" (defined as "strict or theoretically 'correct' judgment").[20] This rabbinic conception of divine law demands that legal procedural truth at times deviate from substantive truth.

My understanding of Exod 22:6–14 suggests that we ought to complicate Halberstam's depiction of biblical law's certainty. Indeed, Deut 17:2–13 appears to portray a justice system wherein one way or another (either through local secular judgment based on unambiguous eyewitness testimony or, when the local secular court is not equipped to reach a verdict,

---

17. Halberstam, *Law and Truth*, 178.

18. Ibid., 84.

19. Ibid., 3.

20. Christine Hayes, *What's Divine about Divine Law? Early Perspectives* (Princeton: Princeton University Press, 2015), 169–245; for these definitions of peace and truth, see 184, 188.

through centralized cultic judgment), a court will always ascertain the truth.[21] But the bailment law's exclusion of cultic fact-finding procedures as an option in some cases where forensic evidence is unavailable (i.e., the borrowed or rented animal's death or injury) means that, for the Covenant Code, substantive truth will not always align with legal procedural truth. The Covenant Code accepts this discrepancy in service to the paradigm of justice that it advances, anteceding the distinction between truth and justice that rabbinic law later develops.[22]

Notions of Negligence

As chapter 2 demonstrated, both biblical and cuneiform bailment laws include explicit references to negligence, in Exodus with the words שלח ידו (Exod 22:7, 10) and in the Laws of Hammurabi with the term *egû* (125, 245, 267). Although neither biblical nor cuneiform law displays as robustly developed a classification of wrongs as Roman law, Roman distinctions may be helpful insofar as they provide a vocabulary and framework for discussing wrongdoing and fault. Three Roman legal terms express ideas of blameworthy or nonblameworthy behavior: *dolus, culpa,* and *casus. Dolus* refers to malicious intent to cause damage; *culpa* entails any blameworthy mindset, and includes failure to behave with an expected standard of care; and *casus* refers to an accident for which no one bears blame.[23] Although *culpa* technically includes both dolose and nondolose acts—that is, any blameworthy act, whether one has behaved maliciously or without ill intent—it has come to be equated with negligence, with

---

21. Regarding these two modes of judgment, see further Levinson, *Deuteronomy and the Hermeneutics of Legal Innovation*, esp. 130–33.

22. If Halberstam is correct, the approach to law and truth found in Deut 17 diverges from the approach I identify in the bailment law (which more closely resembles the later approach that she and Hayes discuss with respect to Tannaitic material). On the other hand, Levinson has argued that the focus in Deut 17:2–13 on the local sphere of law vs. the central sphere—specifically at the Temple, and not the palace—serves in part to eliminate the monarchy from the equation of law, and indeed to make it answerable to the law, in contrast to Mesopotamian law. The law of the king immediately following this law in Deut 17 offers strong supporting evidence for this argument (Levinson, "Right Chorale," 71–79). The depiction of the legal system as thoroughly efficacious and complete in Deut 17 may be incidental to its program of fulfilling this goal (with regard to the king vis-à-vis the law), rather than a reflection of a more widespread biblical conception of truth and justice per se.

23. For definitions and discussion, see recently Eric Descheemaeker, *The Division of Wrongs: A Historical Comparative Study* (Oxford: Oxford University Press, 2009), 70–72. For references to varying definitions of *culpa* in Roman legal literature, see Hayim Lapin, *Early Rabbinic Civil Law and the Social History of Roman Galilee: A Study of Mishnah Tractate Baba² Meṣi'a²,* BJS 307 (Altanta: Scholars Press, 1995), 170 n. 106.

dolus and *casus* corresponding to fraud and accident, respectively.[24] This Roman trichotomy shares equivalents with both biblical and cuneiform law. A bailee may commit fraud (e.g., by stealing bailed property) or negligence (e.g., by taking improper care of the property). In the case of herding, flock animals may die accidental deaths either naturally (e.g., from illness) or through *force majeure* (by predation); Exodus considers these options separately (natural death in Exod 22:9; predation in Exod 22:12), while the Laws of Hammurabi treat at least some forms of natural death (from the "affliction of the god") together with predation (LH 266).[25] Although in contrast to Roman law, neither biblical nor cuneiform law develops these concepts, we find their seeds embedded in the logic of the law.

Like Roman law, modern characterizations of negligence may be useful for describing and circumscribing the scope of negligence in biblical and cuneiform law. Doing so, however, requires careful avoidance of superimposing an anachronistic definition of negligence onto ancient materials. In modern legal parlance, the term *negligence* has more than one possible meaning. First, it may refer to the inadvertence or lack of care that characterizes a person's behavior when that person is obligated to perform, or refrain from performing, a specific task. This meaning applies to modern as well as ancient law. A second meaning defines negligence as a tort in and of itself; that is, it is its own cause for action.[26] This is a strictly modern development; in biblical and cuneiform law, there is no general requirement not to commit negligence, but rather a nascent notion of negligence that emerges in the context of some laws.[27] Moreover, in certain cases, modern law is interested in differentiating between subcategories of negligence in order to establish a legal difference between them—for example, in some contexts, a person who commits active negligence may face a higher degree of liability than one guilty of passive negligence.[28] In exploring the applicability of such distinctions to ancient law, this section will focus on the question of what constitutes negligence in the first place, and not on degrees of negligence as they correspond with liability. Such a goal better suits the laconic primary sources at the center of this

---

24. Descheemaeker, *Division of Wrongs*, 72, 115.

25. Legal systems vary in their treatment of accident and *force majeure*, with some treating them the same and others distinguishing between them. See contemporary examples in Christian Von Bar, *Non-Contractual Liability Arising out of Damage Caused to Another*, Principles of European Law 7 (Munich: Sellier, 2009), 883–90.

26. For these two definitions of negligence, see Percy H. Winfield, "The History of Negligence in the Law of Torts," *Law Quarterly Review* 166 (1926): 184–201, here 196.

27. For examples of negligence-related laws in Exodus, see Fensham, "Liability in Case of Negligence," 284–89; in the Laws of Hammurabi see, e.g., 44, 53, 55, 125, 245, 267.

28. Regarding liability for negligence in indemnities, see David L. Baylard, "Products Liability – Non-Contractual Indemnity – the Effect of the Active-Passive Negligence Theory in Missouri," *Missouri Law Review* 41 (1976): 382–403.

study, from which all details regarding negligence must be inferred and extrapolated. Therefore, this section will focus on the descriptive utility of modern terms, without extensively seeking to map out further ramifications.

Active versus Passive Negligence

Modern law distinguishes between passive negligence, which results from a failure to act, or omission, and active negligence, which results from commission of a positive act.[29] Despite these categories emerging explicitly only in recent centuries, they existed in earlier times.[30] For example, while the concept of negligence is not well developed in the Mishnah, Hayim Lapin has identified in the Mishnah's law of bailment examples of both passive negligence (e.g., failure to prevent death by a single wolf) and active negligence (e.g., leading an animal to a location where it is likely to get hurt) for which a bailee is liable, in contrast to examples of unavoidable accident.[31] Examples of *culpa* in Roman law include playing a dangerous game that inadvertently causes death, which could be termed active negligence, and failing to foresee what the diligent person would foresee, which one may characterize as passive negligence.[32] An examination of whether both of these notions are present in any form also in Mesopotamian and/or biblical law may help delineate further the scope of negligence in the ancient Near Eastern and biblical world.[33]

---

29. Garner, *Black's Law Dictionary*, s.v. "negligence." Note that in this context we are interested in the distinction of passive vs. active negligence only as it serves to describe the kinds of behavior that fall under the scope of the term "negligence." We do not speak of any legal distinction between active and passive negligence, such as varying degrees of liability for those guilty of one or the other. Note that in contrast to Garner, Baylard's treatment of active and passive negligence contends that, while the commission of a negligent act necessarily comprises active negligence, the negligent omission of an act may comprise either active or passive negligence, depending on the circumstances. Thus, according to this definition, one who is unaware of a danger and therefore fails to remedy it may be guilty of passive negligence, but a person who has knowledge of a dangerous condition and either fails to remedy it or remedies it negligently commits active negligence. For this view, see Baylard, "Products Liability," 388–89.

30. See Winfield, "History of Negligence," 190, with reference to the history of English law.

31. M. B. Meṣ. 7:9–10; Lapin, *Early Rabbinic Civil Law*, 166–67, 291. For the underdeveloped concept of negligence in Tannaitic literature, see ibid., 167–68; and Daube, "Negligence," 124–47.

32. See D.9.2.10 (Paul, 22 *ad Edictum*) regarding playing a dangerous game; D.9.2.31 (Paul, 10 *ad Sabinum*) regarding failure to see; along with other examples of *culpa* cited by David Ibbetson, "Wrongs and Responsibility in Pre-Roman Law," *JLH* 25 (2004): 99–127, here 116.

33. On affinities between negligence in biblical and ancient Near Eastern law and modern law, see Fensham, "Liability in Case of Negligence," 283–94.

The Akkadian idiom *aḫa nadû*, discussed in chapter 2, evokes an image of the arms dropping to the sides, or doing nothing. This sense of inactivity is reflected in the scenarios that the idiom describes. LH 44, for example, addresses a case where a man who rents an uncultivated field is negligent (*aḫšu iddīma*) and "does not open the field (for cultivation)." LH 53 speaks of a man who "neglects [*aḫšu iddīma*] to reinforce the embankment of (the irrigation canal of) his field and does not reinforce its embankment." In both cases, the subject's negligence is clearly a case of omission, or failure to do what he should. The same language occurs in other legal contexts, such as a trial record documenting a person's admission that he "neglected [his] father's house and did not appear for many days."[34] Examples of *aḫa nadû* clearly referring to negligence by omission occur in wisdom literature and letters as well.[35]

Other laws that deal with negligence, without using the term *aḫa nadû*, similarly hold the subject liable for omissions, such as not reinforcing the house he has constructed (LH 229–232) or the well he has opened to an irrigation outlet (LNB 3). In one case, however, which contrasts with LH 53, the subject is liable for the act of negligently (*aḫšu iddīma*) opening the branch of a canal and allowing the water to cause damage, so there is at least one example of *aḫa nadû* bearing an active valence.

Whether the Akkadian term *egû* refers to passive negligence alone is less clear. While in some cases there is no indication whether *egû* refers to the omission or commission of an act, one finds many examples of Old Babylonian letters where the addressee is charged "to do x; not to [*egû*] with regard to y" or similar.[36] In these cases, the addressee must not *fail to do something* with regard to y; the omission of an act thus constitutes *egû*.

In laws relating to a negligent boatman, one might wish to read the boatman's negligence (*egû*) as an example of active negligence based on the language the laws use: he "causes the boat to sink" (*uṭṭebbi*; LH 236; cf. LE 5); "causes the boat ... to become lost" (*uḫtalliq*; LH 236; cf. LH 237, LE 5). However, the negligent party of LH 53, who explicitly omits, rather than commits, an act, bears the "loss he caused" (*uḫalliqu*), also in the D-stem, so it is equally possible that the subject has been passively negligent. Both action and inaction may cause the damage or loss. While I have not found an example of *egû* in a legal context that explicitly relates to

---

34. Nbn. 1113:17.

35. For wisdom, see, e.g., BWL 38:17, which speaks of someone who is negligent and "forgets their [the gods'] rites"; for letters, see, e.g., BIN 7 43:23, in which the speaker asks, "would I be careless with what you gave me orders for?"; and many letters in which the recipient is instructed not to neglect a certain matter (e.g., YOS 2 1:36; CT 6 19:21; TCL 18 82:9; Kraus AbB 1 29:8, 16). See references in *CAD* N/1, s.v. "*nadû*."

36. See examples in *CAD* E, s.v. "*egû*," 2': "keep good guard over this silver, do not be careless in guarding the silver" (YOS 2 11:12); "do not be careless about your funds, do not even leave one-sixth (of a sheqel) of silver in your house" (YOS 2 134:17), etc.

active negligence, the word *egītu* ("negligence, carelessness") from the same root occurs in nonlegal contexts in the Middle Babylonian and Standard Babylonian dialects together with the verb *epēšu*, indicating the commission of an act.[37] Thus, while passive negligence predominates in explicit references to negligence in Mesopotamian law, one also finds possible evidence of a conception of active negligence.

If we expand our consideration of negligence in Mesopotamian law to cases that do not use an Akkadian term for negligence, other possible cases of active negligence emerge. LOx 6 and FLP 1287 vi 23–31, for example, hold responsible the ox renter who crosses a river with the animal, thereby causing its death. This is similar to the example of active negligence in the Mishnah cited earlier: in leading the ox to a place where it might get hurt or die, the renter commits active negligence. While the corpus of extant cuneiform texts is admittedly limited, it is interesting to note that these laws, which do not invoke any term expressing "negligence," have no parallel in the extant cuneiform law collections that treat ox rental, nor do any extant contracts consider the possibility of a rental animal drowning.[38] The usual conception of negligence in cuneiform law appears to lean toward passive negligence.[39]

When turning to biblical law, one must decide based on context alone which cases treat negligence, because, with the exception of the idiom שלח ידי, the extant Biblical Hebrew lexicon lacks a negligence vocabulary. An examination of biblical law yields examples of what may aptly be termed both passive and active negligence. The owner of a habitually goring ox is liable when that ox kills because the owner has failed to watch it (Exod 21:29, 36); and the person who uncovers or digs a pit but fails to cover it is liable when an animal falls in—also for a failure to act (Exod 21:33–34). These constitute cases of passive negligence. On the other hand, Exod 22:4–5, which immediately precedes the law of bailment, treats cases that one might view as active negligence: a person is liable for damages resulting from sending out an animal to graze, when that animal then strays and grazes on another's property, or from kindling a fire that then grows out of control.[40] In both of these cases, the liable party is culpable for the commission of a positive act.[41] Although some biblical scholars have

---

37. See examples in *CAD* E, s.v. "*egītu.*"

38. For this point, see Roth, "Scholastic Exercise,'" 140.

39. For a similar understanding of the passive character of negligence in cuneiform law, see Ibbetson, "Wrongs and Responsibility," 108–9.

40. For identification of these verses as cases of negligence, see, e.g., Finkelstein, "Ox That Gored," 26; Houtman, *Exodus*, 3:192–93; Bruce Wells, "Introduction: The Idea of a Shared Tradition," in *Law from the Tigris to the Tiber: The Writings of Raymond Westbrook*, ed. Bruce Wells and F. Rachel Magdalene, 2 vols. (Winona Lake, IN: Eisenbrauns, 2009), 1:xvii.

41. While one might argue that these could be cases of passive negligence—failure to

equated negligence with an "omission" per se,[42] this characterization mis-represents the scope of negligence that Exodus's Covenant Code envi-sions. Negligent behavior in the Covenant Code, more so than in cuneiform law, may include both the commission and omission of an act, even though these ideas are not fully expressed.

Negligence and Duty

In addition to the categories of active and passive negligence, the modern legal concept of "duty" offers a lens through which to character-ize negligence in biblical and cuneiform law. In the nineteenth century, legal scholars argued that negligence includes four elements, the first of which is the element of duty. According to this view, when the court decides whether a defendant is liable, it must first determine whether the defendant owed the plaintiff a duty of care; if not, there could have been no breach of that duty and, therefore, no grounds for liability.[43] "Duty" was typically conceived of as relational—originating in a relationship—either because the defendant undertook to perform a service or, even in the absence of an undertaking, because of a particular social relationship between the two parties. In contrast to this view, a second school of thought championed by Oliver Wendell Holmes and William Prosser emerged in the late nineteenth and early twentieth centuries, which moved to broaden the concept of duty and conceive of negligence as non-relational, based purely in policy and state directives. According to this view, all citizens must act in accordance with a state-directed standard of reasonable care toward all citizens; this standard of care is determined exclusively based on policy concerns of deterrence (deterring harm) and compensation (making up for losses), irrespective of any connection between the concerned parties.[44] Since the late twentieth century, there has been a further move, spearheaded by John Goldberg and Benjamin Zipursky, to reembrace a tighter concept of duty and relational negli-gence.[45]

---

control the fire, failure to watch one's animal properly—these verses ascribe liability for actions.

42. For this language, see Westbrook, "Deposit Law," 371; cf. the exclusion of negli-gence as a candidate for interpreting שלח ידו in the bailment law in Daube, "Negligence," 127–28; Jackson, *Wisdom-Laws*, 340 n. 46.

43. See John C. P. Goldberg and Benjamin C. Zipursky, "The Moral of MacPherson," *University of Pennsylvania Law Review* 146 (1998): 1733–1847, here 1747.

44. See Holmes, *Common Law*, 71–145; Holmes, "The Path of the Law," *Boston Law School Magazine* 1 (1897): 1–17; William L. Prosser, *Handbook of the Law of Torts* (Saint Paul, MN: West Publishing, 1941), §§29–31.

45. See Goldberg and Zipursky, "Moral of MacPherson," 1733–1847.

Does a biblical conception of negligence fit with either of these constructions? Negligence in the Covenant Code includes cases in which there is no undertaking and those in which an undertaking transpires. The owner of the ox, digger of a pit, owner of the grazing animal, and fire kindler do not undertake to avoid harming another party but nonetheless owe that duty to their neighbors. In contrast, cases of bailment involve an undertaking to perform a service, which explicitly creates a duty between parties. The exception to this rule, the case of lost property, poses a conundrum: if there was no undertaking and no duty-creating relationship existed between the loser and finder of the property, why should the defendant bear liability? Goldberg and Zipursky would likely classify this as an essentially fictive "stranger–stranger" relationship, which still generates a duty. In their view, however, the duty generated by "stranger–stranger" relationships is less demanding than in other categories of relationships.[46] In contrast, according to the Holmes-Prosser school of thought, duty could exist between complete strangers just as much as it could between neighbors or parties to an undertaking, with no differentiation between their responsibilities and liability.[47] According to our understanding of the biblical bailment law, the finder of lost property bears identical liability to a bailee who explicitly undertakes to watch the property of the bailor, based on the equation of lost objects with other objects of bailments in Exod 22:8. This equal liability for strangers and consenting parties squares more easily with the Holmes-Prosser view.

The Laws of Hammurabi similarly include cases of negligence arising from undertakings—for example, in cases of bailment, building a house, renting a field, and driving a boat—as well as cases where no undertaking exists, such as reinforcing the embankment of an irrigation canal. In the latter case, the relationship between parties is highlighted by the law's depiction of a "common irrigated area" affected by the subject's negligent behavior; the defendant and plaintiff participate in a relationship by virtue of partaking in a common irrigated area. The relational aspect of negligence cases in the Laws of Hammurabi allows for an analysis through the lens of Goldberg and Zipursky's view that the biblical involuntary bailment law precludes. This analysis likewise coheres with the predominance of passive negligence in Mesopotamian legal literature. When negligence arises in a case where an obvious relationship connects the plaintiff and defendant, the duty of care is higher and so includes even liability for omissions—in contrast to "stranger–stranger" cases where one would expect a less demanding duty of care, which might include

---

46. Goldberg and Zipursky, "Moral of MacPherson," 1733–1847; Holmes, *Common Law*, 71–145.

47. Holmes, *Common Law*, 71–145; Holmes, "Path of the Law," 1–17; Prosser, *Handbook of the Law of Torts*, §§29–31.

only liability for active negligence.[48] In other words, the Laws of Hammurabi contain many examples of liability for passive negligence, and in these cases one can identify a relational basis for this liability. Because of these underlying relationships, even in a Goldberg-and-Zipurskian analysis it is not odd that the law would demand of the passively negligent actor such a high duty of care. Modern legal categories thus allow for the unpacking of subtle jurisprudential differences between our reticent ancient sources.

The classification of duty in the biblical bailment law as nonrelational, in contrast to the Laws of Hammurabi, further underscores the value that the Covenant Code places on responsibility to the disenfranchised. The owner of lost property may not be socially or economically marginalized per se, like the Covenant Code's stranger (Exod 22:20; 23:9, 12), orphan or widow (Exod 22:21), poor (Exod 22:24; 23:6), and bondman (Exod 23:12). Still, insofar as the loss of property disadvantages its owner, the Covenant Code includes such a person within its larger program of a duty of care toward those who might not otherwise receive it.

Contract, Tort, or Property?

Over the last two centuries, scholars of English and American law have repeatedly asked variations of the same question: What is the nature of bailment?[49] Although many theories have been advanced, three approaches dominate the discourse. Bailment, in these views, sounds either in contract, tort, or property.[50] Recently, scholars have displayed greater willingness to view bailment as traversing these categories, or partaking in more than one.[51] It is useful, however, to examine each of these options as background to a consideration of the biblical law.

---

48. See Goldberg and Zipursky, "Moral of MacPherson," 1830.

49. For references and further discussion, see Hamish Dempster, "Clearing the Confusion Surrounding Bailment: Bailment as an Exercise of Legal Power by the Bailor," *Common Law World Review* 33 (2004): 295–331; R. H. Helmholz, "Bailment Theories and the Liability of Bailees: The Elusive Uniform Standard of Reasonable Care," *Kansas Law Review* 41 (1992–1993): 97–135; Thomas W. Merrill and Henry E. Smith, "The Property/Contract Interface," *Columbia Law Review* 101 (2001): 773–852, here 811 nn. 116–17; Norman E. Palmer, "Gratuitous Bailment—Contract or Tort?," *International and Comparative Law Quarterly* 24 (1975): 565–72.

50. The verb "sound" in this legal usage means "to arise from," signifying the substantive basis for liability at work.

51. See, e.g., Norman E. Palmer, *Bailment* (Sydney: Law Book Co., 1979), 1: "In many respects, bailment stands at the point at which contract, property and tort converge" (although he ultimately argues that bailment is "a separate and independent legal entity," for which see Palmer, "Gratuitous Bailment," 572); Merrill and Smith, "Property/Contract Interface," 773–852.

A first school of thought considers bailment contractual in nature.[52] According to this view, rights and duties of a bailee and bailor originate in an agreement between the two parties. That agreement may be express or implied and is highly subject to customization based on the parties' wishes. Thomas Merrill and Henry Smith write that

> contract rights are in personam; that is, they bind only the parties to [the contract]. The contracting parties are in the best position to evaluate the costs and benefits of adopting novel legal terms to govern their relationship, and in the typical bilateral contract there are no significant third-party effects associated with the adoption of idiosyncratic terms.[53]

Those who reject this view frequently cite examples of involuntary bailments, such as cases of lost property, in which the owner becomes a bailor and the finder becomes a bailee, without the two ever forming any agreement.[54] By definition, such an arrangement precludes an agreement or contract between the two parties. Gratuitous bailments, which lack the element of consideration (i.e., the bilateral exchange of one thing of value for another) crucial to the modern contract, have similarly led scholars to question the contract-based view.[55]

A second view situates wrongdoing in bailment within the realm of torts, which include any wrong requiring the offender (or tortfeasor) to pay damages to the injured party. A tort view accounts for involuntary bailments, insofar as it does not require mutual agreement between the bailor and bailee.[56] Unlike a contractual duty, which one person owes to another individual pursuant to an agreement between them, one owes a tortious duty to the world at large by virtue of having entered into a particular situation.[57] Whereas in contracts, duties and rights originate in an agreement, in torts they stem from a general duty to take care.[58] In the tort-based view, as Alice Tay aptly puts it, "[it] is by entering into a

---

52. The term *contract* has multiple valences in legal discourse and so requires clarification. Contracts occur in at least three primary contexts: contracts vs. sale, contracts vs. status, and unilateral vs. bilateral contracts. My interest here falls within the second context of contracts vs. status, which questions the extent to which an arrangement (here, bailments) is customizable or default. As will become evident from the discussion of contract, tort, and property, it is this distinction that drives the question of how best to characterize bailments.

53. Merrill and Smith, "Property/ Contract Interface," 776–77.

54. See, e.g., William K. Laidlaw, "Principles of Bailment," *Cornell Law Quarterly* 16 (1930–1931): 286–310; Williston, *Treatise on the Law of Contracts*, §1032.

55. See especially Palmer, "Gratuitous Bailment," 565–72.

56. Cf. Alice Ehr-Soon Tay, "The Essence of a Bailment: Contract, Agreement or Possession?," *Sydney Law Review* 239 (1965–1967): 239–53, here 243.

57. Ibid., 245.

58. Gerard McMeel, "The Redundancy of Bailment," *Lloyd's Maritime and Commercial Law Quarterly* 2 (2003): 169–200, here 180.

relationship with a thing, and not by entering into a relationship with a person, that the defendant becomes subject to duties."[59] Critics of this view have pointed to its deletion of the bailor's central role in the bail-ment,[60] the possibility of divergences between duties imposed upon par-ties to a bailment and duties imposed by a law of tort,[61] and the lopsided emphasis on the machinery of bailment's enforcement at the expense of its creation and forms.[62]

A third school of thought, which has gained more currency in recent decades, views bailment as property-based, such that rights and duties stem from ownership and possession.[63] In this view, ownership of prop-erty creates rights and duties, and the element of possession effects bail-ments, irrespective of how that possession comes to be. In bailment, what matters is the identity of the property's owner and its lawful possessor: while a contract might create possession, it is not the contract but the pos-session itself that generates a bailment. Therefore, although a contract may accompany the creation of the bailment and help shape the arrange-ment, it is not necessary, in this view, in order to effect the transaction itself. Like the torts-based view, a property-based understanding can eas-ily account for involuntary and gratuitous bailments. A property-based view, however, has the advantage of considering both the bailor's and bailee's roles in the arrangement, and of focusing on issues of ownership and possession, the allocation of which is the defining feature of bail-ments.

The debate surrounding bailments' basis for liability finds an instruc-tive context within the legal discourse of status versus contract.[64] The nineteenth-century legal historian Henry Maine characterized the evolu-tion of progressive societies as a move from status-based to contract-based.[65] Status regimes restrict people to a set of predetermined relationships and regulations, with limited allowance for customizability, because those relationships are understood as bearing some essential, unchanging char-acter. In contrast, contract regimes allow people freely to define their own relationships with minimal outside regulation. Historically, in a common law context, bailments were defined within a status context. The nine-teenth century saw a move toward the contractization of these arrange-

---

59. Tay, "Essence of a Bailment," 244.

60. Dempster, "Clearing the Confusion," 297.

61. Palmer, "Gratuitous Bailment," 570.

62. Percy H. Winfield, *The Province of the Law of Tort* (Cambridge: Cambridge University Press, 1931), 103.

63. See Merrill and Smith, "Property/Contract Interface," 776–77.

64. For the application of this discourse to ancient Near Eastern law, see Westbrook, *History of Ancient Near Eastern Law*, 1:35–36.

65. Henry Sumner Maine, *Ancient Law: Its Connection with the Early History of Society, and Its Relation to Modern Ideas* (London: Murray, 1861), 169–70.

ments. The meeting of status and contract during this period may account for the ongoing disagreement surrounding how best to classify bailments. The "property" view is thus another way of expressing a status-oriented account of bailments, wherein bailments bear an essential character that contracts have minimal room to customize.

A number of legal scholars who discuss the biblical and cuneiform bailment laws have characterized them as contractual in nature. Saul Levmore, for example, speaks of the "close contractual relationship" between bailor and bailee that distinguishes these laws from other rules within their legal systems.[66] Richard Hiers, in contrast, characterizes the law within the sphere of torts, while noting that it involves "elements of contract."[67] Without entering the debate with respect to modern law, we can use it as a lens through which to examine the biblical and cuneiform laws of bailment. While modern legal categories will not necessarily accord well with ancient laws, they may still be useful for an understanding of these laws when applied critically and with appropriate caveats in mind.

Before continuing, a clarification of the term *contract* with respect to ancient sources is in order. The Akkadian term *riksu*, or its oft-used plural form *riksātum* (literally, "bindings"), though commonly translated as "contract," more accurately refers to the stipulations that could accompany and clarify details of a transaction (i.e., the contractual stipulations, rather than a physical record of those stipulations). In order to transact, parties could make these stipulations orally and were not required to record them in writing. A written record, however, could serve an important evidentiary function and so in some cases would have been desirable. The written record itself did not create any legal change but served as a mnemonic device, recording an event that one might need to remember in the future, for example, to counter a legal claim.[68] Many legal actions involving contractual stipulations were also accompanied by symbolic gestures and/or solemn words.[69] Whereas the modern contract

---

66. Levmore, "Rethinking Comparative Law," 252 n. 44; cf. Russ VerSteeg, "Early Mesopotamian Commercial Law," *University of Toledo Law Review* 30 (1999): 183–214, here 196–98.

67. Richard H. Hiers, "Ancient Laws, Yet Strangely Modern: Biblical Contract and Tort Jurisprudence," *University of Detroit Mercy Law Review* 88 (2010–2011): 473–96, here 480; Hiers, *Justice and Compassion in Biblical Law* (New York: Continuum, 2009), 13–24.

68. See Marc Van de Mieroop, "Why Did They Write on Clay?," *Klio* 79 (1997): 1–18; and see the discussion in F. Rachel Magdalene, "Rachel's Betrothal Contract and the Origins of Contract Law," in *Sexuality and Law in the Torah*, ed. Hilary Lipka and Bruce Wells (London: Bloomsbury, 2020), 77–110, here 91–92.

69. For the Old Babylonian contract in particular, see Greengus, "Old Babylonian Marriage Contract," 505–32; cf. Dominique Charpin, *Writing, Law, and Kingship in Old Babylonian Mesopotamia* (Chicago: University of Chicago Press, 2010), 43–48.

by definition can be valid only if it includes consideration, with each party receiving something of value, in the context of biblical and cuneiform law, I will use the term *contract* to refer specifically to the stipulations that two or more parties make while transacting, irrespective of whether both parties receive some benefit.[70] Therefore, when considering whether a law is "contractual" in nature, we have in mind the possibility that the stipulations to which parties agree—as opposed to the more robust modern definition of contract—serve as the source of duties, rights, and penalties.

Although Exodus does not address the procedure for creating bailments, at least two biblical narratives discussed suggest that such arrangements could have involved contractual stipulations tailored by the parties to the transaction: Gen 29–31 features a series of negotiations between shepherd Jacob and flock-owner Laban, including irregular terms such as payment in the form of flock animals of only a particular breed. The parable of 1 Kgs 20 involves an agreement between two parties and the king's declaration that the agreement must be upheld despite its severe consequences and despite his own hypocrisy. These narrative contractual agreements are legally valid, notwithstanding their moral deficiencies. Their high degree of customizability, on the one hand, suggests that the parties' duties originate in their contractual stipulations, and not in property. Conversely, the genre in which these agreements occur casts doubt on the plausibility of such nonstandard terms.

On the other hand, if one views the Covenant Code's inclusion of the case of lost property, the paradigmatic involuntary bailment, as part and parcel of its bailment law, then this inclusion further challenges the premise that it is based in contract. As legal scholars have long noted, involuntary bailments such as lost property cannot possibly involve an agreement between two parties.[71] To frame the finder of lost property as a party to a contract, even an implied one, would require an elephantine legal fiction. Instead, one might prefer a property-based view of the law, according to which the rights, duties, and penalties emerge from the bailee's lawful possession of the owner's property and from the owner's relationship to the property, rather than from a contractual agreement between the bailee and bailor.[72] To frame this in terms of status, the property's lawful possession in the hands of a person other than its owner automatically generates a bailee–bailor relationship, with the status of "bailee," and all that entails,

---

70. For discussion of the problem of the gratuitous bailment and the lack of consideration, see Palmer, "Gratuitous Bailment," 565. Regarding consideration as an important part of one biblical contract, see Magdalene, "Rachel's Betrothal Contract," 77–110.

71. For a classic formulation of this view, see Williston, *Treatise on the Law of Contracts*, §1032.

72. Indeed, this stance has gained popularity among legal scholars, despite the fact that, in practice, modern courts have continued to treat bailments under certain circumstances as contract-based. See Helmholz, "Bailment Theories," 133.

ascribed to one party, and "bailor" ascribed to the other. A property-based view does not preclude the use of contracts in voluntary bailments. It rather claims that, even if parties to a bailment agree to terms and form a contractual relationship, the origin of their rights and duties to one another does not lie in these stipulations. Moreover, one can expect these stipulations to cohere with a limited number of standard forms, in contrast to stipulations relating to a law that is contractual in nature, which will allow for greater customization.[73]

A torts-based understanding of the biblical law of bailment would also account for the case of lost property. However, such an understanding on its own fails to capture essential aspects of bailment, considering the bailee's duty to take care as simply one example of a broader duty to take care in various relationships, and not just in the relationship between bailee and bailor.[74] While the biblical bailment law occurs amid a series of laws relating to treatment of other people and their property, it is the division of ownership and possession among different parties that constitutes its defining feature. The biblical law of bailment is therefore best characterized in terms of property, or as traversing property and tort.

Unlike biblical law, the Laws of Hammurabi emphasize the role of a contract in both deposits of goods and in herding and animal rental arrangements. Witnesses and a contract must accompany the establishment of a bailment of goods (LH 122–123), and a shepherd who allows for losses in the flock is to compensate the owner in accordance with contractual stipulations (LH 264). In addition, unlike Exodus, the Laws of Hammurabi do not incorporate involuntary bailment into their bailment-related laws, although they treat lost property in proximity to the law of deposit (LH 126). Ancient Near Eastern legal documents also use bailment language to describe other involuntary arrangements, such as the judicial sequestration, in which parties are ordered to place property into bailment pending the resolution of their dispute.[75] Yet the fiction of the contract in such a scenario is not quite as great a leap as the one that the case of lost property requires. In the judicial sequestration, while neither party may wish to place the property into bailment, both parties are aware of the transaction and undertake an agreement, if under duress. Such an involuntary bailment does not preclude a contractual origin for the rights and duties of the bailee and bailor.

Whereas the case of lost property does not pose a challenge to a contractual argument for Hammurabi's bailment laws, the very nature of the contract in the Old Babylonian period raises a difficulty. Old Babylonian

---

73. Merrill and Smith, "Property/Contract Interface," 776.

74. For a summary of a tort-based understanding of bailment, see McMeel, "Redundancy of Bailment," 180.

75. See, e.g., OECT 3 82, discussed in chapter 1.

contractual stipulations did not in themselves effect bailments but rather specified the terms of each arrangement.[76] If contractual stipulations could not create bailments, how could duties, rights, and penalties originate in them?[77] On the other hand, Samuel Greengus has argued that the act of deposit was insufficient to create a bailment; contractual stipulations were necessary in order to distinguish the deposit from other transactions, such as gifts or loans, that also involved the transfer of property from one person to another.[78] Although contractual stipulations were insufficient to create a bailment on their own, they were necessary to clarify that the transaction in effect was indeed a bailment, and to specify the terms to which the parties agreed. Without a contract there could be no bailment. In this light, although there is no evidence contradicting a property- or tort-based view of the law, a contractual view remains plausible for Hammurabi's bailment law, albeit not for that of the Covenant Code. A view that considers lost property—the paradigmatic involuntary bailment that cannot have originated in contract or consent—as integral to the biblical bailment law instead recommends a property- (and possibly torts-) based view, according to which the rights, duties, and penalties of the bailor and bailee (including the finder of lost property) stem not from contractual stipulations or agreement between the two parties but from the bailor's ownership and the bailee's lawful possession of the property in question.

Standards of Liability

Related to contractual, tortious, or property-based understandings of bailment is the liability rule or rules that the laws adopt. These include strict liability and fault liability (or negligence) rules. A strict liability rule starts with the premise that the defendant is liable to compensate the plaintiff when a loss occurs. One form of the strict liability rule affords defendants the chance to clear themselves by proving that a plaintiff is at fault; another version of strict liability does not allow defendants this opportunity. In contrast, a fault liability or negligence rule places the burden of proof on the plaintiff; the plaintiff bears the loss unless the plaintiff can demonstrate that the defendant is at fault.[79] Richard Helmholz has argued that a contractual analysis of bailments accords best with a system of strict liability, whereas a property-based understanding better fits with

---

76. Greengus, "Old Babylonian Marriage Contract," 509.

77. Cf. the critique of the contractual view by Dempster, "Clearing the Confusion," 298.

78. Greengus, "Old Babylonian Marriage Contract," 508.

79. This definition follows Jules L. Coleman, *Risks and Wrongs*, Cambridge Studies in Philosophy and Law (Cambridge: Cambridge University Press, 1992), 212–33.

a negligence rule, or fault liability.[80] Merrill and Smith, on the other hand, contend that fault liability is associated with contract, while strict liability is associated with property.[81] This section will consider the standards of liability that the biblical and cuneiform bailment laws adopt, as well as whether they align with contractual or property-based analyses.

The biblical law of deposit requires that the bailee be at fault, whether through negligence or wrongful intent, in order to incur liability. Thus, this law falls under the umbrella of fault liability. Unlike the typical expression of fault liability, however, this law places the burden of proof on the defendant, rather than on the plaintiff. If the bailor accuses the bailee of wrongdoing, the bailee will be responsible for the loss unless the bailee is willing to undergo a cultic procedure to achieve exoneration. The biblical oath was taken only with great trepidation. Although the law establishes a means for the bailee to defeat liability, it rests on the assumption that it will be used sparingly.[82] The law thus places a grave burden upon the defendant in this case, despite requiring fault as a prerequisite for liability.[83] The same standard of liability applies also to the shepherd, with an exception: in cases of theft, the shepherd faces a strict liability standard and must compensate the bailor irrespective of fault, with no opportunity for exoneration. Here we find an example of variety within a legal system. The Covenant Code includes more than one standard of liability within the same legal topic.

Like the standard of liability a shepherd faces in cases of theft, the law of animal borrowing and rental applies a strict liability standard. If the owner is not present—that is, in nearly all cases—then the defendant is liable, regardless of whether the defendant bears fault.[84] Only under the

---

80. Helmholz, "Bailment Theories," 98–99.

81. Merrill and Smith, "Property/Contract Interface," 819–20.

82. See, e.g., Westbrook, "Deposit Law," 364 (and see nn. 7–9): "Such was the fear of the oath's consequences … that it was not infrequent for the defendant to refuse to swear, or for the plaintiff to concede the case rather than let him swear, or for the two parties to reach a compromise rather than proceed to the oath."

83. For an alternative analysis, see Levmore, "Rethinking Comparative Law," 235–87. Levmore, who interprets Exod 22:6–8 as treating gratuitous bailment, likewise identifies a fault liability rule in this law. However, his statement that the bailee "is only liable when at fault; in the case of theft he merely swears his innocence and is then not liable" mischaracterizes the oath.

84. Levmore, in contrast, adopts the talmudic understanding of the owner's presence as referring specifically to the time of borrowing or rental, as opposed to the time that the animal's death or injury occurs. Therefore, if the owner consents to the borrowing or rental, then the borrower or renter will be liable only for negligence and theft. The borrower or renter would thus be subject to a fault liability standard, except in cases of theft, just like the bailee of Exod 22:9–12. This rabbinically inclined reading of Exod 22:13–14, however, does not reflect the plain sense of the text. See Levmore, "Rethinking Comparative Law," 274 n. 14.

limited conditions of the owner's presence at the time of animal death or injury does the defendant earn a chance at exoneration, presumably when the owner has witnessed that the borrower or renter bore no fault. In this regard, the strict liability of the animal borrower and renter law differs from the definition proposed above. In order to defeat liability when the owner is present, the defendant would not have to prove that the other party was at fault, only that the defendant was not.[85]

Like the biblical deposit law, the Laws of Eshnunna (36–37) reflect a standard of fault liability. The defendant is liable only if the defendant bears fault. Otherwise, responsibility for the loss will fall on the plaintiff. However, the Laws of Eshnunna's fault liability differs from a typical understanding of this standard insofar as it places the burden of proof on the defendant, rather than on the plaintiff.[86] It is up to the defendant to take an oath to achieve exoneration; otherwise, the defendant will bear liability. This "atypical" form of fault liability thus occurs in both the Covenant Code and the Laws of Eshnunna, pointing to a slightly different model from that of modern law.

One similarly finds variety in Hammurabi's bailment laws. LH 120, which requires double compensation in cases of loss or fraud, holds the bailee to a strict liability standard of the first type. The defendant (the bailee) is liable, irrespective of fault, and without an opportunity for exoneration. Thus, in the cases envisioned by LH 120, it is not the bailee but the bailor who takes an oath, establishing the quantity of the bailment. In contrast, in cases of gratuitous bailments of silver and goods, the bailee is held to a standard of fault liability; the bailee is liable because the bailee is considered at fault for committing fraud (LH 124) and for negligence (LH 125). The herding law (LH 263–267) similarly assigns liability to the defendant (the shepherd) on the condition of fault.[87]

Finally, Hammurabi's animal rental law (LH 244–249), like the biblical law of animal borrowing and rental, reflects a strict liability standard according to which the renter is liable as long as the renter's conduct has caused the loss (injury or death). Predation, here and in the herding laws

---

85. The understanding of this criterion as the owner's presence signifying his share of blame would cohere with Coleman's definition; in this reading, the borrower is not liable because the owner bears fault.

86. For this point, see Levmore, "Rethinking Comparative Law," 252 n. 44.

87. Levmore argues that LH 265 bears a strict liability standard for all losses that occur in the pen, in contrast to LH 267's fault liability rule for losses in the field ("Rethinking Comparative Law," 261 n. 70; cf. Nelson P. Miller, "An Ancient Law of Care," *Whittier Law Review* 26 [2004–2005]: 3–57, here 26). Yet LH 265 refers specifically to losses incurred through fraudulent brand altering and sale of flock animals, rather than to any pen-set loss. The difference between these paragraphs is therefore one not of setting (pen vs. field) but of intentional wrong vs. negligence. In both cases the shepherd faces a fault liability standard; the liability and resultant penalty are contingent upon the shepherd's level of fault.

of Hammurabi and the Covenant Code, constitutes *force majeure* and is an exceptional case for which the bailee is not liable; in such a scenario, the bailee bears no causal relationship to the loss, let alone fault.

In summary, in both the Laws of Eshnunna and the Covenant Code, the law of deposit of goods and silver adopts a fault liability standard, which deviates from a modern definition of fault liability in placing the burden of proof on the defendant rather than on the plaintiff. The Laws of Hammurabi, the only law collection to distinguish between non-gratuitous and gratuitous deposits of goods and silver, also apply a different standard of liability in each of these cases, with fault liability for the gratuitous bailee and strict liability for the non-gratuitous bailee. Otherwise, the Laws of Hammurabi and the Covenant Code both apply a fault liability standard to the shepherd and a strict liability standard to the renter (and in the Covenant Code's case, the borrower).

SUMMARY: STANDARDS OF LIABILITY IN THE BAILMENT LAWS IN THE COVENANT CODE, THE LAWS OF ESHNUNNA, AND THE LAWS OF HAMMURABI

	The Covenant Code	The Laws of Eshnunna	The Laws of Hammurabi
Deposit of goods, silver	*Fault liability*, with burden of proof on defendant.	*Fault liability*, with burden of proof on defendant.	*Fault liability* for the gratuitous bailee; *strict liability* for the non-gratuitous bailee.
Herding	*Fault liability*, with burden of proof on defendant. Exception: *strict liability* in case of theft.	--	*Fault liability*.
Animal rental (and borrowing in Exodus)	*Strict liability*. Exception: if owner witnessed renter's innocence.	--	*Strict liability*.

In light of the similarities between the Covenant Code and the Laws of Hammurabi's liability rules in cases of herding and rental, and between the Covenant Code and the Laws of Eshnunna's liability rule for deposit, illustrated in the chart above, Hammurabi's distinctive deposit law merits further attention. Unlike the deposit laws in the Laws of Eshnunna and Exodus, Hammurabi's deposit laws (LH 124 and LH 125) do not explicitly afford the defendant an opportunity to take an oath declaring innocence; yet, in holding the bailee liable for fraud or negligence, the law implies that if the bailee were not considered at fault, the bailee would not be liable. In these cases, which do not require an oath of the defendant in order to defeat liability, it appears that the plaintiff indeed bears the burden to prove through other evidentiary means (e.g., physical evidence or eyewitness testimony) that the defendant is at fault. In other words, this version of fault liability matches a modern definition more closely than that of the Covenant Code or the Laws of Eshnunna, which instead place the burden of proof on the defendant. These other law collections' form of fault liability perhaps differs from the modern definition not because of these law collections' antiquity and other features that might distinguish them from modern law, but because the topic that these laws treat is broad enough so as to straddle the line between two liability rules: fault liability, in which the defendant is liable only when at fault, and strict liability, in which the burden of proof lies with the defendant rather than with the plaintiff. Hammurabi's two laws of deposit, which treat more narrowly defined cases than those of the Covenant Code and the Laws of Eshnunna, thus offer a model for fault and strict liability that more closely matches the modern equivalent described above.

The liability rules of both the Covenant Code and the Laws of Hammurabi's bailment laws are characterized by variety: neither legal system adopts a single liability rule for all bailment scenarios. We began this discussion by referring to the ongoing debate surrounding the nature of bailment and further noted that contractual and property-based laws have alternately been associated with either strict or fault liability rules. Some scholars have preferred to understand bailment as standing at the intersection of contract and property, for example, rather than belonging to a single category.[88] The variety in liability rules in both the Covenant Code and the Laws of Hammurabi suggests that we adopt a similar understanding of these laws, rather than see the bailee and bailor's rights, duties, and penalties in either collection as corresponding exclusively to contract, tort, or property.

Modern Jurisprudence, Ancient Laws

The challenge of applying modern legal categories to ancient data recurs throughout this chapter. As Raymond Westbrook has noted, prior to the mid-first millennium, "[the] ability to express the law differently through definition, categorization, broad statements of principle and similar intellectual tools" was absent.[89] The idea of a concept or category

---

88. See, e.g., Helmholz, "Bailment Theories," 134 (also including torts); Merrill and Smith, "Property/Contract Interface," 811–20.

89. Westbrook, *History of Ancient Near Eastern Law*, 1:22–23.

of law does not accurately depict how biblical and ancient Near Eastern legal thinking operated. In fact, as noted from the start of this study, the very use of the term *bailment* to describe the ancient laws under consideration poses a difficulty. Did a concept of bailment exist for the authors of these sources, or is it rather the case that, once a person is familiar with an anachronistic notion of bailment, it is possible to identify elements of this not-yet-crystallized concept in ancient texts? Cuneiform law does not evince a concrete idea of bailment; thus, sections of the Laws of Hammurabi that might be called "bailment laws" are dispersed throughout the law collection, and "bailment-related legal documents" may use a variety of inconsistent forms and terminology. In contrast, biblical law appears to reflect a more developed, albeit not fully expressed, notion of bailment. Therefore, the Covenant Code groups together four laws in Exod 22:6–14, the starkest common feature of which is the defining characteristic of bailment; property lawfully resides in the possession of someone other than the owner. The rabbis, who were heirs to the Bible and also to the highly categorized Roman law, articulate a concept of bailment even more clearly.

We also use the terms *active* and *passive negligence*. As demonstrated above, examples of what one would call active and passive negligence surface in both Mesopotamian and biblical law. Curiously, explicit Akkadian references to negligence (e.g., *aḫa nadû* and *egû*) nearly always have in mind passive negligence. However, if one were to go through all of cuneiform law case by case—as one must do in the case of biblical law, where negligence is not typically identified explicitly—then one can find examples of active negligence as well. This disparity between language and content may reflect one of two options: it is possible that (1) the Akkadian lexicon reflects a conceptual difference from modern law, wherein negligence is by default passive. What a modern person would call "active negligence" would not fall under an ancient Near Eastern conception of negligence. Alternatively, (2) omissions constitute simply one type of negligence, which the Akkadian language happens to have multiple ways of expressing explicitly. However, "active negligence" is also negligence; Akkadian simply does not have a term for it. This omission could be the result of linguistic happenstance, and, further, the line between "active" and "passive" negligence may be arbitrary or subjective; so, for example, one might fail to uphold one's duty (an omission) by committing an action (a commission). It remains unclear whether cuneiform law—and even more so the less explicit biblical law—has a notion of negligence that is the same as or different from the modern conception specifically with regard to passivity and activity, or whether one is merely able to identify the seeds of these ideas in ancient data.

The modern term *contract* likewise diverges from the reality one can cull from ancient sources. By default, a modern contract is written; recording a

Mesopotamian contract was by no means necessary and perhaps not even usual. Whereas the modern contract requires consideration, the *riksātum* (as in LH 122–125) could record and define arrangements in which one party received no benefit. Likewise, a developed notion of contract law, tort law, and property law hardly existed. Still, these terms have proven useful for thinking about the features of bailment, including the scope of bailees' and bailors' rights, duties, and penalties, as long as one acknowledges the anachronism.

With the necessary caveats in mind, the findings of this chapter allow for the following legal characterization of the biblical law of bailment: The bailee may be understood as standing close to the modern category of fiduciary, a person whose burden of accounting for property under fiduciary care is proportionate to the discretion the fiduciary is accorded with respect to the bailed property. Thus, the bailee in a case of deposit has the opportunity to achieve exoneration in more cases than the shepherd, and the animal borrower or renter has the fewest such opportunities. Related to the number of exclusionary rules placed upon the fact-finding procedures allowed in each of these cases is the relationship between substantive and formal legal truth, which are most likely to match in the case of deposit and least likely in the case of animal borrowing or rental. Truth and justice are not the same.

The bailment law includes three primary gradations of fault that may or may not affect the harshness of a penalty; these include fraud, negligence, and *force majeure*. With respect to negligence, although biblical law includes examples of both active and passive negligence, the bailment law offers no indication that it distinguishes between these categories. The biblical bailment law likewise does not determine the severity of liability and compensation based on whether a relationship existed between the plaintiff and defendant, which squares well with an instrumentalist analysis of negligence. Examining the law through the lens of the admittedly anachronistic categories of contract, tort, and property, one finds that the biblical law most closely fits with the modern category of property or both property and tort, and is certainly not contractual in nature. One likewise finds variety in standards of liability within both the biblical and cuneiform laws, with evidence of fault and strict liability in both.

Ultimately, though these findings are not meaningful for the study of operative law in ancient Israel, they inform an understanding of the thinking that shaped biblical law and that biblical law sought to shape. Combining diverse modes of analysis has allowed us to identify a wide range of ideas and values that the Covenant Code negotiates at the meeting ground of biblical law and culture. Thus, exegetical and comparative analysis show that Exod 22:6–14 is less interested in how to establish a bailment than in how to establish justice, through the establishment of facts and consequences for wrongdoing. Beyond this, legal analysis uncovers with terminological precision the logic underlying the organization and details of this law, including how the law conceives of bailments; on what grounds the law assigns liability, and why it offers greater or fewer opportunities for exoneration in different cases; the nonrelational concept of duty that informs the biblical law (in contrast to the Laws of Hammurabi); and a concept of justice that is distinct from substantive truth.

5

From Cuneiform Law
to Classical Judaism

Biblical narrative and prophetic texts, cuneiform law collections, and
Mesopotamian legal documents serve as aids for sketching a picture
of how bailments functioned in biblical and ancient Near Eastern societies, while legal analysis builds on these results to home in on the jurisprudential character of the laws in question. This chapter shifts from a focus
on reconstructing legal practice and thinking in ancient Israel to what
came next in postbiblical, Jewish contexts. Early Jewish texts offer a window into the afterlife of areas of law in communities that saw themselves
as heirs of the Bible but also share aspects of other legal traditions, including Greco-Roman and ancient Near Eastern law. At times, early Jewish
law may preserve aspects of operative law from ancient Israel and Judah
and, as such, merits consideration in conjunction with the practice-ori-
ented study of biblical law, despite the fact that definite conclusions will
typically remain beyond the realm of possibility. The nature of the material is such that we may divide it into two sections, similar to our categorization of diverse legal texts from Mesopotamia: documents of legal
practice reflecting transactions between individuals (or "legal documents"), which have survived from Jewish communities at Elephantine
and the Judean Desert;[1] and law writings from the Tannaitic period,
including the Mishnah and Midrash.

---

1. Of note, however, none of the texts that will be discussed in this chapter is from
Qumran. This is due to the absence of relevant material from the documents discovered
there. In other cases, the availability of pertinent Qumran documents has proven invaluable
for tracing a history of law and interpretation from the Bible down into early rabbinic literature. See especially essays in Moshe J. Bernstein, *Reading and Re-Reading Scripture at Qumran,*
2 vols., STDJ 107 (Leiden: Brill, 2013), vol. 2; Steven Fraade, Aharon Shemesh, and Ruth
Clements, eds., *Rabbinic Perspectives: Rabbinic Literature and the Dead Sea Scrolls: Proceedings of
the Eighth International Symposium of the Orion Center for the Study of the Dead Sea Scrolls and
Associated Literature, 7–9 January, 2003,* STDJ 62 (Leiden: Brill, 2006).

Early Jewish Legal Documents

Legal documents from Elephantine, an Egyptian island with a Jewish presence during the fifth century BCE, and from the Judean Desert in the first two centuries CE, point to a number of uses for bailments. One such example emerges from AP 2, a contract from Elephantine.[2] Neither biblical law nor the cuneiform law collections address bailments for transportation, in which the owner of goods deposits them for safekeeping with a bailee, who is then responsible for delivering them to another location.[3] As examples from chapter 1 demonstrate, however, bailments for transportation find expression in Babylonian contracts and trial records from different periods. AP 2 similarly attests to this practice at Elephantine. According to this document, two men receive a quantity of barley and lentils to deliver to government officials in Aswan, and make an oral declaration:

> You have consigned to us [such and such] ... and our heart is satisfied therewith. We will deliver [this] grain ... [If we do not deliver all of the grain that is] yours in full ... we shall be liable.[4]

The document records the point of view of the bailees, who express their satisfaction upon receipt of the grain in order to confirm the initial quantity of the bailment.[5] Therefore, if they deliver a different quantity at their destination, they can be held accountable.[6]

Although biblical and cuneiform law collections do not treat transportation bailments as part of their primary bailment-related sections of laws, practice documents recording these transactions utilize the same language as other bailments (e.g., *maṣṣartum, paqādu*),[7] and reflect a common legal premise. The Bible offers negligible information about transportation bailments. Yet it is reasonable to imagine that, just as these arrangements

---

2. The extent to which these documents may be considered "Jewish" is under debate. See further Seth Schwartz, "Law in Jewish Society in the Second Temple Period," in *The Cambridge Companion to Judaism and Law*, ed. Christine Hayes (New York: Cambridge University Press, 2017), 57–84. Schwartz considers the colonists at Elephantine to have been "pre-Jewish."

3. But see LH 112, regarding a consignment for transportation, which does not occur together with the primary deposit law in LH.

4. Translation adapted from Yochanan Muffs, *Studies in the Aramaic Legal Papyri from Elephantine*, HdO 66 (Leiden: Brill, 2003), 52.

5. The importance of a clear record in transportation bailments is at issue also in a Hittite lawsuit against a man charged with failing to document his activities in distributing items entrusted to him by a queen and is further suspected of embezzlement. For this text, see William W. Hallo, ed., *Context of Scripture* (Leiden: Brill, 2003), 3:57–60.

6. Muffs, *Studies in the Aramaic Legal Papyri*, 57–58.

7. See, e.g., CT 8 37b; AT 119.

occupied a role in the commercial world of the ancient Near East and at Elephantine, they would also have played a part in the commercial practice of ancient Israel.

Whereas AP 2 illuminates one possible function of bailments in practice, AP 20, a claim settlement from Elephantine, offers insight both into possible contents of a deposit and into recourse for resolving a dispute when something has gone wrong. According to this document, a bailee had not returned the "goods, garments of wool and cotton, vessels of bronze and iron, vessels of wood and ivory, corn" and other unspecified objects to their owner, the bailor.[8] Possibly following the bailee's death, the original bailor's grandsons sued the bailee's sons, and, following an investigation, the sons restored the deposit to the bailor's family. With the deposit restored, they agreed that no one could sue the bailee's family in the future, or else that person would be required to pay a penalty. Of note, this deposit includes objects from a motley range of materials, along with corn, which recalls ancient Near Eastern textual and archaeological evidence of storage of grain and other goods together.

Like cuneiform contracts that fictionally utilize the deposit form to reflect other transactions or transactions that have not yet occurred, both Roman and early Jewish legal documents attest to the fictional use of deposits, albeit in different ways. In the second century CE, Roman soldiers stationed in Egypt were not permitted to marry but could live with a woman on a long-term basis. To bypass the prohibition of marriage, documents characterized the transfer of property from the woman to a Roman soldier as a deposit for safekeeping rather than as a marriage-related transaction.[9] In at least one instance, this legal fiction failed: A woman who had "deposited" property with a soldier was denied the return of her property from his estate upon his death, because, according to the prefect handling the case, "We know that deposits are dowries ... (and) soldiers cannot marry."[10] The legal fiction could only succeed if it went unacknowledged.

A similar fiction is found with dowries in early Jewish texts from a Roman milieu. These texts, however, reflect actual marriages, in contrast to the arrangements into which women entered with Roman soldiers. P. Yadin 17, for example, records Judah son of Eleazar Khthousion's acknowledgment to his wife Babatha that he has received from her three hundred

---

8. For this translation, see AP, p. 58.

9. See Sara Elise Phang, *The Marriage of Roman Soldiers (13 BC–AD 235): Law and Family in the Imperial Army,* Columbia Studies in the Classical Tradition 24 (Leiden: Brill, 2001), 29; Jacobine G. Oudshoorn, *The Relationship between Roman and Local Law in the Babatha and Salome Komaise Archives: General Analysis and Three Case Studies on Law of Succession, Guardianship and Marriage,* STDJ 69 (Leiden: Brill, 2007), 120.

10. See P. Catt. I.5–13 and BGU 114, discussed in Phang, *Marriage of Roman Soldiers,* 29.

denarii of silver as a deposit (*parathēkē*),[11] which he will hold and "owe on deposit" until she desires them in return.[12] In effect, this return clause refers to the possibility of divorce, in which case Judah would be obligated to return the dowry, termed a deposit, to Babatha.[13] As with the Roman soldiers in Egypt, the dowry transactions of these Jewish couples were fictionally cast as deposits.

P. Yadin 5 records yet another kind of fictional deposit. Joseph and Jesus's father (also named Jesus) had been partners in business. After the death of Jesus's father, Joseph states that he owes Jesus money for the deposit (*parathēkē*) of silver, debt contracts, and various other things that Joseph had shared with his deceased partner.[14] In reality, Jesus's father had never created a bailment with Joseph; the deposit rather functions as a tool for fabricating a formal legal relationship between Joseph and his partner's heir. This allows Jesus to inherit his father's share of assets from the partnership while enabling Joseph to maintain his business.[15]

Bailments played a part in a variety of legal and economic processes in early Jewish contexts. These included transportation bailments, like those found in cuneiform documents, as well as transactions that utilized deposits fictionally in order to facilitate a dowry or business partnership.[16] These transactions offer a small aperture into the range of roles that bailments could occupy, typically as one element of varying consequence within a larger process.

---

11. For discussion of the function of this arrangement and its relation to the marriage itself (as e.g., a "marriage loan"), see Oudshoorn, *Relationship between Roman and Local Law*, 132–39.

12. See the Greek text with translation in Hannah M. Cotton, "The Guardian (ἐπίτροπος) of a Woman in the Documents from the Judaean Desert," *Zeitschrift für Papyrologie und Epigraphik* 118 (1997): 267–73, here 267–68. We find here the bleeding together of deposit and loan in the context of a fictively represented transaction; the transfer of property explicitly termed a deposit is "owed"—a term more appropriate to a loan. Note, however, the characterization of the Greek deposit—the term used in P. Yadin 17—as an interest-free loan, which may account for the blurring of categories in this text.

13. Despite the validity of the marriage, marriage-related elements of the transaction—e.g., the dowry and prospect of divorce—are eliminated from Judah's acknowledgment by casting the entire transaction as a deposit.

14. Exactly what English translation best captures the relationship between the money owed and the *parathēkē* is subject to debate. See discussion in Oudshoorn, *Relationship between Roman and Local Law*, 119.

15. Oudshoorn, *Relationship between Roman and Local Law*, 119–21.

16. For a possible fictional use of a deposit in the Mishnah, see Lapin, *Early Rabbinic Civil Law*, 173 n. 111.

Bailment in Tannaitic Law Writings

The pentateuchal law collections have inspired copious debate about their nature and function in ancient Israel and Judah. Despite disagreement about the precise purpose(s) of these collections, most scholars reject the premise that these texts were truly legislative and enforceable, instead considering them as apologia, theological or sapiential texts, or legally descriptive treatises.[17] Regardless of their earlier purpose(s), however, at some point biblical law came to be viewed as prescriptive. This certainly was the case by the time of the Tannaitic rabbis, who authored numerous law writings including the Mishnah and Midrash Halakhah (i.e., law-focused Midrash).[18] A collection of independent legal statements composed during the first to third centuries CE in the land of Israel, the Mishnah generally does not cite the Bible as a source of law, whether or not it has it in mind. In contrast to the Mishnah, two contemporaneous works of Midrash Halakhah on the Book of Exodus—the Mekhilta de-Rabbi Ishmael and Mekhilta de-Rabbi Simon bar Yohai—formulate their legal teachings as a running commentary on Scripture, explicitly engaging the biblical text.[19] Despite not always citing the Bible, the rabbis self-consciously identify themselves as heirs to, and part of the same chain of transmission as, biblical law (see m. ʾAbot 1:1–12). At the same time, both the Mishnah and Midrash Halakhah exhibit points of contact with other sources of law, including earlier legal texts from the Jewish communities at Elephantine and in the Judean Desert; Greco-Roman legal sources; and, perhaps least obviously, the laws and legal documents of the ancient Near East.

The Mishnah sets forth a classification of bailments, introducing four discrete categories of bailees and treating them in a more concentrated, explicit, and systematic way than one finds in biblical or cuneiform texts.

---

17. For an exception that considers biblical law prescriptive, see, e.g., Gregory C. Chirichigno, *Debt-Slavery in Israel and the Ancient Near East*, JSOTSup 141 (Sheffield: JSOT Press, 1993), 354. See further discussion of variations on this position in Wells, "What Is Biblical Law?," 226–27; Michael LeFebvre, *Collections, Codes, and Torah: The Re-characterization of Israel's Written Law*, LHBOTS 451 (New York: T&T Clark, 2006), 48–53.

18. See LeFebvre, *Collections, Codes, and Torah*, 242–48; and see John J. Collins, "The Transformation of the Torah in Second Temple Judaism," *JSJ* 43 (2012): 455–74, regarding a shift during the Second Temple period. For views dating this shift earlier, to the reform of either Josiah or Ezra, see, e.g., Patrick, *Old Testament Law*, 200 (for the period of Josiah); Jackson, *Studies in the Semiotics of Biblical Law*, 141–42.

19. For a recent overview of the dating and differences between the Mishnah and Midrash Halakhah, see Christine Hayes, "Law in Classical Rabbinic Judaism," in *The Cambridge Companion to Judaism and Law*, ed. Christine Hayes (Cambridge: Cambridge University Press, 2017), 98–100.

The halakhic midrashim, though different in their form, adopt the same four categories of bailees as the Mishnah. An examination of continuities and discontinuities between biblical, ancient Near Eastern, and Tannaitic law writings provides an opportunity to see how a system that was heir to both biblical and ancient Near Eastern legal traditions (to varying extents, and among other antecedents) interpreted, internalized, and synthesized eclectic threads of legal writing as well as legal practice in generating its own rabbinic model.

The Ancient Near Eastern Background to Tannaitic Law Writings

Although the legacy of biblical law looms large in the Mishnah and the Midrash, and the Greco-Roman and Second Temple Jewish contexts of these writings have been amply established, relatively little scholarship has attended to a relationship between cuneiform and early Jewish law writings.[20] In the case of the Mishnah (as well as the Tosefta, another body of Tannaitic literature), there are numerous cases where cuneiform and rabbinic laws share features such as legal formulae, premises of cases, and rationale behind legal remedies, with no alternative extant parallel to account for the rabbinic law. Still, very few scholars (with notable exceptions including Yochanan Muffs, Baruch Levine, and Markham Geller) have had the breadth of expertise to bridge the gap between Assyriology and rabbinics, nor is this gap widely recognized as one that merits bridging. Samuel Greengus's 2011 book, *Laws in the Bible and in Early Rabbinic*

---

20. Notable works on the Mesopotamian background to early Jewish law include Muffs, *Studies in the Aramaic Legal Papyri*; Muffs, *Love and Joy: Law, Language, and Religion in Ancient Israel* (New York: Jewish Theological Seminary of America, 1992); Baruch Levine, "*Mulūgu/melûg*: The Origins of a Talmudic Legal Institution," *JAOS* 88 (1968): 271–85; Markham J. Geller, "The Influence of Ancient Mesopotamia on Hellenistic Judaism," in *Civilizations of the Ancient Near East*, ed. Jack M. Sasson (New York: Scribner, 1995), 43–54; Jonathan S. Milgram, *From Mesopotamia to the Mishnah: Tannaitic Inheritance Law in Its Legal and Social Contexts*, TSAJ 164 (Tübingen: Mohr Siebeck, 2016). For the ancient Near Eastern background specifically to the Midrash, see Stephen A. Lieberman, "A Mesopotamian Background for the So-Called Aggadic 'Measures' of Biblical Hermeneutics," *HUCA* 58 (1987): 157–225; Antoine Cavigneaux, "Aux sources du midrash: L'herméneutique babylonienne," *AuOr* 5 (1987): 243–55; Eckart Frahm, *Babylonian and Assyrian Text Commentaries: Origins of Interpretation*, Guides to the Mesopotamian Textual Record 5 (Münster: Ugarit-Verlag, 2011), 368–83; Uri Gabbay, *The Exegetical Terminology of Akkadian Commentaries*, CHANE 82 (Leiden: Brill, 2016), 289–91; Uri Gabbay, "Akkadian Commentaries from Ancient Mesopotamia and Their Relation to Early Hebrew Exegesis," *Dead Sea Discoveries* 19 (2012): 267–312; Steven D. Fraade, "Early Rabbinic Midrash between Philo and Qumran," in *Strength to Strength: Essays in Honor of Shaye J. D. Cohen*, ed. Michael L. Satlow, BJS 363 (Providence, RI: Brown Judaic Studies, 2018), 281–93.

Collections: The Legal Legacy of the Ancient Near East, offers a corrective to the gulf between these fields, demonstrating through multiple cogently developed examples that rabbinic law indeed takes its place within the ancient Near Eastern "legal legacy." Thus, in some cases, an aspect of cuneiform law reappears centuries later in rabbinic law written in the land of Israel, with no counterpart in the Bible or in extrabiblical Jewish texts from the first millennium BCE that might account for the chain of transmission.[21] Greengus adduces several cases of this phenomenon. For example, in a case of a chronically ill wife, the Mishnah and the Tosefta require her husband to support her but also allow him the option of divorcing her. Although the Bible does not address this situation, cuneiform law similarly discusses physical impairment as a basis for divorce.[22] Laws treating agricultural leases and natural disasters likewise appear in cuneiform and rabbinic sources, but not in the Bible.[23]

While Greengus focuses primarily on the Mishnah and Tosefta from the Tannaitic writings, Uri Gabbay and Eckart Frahm have similarly called attention to affinities between cuneiform commentaries from the first millennium BCE and the Midrash. Features in common include the kinds of questions they raise, the methods they employ to solve problems, and even their terminology—a parallel that may support an argument for direct cultural contact between cuneiform and midrashic commentaries.[24] These commonalities often relate more to the mode and form of commentary than to the specifics of the content.

The relationship between cuneiform and rabbinic law writings raises a thorny question: How did the rabbis of the Tannaitic period end up with laws whose likeliest antecedent is from Mesopotamia? Greengus proposes one possibility, arguing that when a connection between Mesopotamian and early rabbinic law is absent from the Bible, one can posit a mediating source in the "oral law" of ancient Israel.[25] In other words, these cases provide an avenue for reconstructing Israelite legal practice or, at the very least, law that was known in ancient Israel. With regard to Midrash, Uri Gabbay points to the exegetical practice common to Babylonian and Judean scholars as evidence for direct, likely oral, contact between these scholars, locating a channel for the transmission of Mesopotamian knowledge in a narrowly scholastic context.[26]

---

21. Greengus, *Laws in the Bible*, 282.

22. See m. Ketub. 4:9; t. Ketub. 4:5; and compare LH 148–149 and LL 28, discussed by Greengus, *Laws in the Bible*, 42–45.

23. See m. B. Meṣ. 9:6 and LH 45–46, discussed by Greengus, *Laws in the Bible*, 245–46.

24. Gabbay, *Exegetical Terminology*, 289. See also Frahm, *Babylonian and Assyrian Text Commentaries*, 369–83.

25. Greengus, *Laws in the Bible*, 282–83.

26. Gabbay, *Exegetical Terminology*, 290.

While acknowledging the difficulty of tracing the course of cultural transfer from Mesopotamia to Jewish Palestine during the first centuries CE,[27] scholars have located a number of possible channels from earlier periods that could account for survivals into the Tannaitic period, aside from a hypothesized oral law in ancient Israel. In a discussion of the transfer of lunar procedures from Mesopotamia to Judaea, Jonathan Ben-Dov argues for at least two waves of transfer during the Second Temple period: A first wave occurred during the fifth-century BCE restoration, when Judeans living the Babylonian exile returned to Jerusalem. A second wave occurred during the third to second centuries BCE, when cultural knowledge from Babylonia reached a restricted circle of scholars in Judea — in a process that could account for the kind of scholarly interaction that Gabbay describes.[28] The fifth-century wave likely would have involved a degree of familiarity with some areas of everyday legal practice in Mesopotamia, while the third- to second-century wave would have been more limited in scope.

The recent publication of documents from the Āl-Yahūdu archive (three years after the publication of Greengus's book) further corroborates the premise that Judeans from the sixth- to fifth-century Babylonian exile (and not only an elite group of scholars) would have been intimately familiar with Mesopotamian practices.[29] The texts from this archive testify to explicit interactions between Judeans and Babylonians, and to Judean absorption of Babylonian legal practices, leading Laurie Pearce to conclude that Judeans "were readily integrated into Babylonian social and economic practices."[30]

---

27. See, e.g., Levine, "*Mulūgu/Melûg*," 271.

28. Jonathan Ben-Dov, *Head of All the Years: Astronomy and Calendars at Qumran in Their Ancient Contexts*, STDJ 78 (Leiden: Brill, 2008), 245–78. In contrast to Gabbay's view that methods of midrashic interpretation reflect direct interactions with Mesopotamian scholars, Cavigneaux has argued for a channel of transmission between Mesopotamian medical and omen literature and rabbinic interpretative methods; these kinds of knowledge were not necessarily limited to elite scholastic circles and thus could have reached the rabbis through a wider range of channels ("Aux sources du midrash," 251–52).

29. See Laurie E. Pearce and Cornelia Wunsch, *Documents of Judean Exiles and West Semites in Babylonia in the Collection of David Sofer*, Cornell University Studies in Assyriology and Sumerology 28 (Bethesda, MD: CDL, 2014). For a list of several archives mentioning Jews in Babylonia, see Caroline Waerzeggers, "Locating Contact in the Babylonian Exile: Some Reflections on Tracing Judean-Babylonian Encounters in Cuneiform Texts," in *Encounters by the Rivers of Babylon: Scholarly Conversations between Jews, Iranians and Babylonians in Antiquity*, ed. Uri Gabbay and Shai Secunda, TSAJ 160 (Tübingen: Mohr Siebeck, 2014), 131–46, here 136–37.

30. Laurie E. Pearce, "'Judean': A Special Status in Neo-Babylonian and Achaemenid Babylonia?," in *Judah and the Judeans in the Achaemenid Period: Negotiating Identity in an International Context*, ed. Oded Lipschits, Gary N. Knoppers, and Manfred Oeming (Winona Lake, IN: Eisenbrauns, 2011), 267–77, here 274.

Although Greengus's proposed Israelite "oral law" remains a plausible candidate for how rabbinic law came to share aspects of cuneiform law, the possibility of alternatives to this theory cautions against reconstructing Israelite legal practice—especially prior to the exilic period—on the basis of a parallel between ancient Near Eastern and Tannaitic literature. Instead, Israelite law remains one possible candidate, among other viable candidates, for explaining features common to (and exclusive to) cuneiform and Tannaitic law.

To be clear, analyses such as Greengus's and those that follow in this chapter trace connections between texts that not only are geographically and linguistically disparate but also originate from periods separated by centuries, sometimes exceeding a millennium. Though one might assume that drawing such connections is academically irresponsible, Greengus has defended comparison of biblical and early rabbinic laws with similar laws from the ancient Near East, arguing,

> To judge from the similarities found between both biblical and ancient Near Eastern law collections, it would appear that these are areas of shared cultural experience that framed them on a large stage. These shared cultural experiences grew out of economic, political, and other interactions that went beyond the conventional borders of language and religion.... Differences in language are overstated as a cultural barrier. Sumerians, Akkadians, Assyrians, Amorites, Arameans, Hebrews (or Canaanites), and speakers of other languages like Eblaite, Ugaritic, Hurrian, and Hittite clearly were shareholders in a common civilization that continued for over two thousand years, touching even upon Egypt, Iran, Anatolia, and the Aegean.[31]

Greengus also acknowledges the importance of considering each text in its immediate cultural context. Indeed, while I agree that casting all of ancient Near Eastern and biblical literature as a monolithic enterprise would constitute a grievous mistake, there is a difference between flattening all signs of diversity to depict falsely a homogeneous culture and identifying markers of a conservative common ground, even over time and space. In this case, the proof is in the pudding: Greengus establishes connections between biblical, cuneiform, and rabbinic texts through many compelling examples, with respect both to ideas and to specific rules.[32] Relying on the evidence that Greengus lucidly adduces, I adopt his methodology in order to demonstrate the meeting of aspects of biblical and cuneiform law in the early Jewish legal literature surrounding bailments.

---

31. Greengus, *Laws in the Bible*, 4.

32. I agree here with Wells's defense of Greengus's diffusionist approach; see Bruce Wells, "The Long View: From Hammurabi to the Bible to the Rabbis," *ZABR* 19 (2013): 171–79, here 172–73.

The Rabbis' Four Bailees

In a series of laws treating bailments in the Mishnah, the rabbis outline four kinds of bailees:

> the gratuitous bailee,
> the borrower,
> the non-gratuitous bailee,
> and the renter (m. B. Meṣ. 7:8; my translation).

As in Exod 22:6–14, though without acknowledging it as a source, the rabbis speak of four kinds of bailments, two of which involve borrowing and rental. Unlike the biblical law, however, the Tannaitic law distinguishes between gratuitous and non-gratuitous bailees, that is, bailees who watch another person's property either free of charge (gratuitously) or for compensation (non-gratuitously). These categories diverge from the biblical differentiation between deposits of goods and animal herding. Efforts at harmonization notwithstanding, the rabbinic categories patently do not align with a plain-sense reading of Exod 22.[33] In contrast to the biblical law, which distinguishes between the bailees of Exod 22:6–12 on the basis of the object of bailment and makes no reference to compensation, the Mishnah distinguishes between the two corresponding categories on the basis of whether the bailee receives payment. Moreover, unlike Exod 22, the Mishnah sets up categories according to which the object of bailment is immaterial.

The Mishnah lays out four categories of bailees without explaining how it arrives at them or noting other options for classification. As a running commentary on biblical law, however, the Midrash Halakhah is forced to deal with the text of the Bible itself. Mekhilta de-Rabbi Shimon and Mekhilta de-Rabbi Ishmael are the legal midrashic products of two schools, that of Rabbi Akiva and that of Rabbi Ishmael, respectively. Azzan Yadin-Israel has argued that Rabbi Akiva midrashim serve in part to provide support for existing, extrascriptural law, thereby allowing the interpreter a wide berth in connecting the law to the biblical text; Rabbi Ishmael midrashim, on the other hand, reflect an understanding of the Bible as the ultimate authority of its own meaning. Thus, in the view of Rabbi Ishmael's school, biblical law is effectively self-interpreting; it provides clues to the reader about how to interpret the law in order to arrive at an intended conclusion, so that the reader must exercise relative interpretative

---

33. For this kind of harmonization, see, e.g., the commentary of Bekhor Shor on Exod 22:6; Nahmanides on Exod 22:6; Cassuto, *Commentary on the Book of Exodus*, 287.

restraint.[34] The commentaries of these two midrashic works on Exod 22:6–14 bear out Yadin-Israel's distinctions.

Similar to the Mishnah, Mekhilta de-Rabbi Shimon assumes four kinds of bailees that include a gratuitous and non-gratuitous bailee. But, whereas the Mishnah states the law independent of its connection to the biblical text, the Midrash identifies a source for the gratuitous/non-gratuitous distinction in the formulation of Exod 22:9–10:

> "… an ass, an ox, a sheep" (Exod 22:9):
> I only know specifically about an ass, an ox, or a sheep. How does one know from Scripture to include the remaining [other] animals?
> Scripture states, "… or any other animal" (Exod 22:9).
> How does one know from Scripture to include the other movable chattel?
> Scripture states, "… to guard … and the owner must acquiesce, and no restitution shall be made" (Exod 22:9–10), [meaning,] concerning that for which owners typically receive [restitution].
> From this you state [that] these [include] the movable chattel!
> I might think that I should include the servants, documents, and immovable property.
> Scripture states, [however,] "… an ass, an ox, a sheep or any other animal" (Exod 22:9).[35]

According to this mining of Exod 22:9–10, one may infer from the words "no restitution shall be made" that the law applies to any case that normally does involve restitution — that is, to the non-gratuitous bailment not only of animals but also of other movable property (to the exclusion of servants, documents, and immovable property). This hardly seems an obvious reading of the law. Instead, it is a case of the Akivan midrash creating a biblical basis for an existing extrabiblical law with which it was familiar, which differentiated between gratuitous and non-gratuitous bailments irrespective of the object bailed.

Mekhilta de-Rabbi Ishmael displays greater anxiety about locating these categories within biblical law:

> "For every matter of trespass" (Exod 22:8):
> Scripture here speaks with regard to the difference between one kind of a bailee and another.

---

34. See Azzan Yadin, *Scripture as Logos: Rabbi Ishmael and the Origins of Midrash*, Divinations (Philadelphia: University of Pennsylvania Press, 2004); Yadin-Israel, *Scripture and Tradition: Rabbi Akiva and the Triumph of Midrash*, Divinations (Philadelphia: University of Pennsylvania Press, 2015).

35. Translation adapted from W. David Nelson, *Mekhilta de-Rabbi Shimon bar Yoḥai*, Edward E. Elson Classic (Philadelphia: Jewish Publication Society of America, 2006), 339.

You say it speaks with regard to the difference between one kind of bailee and another. Perhaps however it comes to make a distinction between silver and vessels (v. 6), and cattle?

But it says: "For raiment." Now, "raiment" has been included in the general statement (v. 6). And it has been singled out for special mention merely to teach that just as when "raiment" is specifically mentioned, Scripture speaks with regard to the difference between the one kind of bailee and the other, so also with all the others mentioned with it, Scripture speaks with regard to the difference between one kind of bailee and the other. Behold, then, Scripture does not come to make a distinction between silver and vessels on the one hand and cattle on the other.[36]

The Ishmaelian midrash acknowledges that one would, at first glance (and in my view, correctly), read the biblical law as differentiating between categories of bailment on the basis of the object bailed. However, the inclusion of the "raiment" (i.e., garment) in Exod 22:8 demonstrates that the Bible does not distinguish between its bailees on this basis. The midrash does not explicate here that the distinction is rather between gratuitous and non-gratuitous bailments. Instead, having established that the object bailed is immaterial to the law, the Mekhilta goes on to assume these other categories in the continuation of its commentary, questioning only which category matches up with which subsection of the biblical bailment law:

"But if it be stolen from him" (Exod 22:11):
This section deals with the bailee for hire and the section above deals with the gratuitous bailee.
You say this deals with the bailee for hire and the above deals with the gratuitous bailee. Perhaps, however, this deals with the gratuitous bailee and the above with the bailee for hire?
Behold you must reason thus:
Since the hirer is liable and the bailee here mentioned is liable, it follows that just as the hirer is one who derives some benefit, also the bailee here mentioned must be one who derives some benefit.
Hence it is impossible for you to argue as in the latter version, but you must argue as in the former version: This one deals with the bailee for hire and the above deals with the gratuitous bailee.[37]

After demonstrating that the law does not distinguish between goods and animals, but without spelling out how it connects the dots between these arguments, Mekhilta de-Rabbi Ishmael reveals its view that the two cate-

---

36. Translation adapted from Jacob Z. Lauterbach, *Mekhilta de-Rabbi Ishmael: A Critical Edition*, 2nd ed. (Philadelphia: Jewish Publication Society, 2004), 438.
37. Translation adapted from Lauterbach, *Mekhilta de-Rabbi Ishmael*, 442.

gories implicit in Exod 22:6–12 are gratuitous and non-gratuitous bailments.

If the Tannaitic categories of gratuitous and non-gratuitous bailment do not stem from the Bible, do they reflect a rabbinic innovation, or might they have some other antecedent? The Greco-Roman legal tradition does not offer a compelling source. Classical Roman law, for example, required that the *depositum* always be gratuitous, eliminating it as a candidate for a tradition to which the rabbis were heir in this particular case.[38] The Greek *parakatathēkē*, parallel to Roman law's *depositum*, more commonly functioned as an interest-free loan, often in the context of banks.[39]

Although Greco-Roman law differs from the Tannaitic writings in this regard, my analysis of Hammurabi's deposit law (LH 120–125), in conjunction with practice documents from the ancient Near East, allows us to locate a Mesopotamian antecedent to the rabbinic distinction between gratuitous and non-gratuitous bailment.

> 120. If a man puts his grain in storage in another man's house, and in the storage bin a loss occurs; or the owner of the house opens the granary and takes the grain; or he completely denies (receiving) the grain which was stored in his house—the owner of the grain will establish his grain before the god, and the owner of the house will restore double the grain which he accepted and give it to the grain owner.
>
> 121. If a man stores grain in another man's house, he shall pay 5 silas of grain per gur of grain per year as rent for storage.
>
> 122. If a man gives silver, gold, or anything else to another man for a deposit, whatever he gives he shall show to witnesses; he shall set forth contractual stipulations; (thus) he shall give (it) for a deposit.
>
> 123. If he gives it for a deposit without witnesses or contractual stipulations, and with respect to the place where he gave (it) it is denied, that case has no grounds for a claim.
>
> 124. If a man gives silver, gold, or anything else to another man for a deposit before witnesses and then he denies it, they shall convict that man; whatever he denied he shall give back double.
>
> 125. If a man gives his property for a deposit, and at the place where he gave it—either through a breach or through scaling a wall—his property along with the property of the owner of the house is lost, the owner of the house who was negligent shall restore that which was given to him for a

---

38. See Reinhard Zimmermann, *The Law of Obligations: Roman Foundations of the Civilian Tradition* (New York: Oxford University Press, 1996), 213; Oudshoorn, *Relationship between Roman and Local Law*, 131. An arrangement involving remuneration was not considered deposit, but letting and hiring (*locatio et conductio*).

39. See Richard A. Billows, *Kings and Colonists: Aspects of Macedonian Imperialism*, Columbia Studies in the Classical Tradition 22 (Leiden: Brill, 1995), 141, with further references in n. 62.

deposit and which he allowed to be lost; he shall replace it for the owner of the property. The owner of the house shall continue to search for his lost property; he shall take it from the one who stole it from him.

As discussed in chapter 1, LH 120–121 appear to address deposits of grain, while LH 122–125 appear to address silver, gold, or "anything else." These two sections of the deposit law diverge with respect to the procedure for setting up the transaction (with the first section stipulating an annual rate to pay for storage, and the second requiring witnesses and contractual stipulations) and in whether they differentiate between negligent and fraudulent wrongdoing in establishing a penalty (with the first section requiring double compensation irrespective of fault, and the second section requiring only single compensation for negligence and double for fraud). There is no obvious reason that the law should differ in these regards due to some difference between grain, on the one hand, and silver, gold, or anything else, on the other hand. In fact, legal documents from Mesopotamia, along with archaeological evidence, clarify that grain and precious metals, and the like, could take part in the same bailment transactions—without any distinction between how they would be deposited and what was expected of the bailee—and could even be stored in an identical fashion.[40] In practice, then, one could give grain and goods in bailment as part of the same transaction, without any difference between the responsibilities of a bailee of grain and a bailee of goods.

As argued in chapter 1, the primary difference between LH 120–121 and LH 122–125 is not whether they treat grain or goods but whether the bailee receives compensation. Because LH 121 sets a rate of compensation for storage, the bailee of LH 120–121 bears a higher degree of liability than the bailee of LH 122–125, which do not mention compensation. The drafters' choice of objects of the deposit—grain in the first section and silver, gold, or anything else in the second—is likely representative rather than determinative. This understanding of LH 120–121 and LH 122–125 as treating non-gratuitous and gratuitous deposits, respectively, accords with textual and archaeological data and accounts for differences between the two sections in procedure and liability.[41]

---

40. These have been discussed in chapter 1. For deposits of grain and precious metals together see JEN 545; ARM 8 74; for storage of grain in sealed containers, similar to storage of other goods and metals, see HSS 9 108; Szlechter TJA p. 153 UMM G 45:3; ARM 10 136; JEN 381; and see discussion of archaeological evidence in Creekmore, "Kazane Höyük," 258; Pfälzner, "Modes of Storage," 276–78.

41. Admittedly, this reading of the Laws of Hammurabi is similar to the midrashic reading of Exod 22 that I reject. In the case of Exod 22, however, the distinction is not between grain and goods—which may be stored similarly and even as parts of the same transaction—but between goods and animals, which the Laws of Hammurabi also treat separately and between which the biblical law understandably also differentiates. The distinction between

Although the rabbis of the Tannaitic period surely would not have had access to a copy of the Laws of Hammurabi, it is reasonable to imagine that this distinction between gratuitous and non-gratuitous bailments persisted in practice in Mesopotamia. Like the many examples adduced by Greengus and scholars before him, this is yet another case of an aspect of Tannaitic law that we can trace back to Mesopotamia, whether it found its way into rabbinic law via Israelite "oral law" or by way of the sixth-century BCE restoration.

A stark difference remains, however, between the biblical and cuneiform laws, on the one hand, and the rabbis' treatment of bailment in the Mishnah and the Midrash, on the other. Both biblical law and the Laws of Hammurabi distinguish clearly between deposits of goods or silver and bailments of animals, such as herding arrangements and animal borrowing or rental. The Mishnah and Midrash collapse these distinctions entirely, introducing four categories—the gratuitous and non-gratuitous bailees, the renter, and the borrower—with no differentiation between bailments of animals and nonanimals. This collapsing of categories with respect to objects of bailment is further evident in m. B. Meṣ. 3:1, which addresses a person who "deposits with his fellow an animal or goods" that are then "stolen or lost." For the Tannaitic rabbis, the law is the same whether the objects stolen or lost were animal or goods.

In this case as well, Mesopotamian legal documents offer a perspective that complicates the picture emerging from the law collections in isolation. LIH 79 is a letter from King Samsu-iluna of Babylon to city administrators at Sippar concerning a family that owed barley in arrears.[42] The family was allowed the opportunity to settle the debt through payment of three cows and one-half mina of silver. Although they were required to pay this amount immediately, it would take some time for a messenger to arrive in order to transport the cows and silver to Babylon. In the interim, the family received instructions to "give those three cows and the one-half mina of silver to the envoy whom I sent to you." The debt was to be entrusted for safekeeping with a specific third party, effectively in escrow. LIH 79 thus refers to a bailment of both animals and silver, demonstrating that, in practice, animals and nonanimals could be deposited as part of the same arrangement, just as silver and grain could be.

Mesopotamian legal documents and archaeological evidence bear out the following two characterizations of bailments:

---

grain and goods falls apart in Hammurabi in contrast to the distinction between goods and animals in Exod 22, which holds up to scrutiny. Further, whereas no part of the biblical law mentions compensation (or lack thereof), the Laws of Hammurabi do include mention of compensation in one law (but not the other).

42. Regarding this letter, see Harris, *Ancient Sippar*, 41.

1. Animals could be deposited for safekeeping in the same way as goods, grain, and silver, and not just given to a bailee for herding or for labor.
2. A deposit could be either non-gratuitous, with the bailee receiving compensation, or gratuitous, with the bailee receiving no compensation.

Taken together, these findings point to bailment practices in Mesopotamia as an antecedent to the rabbinic conceptualization of bailment in Tannaitic law writings, which distinguish between gratuitous and non-gratuitous arrangements irrespective of the kind of object that has been bailed. The absence of another compelling candidate for a precursor to the rabbinic conceptualization of bailment further recommends the ancient Near Eastern legal tradition as an antecedent.

From Cuneiform Law to Classical Judaism: Two Roads

Did aspects of Mesopotamian bailments make their way into Tannaitic literature by way of an Israelite "oral law" or through the Judeans who returned to Judea from their Babylonian homes during the restoration? The latter possibility offers a strong candidate for the channel of transmission between Mesopotamian legal practice—especially pertaining to agriculture—and Tannaitic law writings. Yet, with respect to the former possibility, this particular case diverges from the typical situation in which Greengus posits an Israelite oral law mediating between Mesopotamian and rabbinic sources: Greengus discusses this possibility in the context of laws that do not have a counterpart in the Bible. In this case, however, Exod 22:6–14 indeed addresses a law of bailment. But this law conflicts with evidence from Mesopotamia and from the Tannaitic rabbis, insofar as it does not reflect a distinction between gratuitous and non-gratuitous bailments.

Is it still possible, then, that Israelite law could have served as an antecedent to the Tannaitic conceptualization of bailment? The answer to this question depends on an understanding of the relationship between biblical law writings and legal practice in ancient Israel. The study of the biblical bailment law in connection with narrative, cuneiform law, and Mesopotamian legal documents bears out the likelihood that at least several aspects of Exod 22:6–14 may offer an accurate window into legal practice. The interest in negligence (as demonstrated through a new interpretation of שלח ידו in Exod 22:7, 10) finds a parallel both in cuneiform law and in legal documents.[43] The scenarios that the biblical herding law

---

43. For example, the bailee of JEN 335 negligently causes the death of the cow in his

addresses are common also to biblical narrative (e.g., Gen 29–31) and Mesopotamian legal documents as well. Although the penalty for predation (in Exod 22:12) does not mention the possibility of a maximum percentage of the flock for which the shepherd might achieve exoneration, the general principle of exoneration in cases of predation matches that found in cuneiform law and in herding contracts, consignment texts, trial records, and debt statements.[44] The connection between deposits of goods and animal herding is supported by a cuneiform record of deposit, in which a shepherd requires a bailee for his personal possessions due to his herding obligations.[45] The setting of the biblical deposit in the home also finds a parallel in biblical narrative (e.g., 2 Kgs 5:24), the Laws of Hammurabi, and Mesopotamian trial records.[46] The overall impression that biblical narrative, cuneiform law, and Mesopotamian legal documents create is that the biblical bailment law is generally plausible and probably realistic.

What, then, of the possibility of an oral law reflecting a classification of bailments distinct from the one found in Exod 22? Ultimately, such a divergence would be interesting, but not surprising. The focus of the biblical law on methods of fact-finding and means of establishing justice, in favor of other possible foci such as the procedure for setting up valid bailments, supports the view that the primary purpose of the Covenant Code is not to offer an accurate portrayal of legal practice, irrespective of whether it succeeds in doing so. In fact, the biblical law's lack of interest in the formation of bailments—a lack of interest that the corresponding cuneiform laws, especially the Laws of Hammurabi with its terms regarding witnesses and contractual stipulations, throw into relief—further makes room for an alternate extrabiblical model focused on whether or not a bailee receives compensation.

Ultimately, the affinities between the Covenant Code's bailment law and reconstructed operative law do not preclude the possibility of dissonance, to whatever degree, between other aspects of the law and Israelite legal practice. We are left, then, with two plausible candidates for a channel of transmission but without a single clear answer regarding how the Tannaitic law writings came to conceptualize bailments in a manner that intimates a Mesopotamian antecedent.

---

care for safekeeping, and numerous letters include directives not to be negligent in contexts of bailment; see, e.g., CT 52 183; UMBS I 2 90; YOS 2 11:9–11.

44. Although Ezek 34 presents a scenario in which a shepherd bears liability for predation, this appears to be a divergence from the norm based on the particular behavior of Ezekiel's shepherd, who acts with unabashed, deliberate negligence.

45. See CT 4 30a.

46. See HSS 9 108; MVAG 35/3 330; and cf. CT 6 35b.

Conclusion

How can we access ancient Israelite legal practice and thinking in the absence of texts that might offer a more direct avenue into uncovering these aspects of life in ancient Israel? This study has brought together a wide swath of texts—biblical and cuneiform law collections, biblical narrative and prophecy, and Mesopotamian legal documents—and mined them for points of convergence and divergence in order to reconstruct, to the best of our ability, how the institution of bailment operated in the world of the Bible. Extralegal biblical texts—narrative and prophecy—played an especially important role for identifying and strengthening points of contact between biblical law and Mesopotamian legal documents. The fruitful use of these generically complicated texts demanded that we assess the extent to which the verisimilitude of any details was limited to specific temporal, geographic, or social settings, and that we avoid equating elements of fiction or hyperbole with reality. I have attempted to navigate these methodological landmines with special care, in order to salvage biblical narrative and prophecy as usable, if not ideal, sources of legal practice, to be compared with law collections and with documents of legal practice from Israel's neighboring societies. In doing so, I have pointed to a range of socioeconomic contexts for bailments, which together highlight the extent to which bailments were a crucial and commonplace arrangement, particularly in the largely agrarian societies of ancient Israel and Judah. This methodology may be replicated with respect to other areas of law, and I hope it will prove profitable for others who wish to learn more about everyday life in parts of ancient Israel, and how this compares with biblical writings.

My reconstruction of aspects of bailments in ancient Israel and Judah, coupled with original philological analysis of the bailment law in Exod 22:6–14, offers a new way to approach an old question: What is the nature of the Covenant Code, the laws in Exodus in which the bailment law appears? There are many ways to approach answering this question, and I have focused primarily on two such avenues. First, what does the law itself focus on, and what does this say about what it is trying to accomplish? Second—and this question relies on reconstruction of operative law in ancient Israel and Judah—how closely related is the law in the Covenant Code to legal practice?

With regard to the first question, through close examination of the biblical bailment law, especially in comparison with related cuneiform laws, I pointed to the biblical law's particular interest in fact-finding methods, including when any given method is appropriate or not appropriate, who may engage in these methods, and what are their results. This focus becomes even starker in comparison with the treatment of related cases in the Laws of Hammurabi, which are more interested than the Covenant Code in the procedures for setting up bailments. Likewise, the biblical bailment law—also in contrast to the Laws of Hammurabi— establishes an equal penalty for wrongdoing regardless of whether the offender acts fraudulently or negligently, whether for voluntary and involuntary bailments, and whether with respect to an offending bailee or a falsely accusing bailor. Comparison with other laws has demonstrated the extent to which the biblical bailment law ignores important aspects of what one might expect to find in a "bailment law" in favor of promoting a standard of justice, by emphasizing the use of fact-finding methods and establishing an equally harsh penalty for different offenses in order to create protections for vulnerable parties. The skewed focus of this law suggests that it does not aim to legislate actual practice; if it did, it might address further aspects of bailments, such as how to create them in the first place.

With regard to the connection between the law of Exodus and legal practice, my reconstruction of aspects of bailments in ancient Israel and Judah suggests that, to a large degree, the biblical bailment law is grounded in reality. That is, we uncovered multiple points of contact between the biblical law and other sources (as delineated above) and also did not discover major discrepancies between these texts. Although not every detail of the biblical law finds a corresponding reconstructed practice for comparison, the overall picture emerging from this analysis is one of coherence. This conclusion is a modest one, given the absence of correspondences in my reconstruction to fact-finding procedures, which occupy a central place in the law. Still, the parallels I was able to establish suggest that the biblical law is, at the very least, not unrealistic. To whatever extent, the bailment law appears to cohere with legal practice. At the same time, the law's thorough disregard of procedures for creating bailments coupled with its spotlight on establishing justice makes it highly unlikely that the goal of the law is to legislate. Instead, while the law appears to be descriptively accurate, its purpose appears to be more apologetic in nature, driving home to its audience a notion of divine justice that both elevates the God who establishes it and demands that this standard be emulated. The law is perhaps normative with respect to an ethical or religious standard, but not with respect to actual legal practice.

This understanding of the law's goals further informs another undertaking of this book: to reconstruct not only legal practice but also the legal thinking underlying the formulation of the biblical law. The application of concepts from legal studies has proven useful for analyzing our ancient sources with a vocabulary and precision that otherwise would not be possible. We have been able to trace distinct ideas about justice and truth, fault, liability, and negligence, in addition to demonstrating how a nascent concept of bailment existed in biblical Israel, well before the more systematic legal systems of Greco-Roman and rabbinic circles. This analysis also brings biblical and ancient Near Eastern bailment law into conversation with later legal systems in a way that is accessible both to humanists and to legal historians.

In my examination of the bailment law from a legal perspective, I proposed adopting a framework that understands law in connection with culture. In my view, the biblical bailment law performs what we might call an essentially cultural function, where culture involves practices through which members of a society create, adapt, challenge, and otherwise interact with meaning. Austin Sarat and Thomas Kearns have argued that

> [from] the perspective of law's cultural lives, law operates largely by influencing modes of thought rather than by determining conduct in any specific case. It enters social practices and is, indeed, "imbricated" in them, by shaping consciousness, by making law's concepts and commands seem, if not invisible, then perfectly natural and benign. Law is, in this sense, constitutive of culture.[1]

Although Sarat and Kearns had in mind "law" in the more modern, prescriptive sense of the word, their claims hold relevance for the generically amorphous biblical law as well. Whether law is prescriptive or not, one of its primary functions is to influence "modes of thought," constituting culture by affecting how people think, perceive, and value. The biblical bailment law bears out this model for thinking about law, with all of its details from everyday practices and ideas about truth, liability, and other concerns coming together to advance a vision of justice. While there remain multiple theoretically valid ways to think about the pentateuchal law collections, I believe that this approach may help move the study of biblical law forward by freeing us (if we wish) from the age-old question of what law *is*, and instead allowing us to focus on what and how law *does* as an object and subject of culture.

In addition to illuminating biblical law by using the language and insights of legal studies, I have brought biblical and cuneiform legal texts into conversation with early Jewish law from rabbinic and nonrabbinic

---

1. Sarat and Kearns, "Cultural Lives of Law," 7.

contexts. This analysis not only has shown continuity between biblical and early Jewish law, which is to be expected, but also has pointed to previously unidentified points of continuity between—and exclusive to—ancient Near Eastern and early Jewish law. While independent innovations within unrelated legal systems remain a possibility for how these similarities came to be, it is more likely, given the identifiable channels of transmission between the different societies from which these aspects of law emerged, that early Jewish law was indeed heir to aspects of Mesopotamian bailment law, just as it inherited other aspects of cuneiform law that scholars such as Greengus and Milgram have already identified. While it is possible that early Jewish law also preserves aspects of ancient Israelite or Judahite legal practice that is not recorded in the Bible, and was similar to Mesopotamian legal practice, it is impossible at this point to substantiate this hypothesis.

While the limitations facing any study of Israelite law are many and frustrating, this study has been able to create a sketch of bailment practice in ancient Israel that plausibly could apply to a range of periods and settings from ancient Israel, and to probe connections between legal writing, legal practice, and legal thinking. These methods may be applied fruitfully to other areas of law that, like bailment, are addressed in generically diverse sources from ancient Israel and neighboring societies. The word *bailment* may remain obscure to legal nonspecialists, but I hope this study has shown that behind this dusty legal term is an institution that was pervasive in ancient Israel and deeply embedded in the socioeconomic fabric of everyday life, and that tapping into a single legal institution may tell us quite a bit about the societies in which it operated.

Bibliography

Adam, Klaus-Peter, Friedrich Avemarie, and Nili Wazana, eds. *Law and Narrative in the Bible and in Neighbouring Ancient Cultures*. FAT 2/54. Tübingen: Mohr Siebeck, 2012.

Alter, Robert. *The David Story: A Translation with Commentary of 1 and 2 Samuel*. New York: Norton, 1999.

Amihay, Aryeh. *Theory and Practice in Essene Law*. New York: Oxford University Press, 2017.

Annus, Amar. "On the Beginnings and Continuities of Omen Sciences in the Ancient World." Pages 1-18 in *Divination and Interpretation of Signs in the Ancient World*. Edited by Amar Annus. University of Chicago Oriental Institute Seminars 6. Chicago: Oriental Institute of the University of Chicago, 2010.

Baden, Joel S. *The Historical David: The Real Life of an Invented Hero*. New York: HarperCollins, 2013.

Baker, David L. "Finders Keepers? Lost Property in Ancient Near Eastern and Biblical Law." *BBR* 17 (2007): 207–14.

———. "Safekeeping, Borrowing, and Rental." *JSOT* 31 (2006): 27–42.

Balkin, Jack M. "The Proliferation of Legal Truth." *Harvard Journal of Law and Public Policy* 26 (2003): 5–16.

Bar-Efrat, Shimon. *1 Samuel: Introduction and Commentary*. 2nd ed. Miqra le-Yisra'el. Tel Aviv: Am Oved; Jerusalem: Magnes, 2008.

Barmash, Pamela. "Achieving Justice through Narrative in the Hebrew Bible: The Limitations of Law in the Legal Potential of Literature." *ZABR* 20 (2014): 181–99.

———. *Homicide in the Biblical World*. Cambridge: Cambridge University Press, 2005.

———. "The Narrative Quandary: Cases of Law in Literature." *VT* 54 (2004): 1–16.

Bartor, Assnat. "The 'Juridical Dialogue': A Literary-Judicial Pattern." *VT* 53 (2003): 445–64.

———. *Reading Law as Narrative: A Study in the Casuistic Laws of the Pentateuch*. AIL 5. Atlanta: Society of Biblical Literature, 2010.

————. "The Representation of Speech in the Casuistic Laws of the Pentateuch: The Phenomenon of Combined Discourse." *JBL* 126 (2007): 231–49.

Baylard, David L. "Products Liability – Non-Contractual Indemnity – the Effect of the Active-Passive Negligence Theory in Missouri." *Missouri Law Review* 41 (1976): 382–403.

Ben-Dov, Jonathan. *Head of All the Years: Astronomy and Calendars at Qumran in Their Ancient Contexts.* STDJ 78. Leiden: Brill, 2008.

Bernstein, Moshe J. *Reading and Re-Reading Scripture at Qumran.* 2 vols. STDJ 107. Leiden: Brill, 2013.

Biddle, Mark E. "Ancestral Motifs in 1 Samuel 25: Intertextuality and Characterization." *JBL* 121 (2002): 617–38.

Blank, Sheldon H. "The Curse, Blasphemy, the Spell, and the Oath." *HUCA* 23 (1950–1951): 73–95.

Boer, Roland. *The Sacred Economy of Ancient Israel.* LAI. Louisville: Westminster John Knox, 2015.

Bottéro, Jean. "Le 'Code' de Hammu-rabi." *Annali della Scola Normale Superiore di Pisa* 12 (1982): 409–44.

Bovati, Pietro. *Re-establishing Justice: Legal Terms, Concepts and Procedures in the Hebrew Bible.* Translated by Michael J. Smith. JSOTSup 105. Sheffield: JSOT Press, 1994.

Breckwoldt, Tina. "Management of Grain Storage in Old Babylonian Larsa." *AfO* 42/43 (1995/1996): 64–88.

Butz, Kilian. "Ur in altbabylonischer Zeit als Wirtschaftsfaktor." Pages 258–409 in *State and Temple Economy in the Ancient Near East: Proceedings of the International Conference Organized by the Katholieke Universiteit Leuven from the 10th to the 14th of April 1978.* Edited by Edward Lipiński. 2 vols. OLA 5–6. Leuven: Departement Oriëntalistiek, 1979.

Cassuto, Umberto. *A Commentary on the Book of Exodus.* Translated by Israel Abrahams. Jerusalem: Magnes, 1967.

Cavigneaux, Antoine. "Aux sources du midrash: L'herméneutique babylonienne." *AuOr* 5 (1987): 243–55.

Cazelles, Henri. *Études sur le code de l'alliance.* Paris: Letouzey et Ané, 1946.

Chiera, Edward, and Ephraim A. Speiser. "Selected 'Kirkuk' Documents." *JAOS* 47 (1927): 36–60.

Childs, Brevard S. *The Book of Exodus: A Critical, Theological Commentary.* OTL. Philadelphia: Westminster, 1974.

Chirichigno, Gregory C. *Debt-Slavery in Israel and the Ancient Near East.* JSOTSup 141. Sheffield: Sheffield Academic, 1993.

Claassens, S. J. [Van Wyk]. "The So-Called 'Mesopotamian Law Codes': What's in a Name?" *JSem* 19 (2010): 461–78.

Cocquerillat, Denise. "Aperçus sur la phéniciculture en Babylonie à l'époque de la Ière dynastie de Babylone." *JESHO* 10 (1967): 161–223.

Cogan, Mordechai, and Hayim Tadmor. *II Kings: A New Translation.* AB 11. Garden City, NY: Doubleday, 1988.

Coleman, Jules L. *Risks and Wrongs.* Cambridge: Cambridge University Press, 1992.

Collins, John J. "The Transformation of the Torah in Second Temple Judaism." *JSJ* 43 (2012): 455–74.

Conklin, Blane. *Oath Formulas in Biblical Hebrew.* Linguistic Studies in Ancient West Semitic 5. Winona Lake, IN: Eisenbrauns, 2011.

Corner-Thomas, R. A., et al. "Ewe Lamb Live Weight and Body Condition Scores Affect Reproductive Rates in Commercial Flocks." *New Zealand Journal of Agricultural Research* 58 (2015): 26–34.

Cotton, Hannah M. "The Guardian (ἐπίτροπος) of a Woman in the Documents from the Judaean Desert." *Zeitschrift für Papyrologie und Epigraphik* 118 (1997): 267–73.

Cover, Robert M. "*Nomos* and Narrative." *Harvard Law Review* 97 (1983): 4–68.

Cowley, A. E. *Aramaic Papyri of the Fifth Century B.C.* Oxford: Clarendon, 1923. Repr., Osnabrück: Zeller, 1967.

Creason, Stuart. "*PQD* Revisited." Pages 27–42 in *Studies in Semitic and Afroasiatic Linguistics Presented to Gene B. Gragg.* Edited by Cynthia L. Miller. SAOC 60. Chicago: Oriental Institute of the University of Chicago, 2007.

Creekmore, Andrew T. "Kazane Höyük and Urban Life Histories in Third Millennium Upper Mesopotamia." PhD diss., Northwestern University, 2008.

Culbertson, Laura E. "Dispute Resolution in the Provincial Courts of the Third Dynasty of Ur." PhD diss., University of Michigan, 2009.

Cuq, Edouard. "Commentaire juridique d'un jugement sous Ammi-Ditana." *RA* 7 (1910): 129–38.

Damaška, Mirjan R. "Truth in Adjudication." *Hastings Law Journal* 49 (1998): 289–308.

Daube, David. "Negligence in the Early Talmudic Law of Contract (*Peshi'ah*)." Pages 124–47 in vol. 1 of *Festschrift Fritz Schulz.* Edited by H. Niedermeyer and W. Flume. Weimar: H. Böhlaus Nachfolger, 1951.

———. *Studies in Biblical Law.* Cambridge: Cambridge University Press, 1969.

De Roche, "Yahweh's Rîb against Israel: A Reassessment of the So-Called 'Prophetic Lawsuit' in the Preexilic Prophets." *JBL* 102 (1983): 563–74.

De Vries, Simon J. *1 Kings.* WBC 12. Waco, TX: Word, 1985.

Del Mar, Maksymilian. "Legal Fictions and Legal Change in the Common Law Tradition." Pages 225–54 in *Legal Fictions in Theory and Practice.* Edited by Maksymilian Del Mar and William Twining. Cham: Springer, 2015.

Dempster, Hamish. "Clearing the Confusion Surrounding Bailment: Bailment as an Exercise of Legal Power by the Bailor." *Common Law World Review* 33 (2004): 295–331.

Descheemaeker, Eric. *The Division of Wrongs: A Historical Comparative Study.* Oxford: Oxford University Press, 2009.

Draffkorn, Anne. "Ilāni/Elohim." *JBL* 76 (1957): 216–24.

Driver, G. R., and John C. Miles. *The Babylonian Laws.* 2 vols. Oxford: Clarendon, 1968.

Dryer, M. S., and M. Haspelmath, eds. *The World Atlas of Language Structures Online.* Leipzig: Max Planck Institute for Evolutionary Anthropology, 2013.

Dworkin, Ronald. *Law's Empire.* Cambridge: Harvard University Press, 1986.

Eichler, Barry L. "Exodus 21:22–25 Revisited: Methodological Considerations." Pages 11–29 in *Birkat Shalom: Studies in the Bible, Ancient Near Eastern Literature, and Postbiblical Judaism Presented to Shalom M. Paul on the Occasion of His Seventieth Birthday.* Edited by Chaim Cohen et al. Winona Lake, IN: Eisenbrauns, 2008.

———. "Literary Structure in the Laws of Eshnunna." Pages 71–84 in *Language, Literature, and History: Philological and Historical Studies Presented to Erica Reiner.* Edited by Francesca Rochberg-Halton. AOS 67. New Haven: American Oriental Society, 1987.

Ehrlich, Arnold B. *Randglossen zur hebräischen Bibel.* 7 vols. Leipzig: Hinrichs, 1908–1914.

Fensham, F. Charles. "Liability in Case of Negligence in the Old Testament Covenant Code and Ancient Legal Traditions." Pages 283–94 in vol. 1 of *Essays in Honour of Ben Beinart: Jura Legesque Antiquiores necnon Recentiores,* ed. Wouter De Vos, *Acta Juridica, 1976–1978,* 3 vols. (Cape Town: Juta, 1979).

———. "The Mišpāṭîm in the Covenant Code." PhD diss., John Hopkins University, 1958.

Fernandez, Joseph M. "An Exploration of the Meaning of Truth in Philosophy and Law." *University of Notre Dame Australia Law Review* 11 (2009): 53–83.

Finkelstein, J. J. "An Old Babylonian Herding Contract and Genesis 31:38f." *JAOS* 88 (1968): 30–36.

———. "On Some Recent Studies in Cuneiform Law." *JAOS* 90 (1970): 243–56.

———. *The Ox That Gored.* TAPS 71.2. Philadelphia: American Philosophical Society, 1981.

———. "Sex Offenses in Sumerian Laws." *JAOS* 86 (1966): 355–72.

———. "Some New *Misharum* Material and Its Implications." Pages 233–46 in *Studies in Honor of Benno Landsberger on His Seventy-Fifth Birthday, April 21, 1965.* Edited by Hans Gustav Güterbock and Thorkild

Jacobsen. Assyriological Studies 16. Chicago: University of Chicago Press, 1965.

Fishbane, Michael A. "Accusations of Adultery: A Study of Law and Scribal Practice in Numbers 5:11–31." Pages 487–502 in *Women in the Hebrew Bible: A Reader*. Edited by Alice Bach. New York: Routledge, 1999.

Fraade, Steven D. "Early Rabbinic Midrash between Philo and Qumran." Pages 281–93 in *Strength to Strength: Essays in Honor of Shaye J. D. Cohen*. Edited by Michael L. Satlow. BJS 363. Providence, RI: Brown Judaic Studies, 2018.

Fraade, Steven D., Aharon Shemesh, and Ruth Clements. *Rabbinic Perspectives: Rabbinic Literature and the Dead Sea Scrolls; Proceedings of the Eighth International Symposium of the Orion Center for the Study of the Dead Sea Scrolls and Associated Literature, 7–9 January, 2003*. STDJ 62. Leiden: Brill, 2006.

Frahm, Eckart. *Babylonian and Assyrian Text Commentaries: Origins of Interpretation*. Guides to the Mesopotamian Textual Record 5. Münster: Ugarit-Verlag, 2011.

Fritz, Volkmar. *1 & 2 Kings: A Continental Commentary*. Translated by Anselm Hagedorn. Minneapolis: Fortress, 2003.

Frymer-Kensky, Tikva. "The Strange Case of the Suspected Sotah (Numbers V 11-31)." *VT* 34 (1984): 11–26.

Fuller, Lon L. *Legal Fictions*. Stanford, CA: Stanford University Press, 1967.

Gabbay, Uri. "Akkadian Commentaries from Ancient Mesopotamia and Their Relation to Early Hebrew Exegesis." *Dead Sea Discoveries* 19 (2012): 267–312.

———. *The Exegetical Terminology of Akkadian Commentaries*. CHANE 82. Leiden: Brill, 2016.

Ganzel, Tova, and Shalom E. Holtz. "Ezekiel's Temple in Babylonian Context." *VT* 64 (2014): 211–26.

Garner, Bryan A., ed. *Black's Law Dictionary*. 9th ed. Saint Paul, MN: Thomson Reuters, 2009.

Gaskins, C. T., et al. "Influence of Body Weight, Age, and Weight Gain on Fertility and Prolificacy in Four Breeds of Ewe Lambs." *Journal of Animal Science* 83 (2005): 1680–89.

Geller, Markham J. "The Influence of Ancient Mesopotamia on Hellenistic Judaism." Pages 43–54 in *Civilizations of the Ancient Near East*. Edited by Jack M. Sasson. New York: Scribner, 1995.

Geller, Stephen A. "A Poetic Analysis of Isaiah 40:1–2." *HTR* 77 (1984): 413–20.

Goetze, Albrecht. "The Laws of Eshnunna." *AASOR* 31 (1951–1952): 1–197.

Goldberg, John C. P., and Benjamin C. Zipursky. "The Moral of MacPherson." *University of Pennsylvania Law Review* 146 (1998): 1733–1847.

Gordon, Cyrus. "אלהים in Its Reputed Meaning of Rulers, Judges." *JBL* 54 (1935): 139–44.

Greenberg, Moshe. *Ezekiel 21–37: A New Translation with Introduction and Commentary.* AB 22A. New York: Doubleday, 1997.

———. "Some Postulates of Biblical Criminal Law." Pages 5–28 in *Yehezkel Kaufmann Jubilee Volume.* Edited by M. Haran. Jerusalem: Magnes, 1960.

Greengus, Samuel. *Laws in the Bible and in Early Rabbinic Collections: The Legal Legacy of the Ancient Near East.* Eugene, OR: Cascade, 2011.

———. "The Old Babylonian Marriage Contract." *JAOS* 89 (1969): 505–32.

Greenstein, Edward L. "Trans-Semitic Idiomatic Equivalency and the Derivation of Hebrew *ml'kh.*" *UF* 11 (1979): 329–36.

Grice, Ettalene Mears. *Records from Ur and Larsa Dated in the Larsa Dynasty.* YOS 5. New Haven: Yale University Press, 1919.

Halberstam, Chaya T. "The Art of Biblical Law." *Prooftexts* 27 (2007): 345–64.

———. *Law and Truth in Biblical and Rabbinic Literature.* Bloomington: Indiana University Press, 2010.

Hallo, William W., and K. Lawson Younger Jr., eds. *The Context of Scripture.* 4 vols. Leiden: Brill, 1997–2016.

Halpern, Baruch. *David's Secret Demons: Messiah, Murderer, Traitor, King.* Bible in Its World. Grand Rapids: Eerdmans, 2001.

Harris, Rivkah. *Ancient Sippar: A Demographic Study of an Old Babylonian City (1894-1595 B.C.).* Uitgaven van het Nederlands Historisch-Archaeologisch Instituut te Istanbul 36. Leiden: Nederlands Historisch-Archaeologisch Instituut te Istanbul, 1975.

———. "Biographical Notes on the *naditu* Women of Sippar." *JCS* 16 (1962): 1–12.

———. *Gender and Aging in Mesopotamia: The Gilgamesh Epic and Other Ancient Literature.* Norman: University of Oklahoma Press, 2000.

Hayes, Christine. "Law in Classical Rabbinic Judaism." Pages 98–100 in *The Cambridge Companion to Judaism and Law.* Edited by Christine Hayes. New York: Cambridge University Press, 2017.

———. *What's Divine about Divine Law?: Early Perspectives.* Princeton: Princeton University Press, 2015.

Helmholz, R. H. "Bailment Theories and the Liability of Bailees: The Elusive Uniform Standard of Reasonable Care." *Kansas Law Review* 41 (1992–1993): 97–135.

Hess, Christian W. "Oblique Core Arguments in Akkadian." Pages 729–49 in *Proceedings of the 53e Rencontre Assyriologique Internationale,* vol. 1, *Language in the Ancient Near East.* Edited by L. Kogan et al. Babel und Bibel 4. Orientalia et classica 30. Winona Lake, IN: Eisenbrauns, 2010.

Hiers, Richard H. "Ancient Laws, Yet Strangely Modern: Biblical Contract and Tort Jurisprudence." *University of Detroit Mercy Law Review* 88 (2010–2011): 473–96.

——. *Justice and Compassion in Biblical Law.* New York: Continuum, 2009.

Hight, G. K., and K. E. Jury. "Hill Country Sheep Production." *New Zealand Journal of Agricultural Research* 16 (1973): 447–56.

Hobbs, T. R. *2 Kings.* WBC 13. Waco, TX: Word, 1985.

Hoffman, Yair. "The Root *QRB* as a Legal Term." *JNSL* 10 (1983): 67–73.

Hoffner, Harry A. "The *Arzana* House." Pages 113–21 in *Anatolian Studies Presented to Hans Gustav Güterbock on the Occasion of His 65th Birthday.* Edited by K. Bittel, Ph. H. J. Houwink ten Cate, and E. Reiner, Publications de l'Institut historique et archéologique néerlandais de Stamboul 35. Istanbul: Nederlands Historisch-Archaeologisch Instituut, 1974.

Holmes, Oliver Wendell. *The Common Law.* Edited by Paulo J. S. Pereira and Diego M. Beltran. Toronto: University of Toronto Law School Typographical Society, 2011. Originally published, 1881.

——. "The Path of the Law." *Boston Law School Magazine* 1 (1897): 1–17.

Holtz, Shalom E. *Neo-Babylonian Trial Records.* WAW 35. Atlanta: Society of Biblical Literature, 2014.

Houtman, Cornelis. *Exodus.* 4 vols. Kampen: Kok, 1993.

Humbert, Paul. "'Étendre la main' (Note de lexicographie hébraïque)." *VT* 12 (1962): 383–95.

Ibbetson, David. "Wrongs and Responsibility in Pre-Roman Law." *JLH* 25 (2004): 99-127.

Jackson, Bernard S. *Essays in Jewish and Comparative Legal History.* SJLA 10. Leiden: Brill, 1975.

——. *Essays on Halakhah in the New Testament.* Jewish and Christian Perspectives 16. Leiden: Brill, 2008.

——. "Modelling Biblical Law: The Covenant Code." *Chicago-Kent Law Review* 70 (1995): 1745–1827.

——. *Studies in the Semiotics of Biblical Law.* JSOTSup 314. Sheffield: Sheffield Academic, 2000.

——. *Theft in Early Jewish Law.* Oxford: Clarendon, 1972.

——. *Wisdom-Laws: A Study of the Mishpatim of Exodus 21:1–22:16.* Oxford: Oxford University Press, 2006.

Jeon, Jaeyoung. "Two Laws in the Sotah Passage (Num. v 11–31)." *VT* 57 (2007): 181–207.

Joannès, Francis, and André Lemaire. "Contrats babyloniens d'époque achéménide du Bît-Abî-Râm avec une épigraphe araméenne." *RA* 90 (1996): 41–60.

Jursa, Michael. "Agricultural Management, Tax Farming and Banking: Aspects of Entrepreneurial Activity in Babylonia in the Late Achaemenid and Hellenistic Periods." Pages 137–222 in *La transition entre l'empire achéménide et les royaumes hellénistiques, vers 350–300 av. J.-C.: Actes du colloque organisé au Collège de France par la chaire d'his-*

toire et civilisation du monde achéménide et de l'empire d'Alexandre et le Réseau international d'études et de recherches achéménides, 22–23 novembre 2004. Edited by Pierre Briant and Francis Joannès. Persika 9. Paris: De Boccard, 2006.

———. "Economic Change and Legal Innovation: On Aspects of Commercial Interaction and Land Tenure in Babylonia in the First Millennium BC." Pages 601–28 in *I diritti del mondo cuneiforme (Mesopotamia e regioni adiacenti, ca. 2500–500 a.C.).* Edited by Mario Liverani and Clelia Mora. Pubblicazioni del CEDANT 4. Pavia: IUSS Press, 2008.

King, L. W. *The Letters and Inscriptions of Hammurabi, King of Babylon, about B.C. 2200 to which Are Added a Series of Letters of Other Kings of the First Dynasty of Babylon.* 3 vols. London: Luzac, 1898–1900.

Kitz, Anne Marie. "Effective Simile and Effective Act: Psalm 109, Numbers 5, and *KUB* 26." *CBQ* 69 (2007): 440–56.

Knierim, Rolf. *Die Hauptbegriffe für Sünde im Alten Testament.* Gütersloh: Gütersloher Verlagshaus Gerd Mohn, 1965.

Kohler, Josef, and Arthur Ungnad. *Hammurabis Gesetz.* 6 vols. Leipzig: Pfeiffer, 1904–1923.

Kozuh, Michael. *The Sacrificial Economy: Assessors, Contractors, and Thieves in the Management of Sacrificial Sheep at the Eanna Temple of Uruk (ca. 625–520 B.C.).* Explorations in Ancient Near Eastern Civilizations 2. Winona Lake, IN: Eisenbrauns, 2014.

Kraus, F. R. "Akkadische Wörter und Ausdrücke, X–XI." *RA* 70 (1976): 165–79.

———. *Ein Edikt des Königs Ammi-Ṣaduqa von Babylon.* Leiden: Brill, 1958.

———. *Staatliche Viehhaltung im altbabylonischen Lande Larsa.* Amsterdam: Noord-Hollandsche, 1966.

Lafont, Sophie. "La procédure par serment au Proche-Orient ancien." Pages 185–98 in *Jurer et maudire: Pratiques politiques et usages juridiques du serment dans le Proche-Orient ancien.* Edited by Sophie Lafont. Paris: L'Harmattan, 1996.

———. "Le roi, le juge et l'étranger à Mari et dans la Bible." *RA* 92 (1998): 161–81.

Laidlaw, William K. "Principles of Bailment." *Cornell Law Quarterly* 16 (1930–1931): 286–310.

Lambert, David A. *How Repentance Became Biblical: Judaism, Christianity, and the Interpretation of Scripture.* New York: Oxford University Press, 2016.

Lambert, W. G. "Interchange of Ideas between Southern Mesopotamia and Syria-Palestine as Seen in Literature." Pages 311–16 in *Mesopotamien und seine Nachbarn: Politische und kulturelle Wechselbeziehungen im alten Vorderasien vom 4. bis 1. Jahrtausend v. Chr.* Edited by Hans-Jörg Nissen and Johannes Renger. Berlin: D. Reimer, 1982.

Landman, Yael. "Herding in Haran: A Note on Jacob's Claim in Genesis 31:39." *ZABR* 25 (2019): 173–80.

Landsberger, Benno. *The Date Palm and Its By-Products according to the Cuneiform Sources.* AfO Beiheft 17. Graz: Weidner, 1967.

———. "Jungfräulichkeit: Ein Beitrag zum Thema 'Beilager und Eheschliessung.'" Pages 41–105 of vol. 2 of *Symbolae Iuridicae et Historicae Martino David Dedicatae.* Edited by J. A. Ankum, R. Feenstra, and W. F. Leemans. 2 vols. Leiden: Brill, 1968.

———. "Tin and Lead: The Adventure of Two Vocables." *JNES* 24 (1965): 285–96.

Lapin, Hayim. *Early Rabbinic Civil Law and the Social History of Roman Galilee: A Study of Mishnah Tractate Baba' Meṣi'a'.* BJS 307. Altanta: Scholars Press, 1995.

Lauterbach, Jacob Z. *Mekhilta de-Rabbi Ishmael: A Critical Edition.* 2nd ed. Philadelphia: Jewish Publication Society, 2004.

Leemans, W. F. *Foreign Trade in the Old Babylonian Period.* Studia et documenta ad iura Orientis antiqui pertinentia 6. Leiden: Brill, 1960.

———. "Old Babylonian Letters and Economic History: A Review Article with a Digression on Foreign Trade." *JESHO* 11 (1968): 171–226.

LeFebvre, Michael. *Collections, Codes, and Torah: The Re-characterization of Israel's Written Law.* LHBOTS 451. New York: T&T Clark, 2006.

Levenson, Jon D. "1 Samuel 25 as Literature and as History." *CBQ* 40 (1978): 11–28.

Levenson, Jon D., and Baruch Halpern. "The Political Import of David's Marriages." *JBL* 99 (1980): 507–18.

Levine, Baruch A. "*Mulūgu/ Melûg*: The Origins of a Talmudic Legal Institution." *JAOS* 88 (1968): 271–85.

Levinson, Bernard M. *Deuteronomy and the Hermeneutics of Legal Innovation.* New York: Oxford University Press, 1997.

———. "Is the Covenant Code an Exilic Composition? A Response to John Van Seters." Pages 272–325 in *In Search of Pre-Exilic Israel: Proceedings of the Oxford Old Testament Seminar.* Edited by John Day. JSOTSup 406. London: T&T Clark, 2004.

———. *"The Right Chorale": Studies in Biblical Law and Interpretation.* FAT 54. Tübingen: Mohr Siebeck, 2008.

Levmore, Saul. "Rethinking Comparative Law: Variety and Uniformity in Ancient and Modern Tort Law." *Tulane Law Review* 61 (1986): 235–87.

Lieberman, Stephen A. "A Mesopotamian Background for the So-Called Aggadic 'Measures' of Biblical Hermeneutics." *HUCA* 58 (1987): 157–225.

Long, Jesse C. *1 & 2 Kings.* College Press NIV Commentary. Joplin, MO: College Press, 2002.

Magdalene, F. Rachel. *On the Scales of Righteousness: Neo-Babylonian Trial*

Law and the Book of Job. BJS 348. Providence, RI: Brown Judaic Studies, 2007.

———. "Rachel's Betrothal Contract and the Origins of Contract Law." Pages 77–110 in *Sexuality and Law in the Torah*. Edited by Hilary Lipka and Bruce Wells. London: Bloomsbury, 2020.

———. "Trying the Crime of Abuse of Royal Authority in the Divine Courtroom and the Incident of Naboth's Vineyard." Pages 167–245 in *The Divine Courtroom in Comparative Perspective*. Edited by Ari Mermelstein and Shalom E. Holtz. Biblical Interpretation Series 132. Leiden: Brill, 2014.

Maine, Henry Sumner. *Ancient Law: Its Connection with the Early History of Society, and Its Relation to Modern Ideas*. London: Murray, 1861.

Malul, Meir. *The Comparative Method in Ancient Near Eastern and Biblical Legal Studies*. AOAT 227. Kevelaer: Butzon & Bercker; Neukirchen-Vluyn: Neukirchener Verlag, 1990.

———. "*Susapinnu*: The Mesopotamian Paranymph and His Role." *JESHO* 32 (1989): 241–78.

McEwan, Jenny. "Ritual, Fairness and Truth: The Adversarial and Inquisitorial Models of Criminal Trial." Pages 51–70 in *The Trial on Trial: Truth and Due Process*. Edited by Antony Duff et al. Oxford; Portland, OR: Hart, 2004.

McMeel, Gerard. "The Redundancy of Bailment." *Lloyd's Maritime and Commercial Law Quarterly* 2 (2003): 169–200.

Merrill, Thomas W., and Henry E. Smith. "The Property/Contract Interface." *Columbia Law Review* 101 (2001): 773–852.

Mezey, Naomi. "Law as Culture." *Yale Journal of Law and the Humanities* 13 (2001): 35–68.

Milgram, Jonathan S. *From Mesopotamia to the Mishnah: Tannaitic Inheritance Law in Its Legal and Social Contexts*. TSAJ 164. Tübingen: Mohr Siebeck, 2016.

Milgrom, Jacob. *Leviticus 1–16: A New Translation with Introduction and Commentary*. AB 3. New York: Doubleday, 1991.

Miller, Nelson P. "An Ancient Law of Care." *Whittier Law Review* 26 (2004–2005): 3–57.

Moorey, P. R. S. *Ancient Mesopotamian Materials and Industries: The Archaeological Evidence*. Oxford: Clarendon, 1994.

Morrison, M. A. *The Eastern Archives of Nuzi*. SCCNH 4 Part 1. Winona Lake, IN: Eisenbrauns, 1993.

———. "Evidence for Herdsmen and Animal Husbandry in the Nuzi Documents." Pages 257–96 in *Studies on the Civilization and Culture of Nuzi and the Hurrians in Honor of Ernest R. Lacheman on His Seventy-Fifth Birthday*. Edited by M. A. Morrison and D. I. Owen. Winona Lake, IN: Eisenbrauns, 1981.

————. "The Jacob and Laban Narrative in Light of Near Eastern Sources." *BA* 46 (1983): 155–64.

Muffs, Yochanan. *Love and Joy: Law, Language, and Religion in Ancient Israel.* New York: Jewish Theological Seminary of America, 1992.

————. *Studies in the Aramaic Legal Papyri from Elephantine.* HdO 66. Leiden: Brill, 2003.

Mulder, Martin J. *1 Kings.* Translated by John Vriend. HCOT 7. Leuven: Peeters, 1998.

Nelson, W. David. *Mekhilta de-Rabbi Shimon bar Yoḥai.* Edward E. Elson Classic. Philadelphia: Jewish Publication Society of America, 2006.

Nevader, Madhavi. "Picking up the Pieces of the Little Prince: Refractions of Neo-Babylonian Kingship Ideology in Ezekiel 40–48?" Pages 268–91 in *Exile and Return: The Babylonian Context.* Edited by Jonathan Stökl and Caroline Waerzeggers. BZAW 478. Berlin: de Gruyter, 2015.

Noonan, Benjamin J. "There and Back Again: 'Tin' or 'Lead' in Amos 7:7–9?" *VT* 63 (2013): 299–307.

Noth, Martin. *Exodus: A Commentary.* Translated by John S. Bowden. OTL. Philadelphia: Westminster, 1962.

Ochsenschlager, Edward L. *Iraq's Marsh Arabs in the Garden of Eden.* Philadelphia: University of Pennsylvania Museum of Archaeology and Anthropology, 2004.

Oppenheim, A. Leo. *Catalogue of the Cuneiform Tablets of the Wilberforce Eames Babylonian Collection in the New York Public Library.* AOS 32. New Haven: American Oriental Society, 1948.

————. "Idiomatic Accadian (Lexicographical Researches)." *JAOS* 61 (1941): 251–271.

Osumi, Yuichi. *Die Kompositionsgeschichte des Bundesbuches Exodus 20, 22b–23, 33.* OBO 105. Freiburg, Switzerland: Universitätsverlag; Göttingen: Vandenhoeck & Ruprecht, 1991.

Otto, Eckart. "Diachronie und Synchronie im Depositenrecht des 'Bundesbuches': Zur jüngsten literatur- und rechtshistorischen Diskussion von Exodus 22:6–14." *ZABR* 2 (1996): 76–85.

————. *Rechtsgeschichte der Redaktionen im Kodex Ešnunna und im "Bundesbuch": Eine redaktionsgeschichtliche und rechtsvergleichende Studie zu altbabylonischen und altisraelitischen Rechtsüberlieferungen.* OBO 85. Freiburg, Switzerland: Universitätsverlag; Göttingen: Vandenhoeck & Ruprecht, 1989.

————. "Die rechtshistorische Entwicklung des Depositenrechts in altorientalischen und altisraelitischen Rechtskorpora." *Zeitschrift der Savigny-Stiftung für Rechtsgeschichte: Romanitische Abteilung* 105 (1988): 1–31. Reprinted, pages 139–63 in Otto, *Kontinuum und Proprium: Studien zur Sozial- und Rechtsgeschichte des Alten Orients und des Alten Testaments.* Orientalia Biblica et Christiana 8. Wiesbaden: Harrassowitz, 1996.

————. *Wandel der Rechtsbegründungen in der Gesellschaftsgeschichte des anti-ken Israel: Eine Rechtsgeschichte des "Bundesbuches" Ex XX 22–XXIII 13.* Studia Biblica 3. Leiden: Brill, 1988.

Oudshoorn, Jacobine G. *The Relationship between Roman and Local Law in the Babatha and Salome Komaise Archives: General Analysis and Three Case Studies on Law of Succession, Guardianship, and Marriage.* STDJ 69. Leiden: Brill, 2007.

Palmer, Norman E. *Bailment.* Sydney: Law Book Co., 1979.

————. "Gratuitous Bailment – Contract or Tort?" *International and Comparative Law Quarterly* 24 (1975): 565–72.

Patrick, Dale. *Old Testament Law.* Atlanta: John Knox, 1985.

Pearce, Laurie E. "Cuneiform Sources for Judeans in Babylonia in the Neo-Babylonian and Achaemenid Periods: An Overview." *Religion Compass* 10 (2016): 230–43.

————. "'Judean': A Special Status in Neo-Babylonian and Achaemenid Babylonia?" Pages 267–77 in *Judah and the Judeans in the Achaemenid Period: Negotiating Identity in an International Context.* Edited by Oded Lipschits, Gary N. Knoppers, and Manfred Oeming. Winona Lake, IN: Eisenbrauns, 2011.

Pearce, Laurie E., and Cornelia Wunsch. *Documents of Judean Exiles and West Semites in Babylonia in the Collection of David Sofer.* Cornell University Studies in Assyriology and Sumerology 28. Bethesda, MD: CDL, 2014.

Petroski, Karen. "Fictions of Omniscience." *Kentucky Law Review* 103 (2014–2015): 447–528.

Petschow, Herbert. "Zur 'Systematik' in den Gesetzen von Eshnunna." Pages 131–43 of vol. 2 in *Symbolae Iuridicae et Historicae Martino David Dedicatae.* Edited by J. A. Ankum et al. Leiden: Brill, 1968.

————. "Zur Systematik und Gesetzestechnik im Codex Hammurabi." *Zeitschrift für Assyriologie und Vorderasiatische Archäologie* 57 (1965): 146–72.

Pfälzner, Peter. "Modes of Storage and the Development of Economic Systems in the Early Jezireh-Period." Pages 259–86 in *Of Pots and Pans: Papers on the Archaeology and History of Mesopotamia and Syria Presented to David Oates in Honour of His 75th Birthday.* Edited by Lamia al-Gailani Werr et al. London: NABU, 2002.

Phang, Sara Elise. *The Marriage of Roman Soldiers (13 BC – AD 235): Law and Family in the Imperial Army.* Columbia Studies in the Classical Tradition 24. Leiden: Brill, 2001.

Phillips, Anthony. *Essays on Biblical Law.* JSOTSup 344. London: Sheffield Academic, 2002.

Postgate, J. N. *Bronze Age Bureaucracy: Writing and the Practice of Government in Assyria.* Cambridge: Cambridge University Press, 2013.

———. *Early Mesopotamia: Society and Economy at the Dawn of History.* London: Routledge, 1994.

———. "Some Old Babylonian Shepherds and Their Flocks." *JSS* 20 (1975): 1–18.

Price, Ira M. "The Laws of Deposit in Early Babylonia and the Old Testament." *JAOS* 47 (1927): 250–55.

Propp, William H. C. *Exodus 19–40: A New Translation with Introduction and Commentary.* New York: Doubleday, 2006.

Prosser, William L. *Handbook of the Law of Torts.* Saint Paul, MN: West Publishing, 1941.

Rendsburg, Gary A. "Repetition with Variation in Legal-Cultic Texts of the Torah." Pages 435–63 in *Marbeh Ḥokmah: Studies in the Bible and the Ancient Near East in Loving Memory of Victor Avigdor Hurowitz.* Edited by S. Yona et al. Winona Lake, IN: Eisenbrauns, 2015.

Renger, Johannes. "The Role and the Place of Money and Credit in the Economy of Ancient Mesopotamia." Pages 15–36 in *New Approaches to Monetary Theory: Interdisciplinary Perspectives.* Edited by Heiner Ganssmann. Routledge International Studies in Money and Banking 63. London: Routledge, 2011.

Röllig, Wolfgang. *Land- und Viehwirtschaft am Unteren Habur in mittelassyrischer Zeit.* BATSHDK 9. Wiesbaden: Harrassowitz, 2008.

Rom-Shiloni, Dalit. "'How can you say, "I am not defiled…"?' (Jeremiah 2:20–25): Allusions to Priestly Legal Traditions in the Poetry of Jeremiah." *JBL* 133 (2014): 757–75.

Rosen, Lawrence. *Law as Culture: An Invitation.* Princeton: Princeton University Press, 2006.

Rosenfeld, Michel. "Dworkin and the One Law Principle: A Pluralist Critique." *Revue internationale de philosophie* 3 (2005): 363–92.

Roth, Martha T. *Law Collections from Mesopotamia and Asia Minor.* 2nd ed. SBLWAW 6. Atlanta: Scholars Press, 1997.

———. "The Scholastic Exercise 'Laws about Rented Oxen.'" *JCS* 32 (1980): 127–46.

Rothenbusch, Ralf. *Die kasuistische Rechtssammlung im "Bundesbuch" (Ex 21,2–11.18–22,16) und ihr literarischer Kontext im Licht altorientalischer Parallelen.* AOAT 259. Münster: Ugarit-Verlag, 2000.

Sandowicz, Małgorzata. "Depositaries, Depositors and Courthouse in Sixth-Century B.C. Babylon." *Palamedes* 4 (2009): 15–25.

———. "'Fear the Oath!' Stepping Back from Oath Taking in First Millennium B.C. Babylonia." *Palamedes* 6 (2011): 17–36.

———. *Oaths and Curses: A Study in Neo- and Late Babylonian Legal Formulary.* Münster: Ugarit-Verlag, 2012.

Sarat, Austin, and Thomas R. Kearns. "The Cultural Lives of Law." Pages 1–20 in *Law in the Domains of Culture.* Edited by Austin Sarat and

Thomas R. Kearns. Amherst Series in Law, Jurispridence, and Social Thought. Ann Arbor: University of Michigan Press, 1998.

Schipper, Jeremy. *Parables and Conflict in the Hebrew Bible*. New York: Cambridge University Press, 2009.

Schorr, Moses. *Urkunden des altbabylonischen Zivil- und Prozessrechts*. Vorderasiatische Bibliothek 5. Leipzig: Hinrichs, 1913.

Schwartz, Seth. "Law in Jewish Society in the Second Temple Period." Pages 57–84 in *The Cambridge Companion to Judaism and Law*. Edited by Christine Hayes. New York: Cambridge University Press, 2017.

Schwienhorst-Schönberger, Ludger. *Das Bundesbuch (Ex 20,22–23,33): Studien zu seiner Entstehung und Theologie*. BZAW 188. Berlin: de Gruyter, 1990.

Seebass, Horst. "Noch einmal zum Depositenrecht Ex 22, 6–14." Pages 21–31 in *Gottes Recht als Lebensraum: Festschrift für Hans Jochen Boecker*. Edited by Peter Mommer, Werner H. Schmidt, and Hans Strauss. Neukirchen-Vluyn: Neukirchener Verlag, 1993.

Shectman, Sarah. "Bearing Guilt in Numbers 5:12–31." Pages 479–93 in *Gazing on the Deep: Ancient Near Eastern and Other Studies in Honor of Tzvi Abusch*. Edited by Jeffrey Stackert, Barbara Nevling Porter, and David P. Wright. Bethesda, MD: CDL, 2010.

Speiser, E. A. "Notes to Recently Published Nuzi Texts." *JAOS* 55 (1935): 432–43.

Sprinkle, Joe M. *"The Book of the Covenant": A Literary Approach*. JSOTSup 174. Sheffield: JSOT Press, 1994.

Stökl, Jonathan. "'A Youth without Blemish, Handsome, Proficient in All Wisdom, Knowledgeable and Intelligent': Ezekiel's Access to Babylonian Culture." Pages 223–52 in *Exile and Return: The Babylonian Context*. Edited by Jonathan Stökl and Caroline Waerzeggers. BZAW 478. Berlin: de Gruyter, 2015.

Stol, Marten, ed. *Letters from Yale Transliterated and Translated*. AbB 9. Leiden: Brill, 1981.

Stone, Elizabeth C. *Nippur Neighborhoods*. SAOC 44. Chicago: Oriental Institute of the University of Chicago, 1987.

Summers, Robert S. "Formal Legal Truth and Substantive Truth in Judicial Fact-Finding – Their Justified Divergence in Some Particular Cases." *Law and Philosophy* 18 (1999): 497–511.

Szlechter, Emile. *Les Lois d'Ešnunna: Transcription, traduction et commentaire*. Paris: Recueil Sirey, 1954.

———, ed. *Tablettes juridiques et administratives de la IIIe dynastie d'Ur et de la Ire dynastie de Babylone conservées au Musée de l'Université de Manchester et, à Cambridge, au Musée Fitz-William, à l'Institut d'études orientales et à l'Institut d'egyptologie*. Publications de l'Institut de droit romain de l'Universitéde Paris 21a. Paris: Recueil Sirey, 1963.

Talstra, Eep. *Solomon's Prayer: Synchrony and Diachrony in the Composition of 1 Kings 8, 14-61.* CBET 3. Kampen: Kok, 1993.

Tay, Alice Ehr-Soon. "The Essence of a Bailment: Contract, Agreement or Possession?" *Sydney Law Review* 239 (1965–1967): 239–53.

Tigay, Jeffrey H. *The JPS Torah Commentary: Deuteronomy.* Philadelphia: Jewish Publication Society of America, 1996.

Toorn, Karel Van der. *Family Religion in Babylonia, Syria, and Israel: Continuity and Change in the Forms of Religious Life.* SHCANE 7. Leiden: Brill, 1996.

Van de Mieroop, Marc. "Why Did They Write on Clay?" *Klio* 79 (1997): 1–18.

van Driel, G. "Neo-Babylonian Sheep and Goats." *Bulletin of Sumerian Agriculture* 7 (1993): 219–58.

Van Koppen, Frans, and Denis Lacambre. "Sippar and the Frontier between Ešnunna and Babylon: New Sources for the History of Ešnunna in the Old Babylonian Period." *Jaarbericht "Ex Oriente Lux"* 41 (2008–2009): 151–77.

Van Selms, A. "The Goring Ox in Babylonian and Biblical Law." *ArOr* 18 (1950): 321–30.

Van Seters, John. *A Law Book for the Diaspora: Revision in the Study of the Covenant Code.* Oxford: Oxford University Press, 2003.

VerSteeg, Russ. "Early Mesopotamian Commercial Law." *University of Toledo Law Review* 30 (1999): 183–214.

Von Bar, Christian. *Non-Contractual Liability Arising out of Damage Caused to Another.* Principles of European Law 7. Munich: Sellier, 2009.

Von Soden, Wolfram. "Kleine Beiträge zum Verständnis der Gesetze Hammurabis und Bilalamas." *ArOr* 17 (1949): 359–73.

Waerzeggers, Caroline. "Locating Contact in the Babylonian Exile: Some Reflections on Tracing Judean-Babylonian Encounters in Cuneiform Texts." Pages 131–46 in *Encounters by the Rivers of Babylon: Scholarly Conversations between Jews, Iranians, and Babylonians in Antiquity.* Edited by Uri Gabbay and Shai Secunda. TSAJ 160. Tübingen: Mohr Siebeck, 2014.

Weigend, Thomas. "Is the Criminal Process about Truth?: A German Perspective." *Harvard Journal of Law & Public Policy* 26 (2003): 157–74.

Wells, Bruce. "The Covenant Code and Near Eastern Legal Traditions: A Response to David P. Wright." *Maarav* 13 (2006): 85–118.

———. "The Cultic Versus the Forensic: Judahite and Mesopotamian Judicial Procedures in the First Millennium B.C.E." *JAOS* 128 (2008): 205–32.

———. "Law and Practice." Pages 183–95 in *A Companion to the Ancient Near East.* Edited by Daniel C. Snell. Malden, MA: Blackwell, 2005.

———. *The Law of Testimony in the Pentateuchal Codes.* BZABR 4. Wiesbaden: Harrassowitz, 2004.

———. "The Long View: From Hammurabi to the Bible to the Rabbis." *ZABR* 19 (2013): 171–79.

———. "What Is Biblical Law? A Look at Pentateuchal Rules and Near Eastern Practice." *CBQ* 70 (2008): 223–43.

Wells, Bruce, and F. Rachel Magdalene, eds. *Law from the Tigris to the Tiber: The Writings of Raymond Westbrook.* 2 vols. Winona Lake, IN: Eisenbrauns, 2009.

Wells, Bruce, Cornelia Wunsch, and F. Rachel Magdalene. "The Assertory Oath in Neo-Babylonian and Persian Administrative Texts." *Revue Internationale des droits de l'Antiquité* 57 (2010): 13–29.

Westbrook, Raymond. "The Deposit Law of Exodus 22, 6–12." *ZAW* 106 (1994): 390–403. Reprinted, pages 361–77 in vol. 2 of *Law from the Tigris to the Tiber: The Writings of Raymond Westbrook.* Edited by Bruce Wells and F. Rachel Magdalene. Winona Lake, IN: Eisenbrauns, 2009.

———, ed. *A History of Ancient Near Eastern Law.* 2 vols. HdO 1.72. Leiden: Brill, 2003.

———. "A Matter of Life and Death." *JANES* 25 (1997): 61–70.

———. *Studies in Biblical and Cuneiform Law.* Paris: Gabalda, 1988.

———. "The Laws of Biblical Israel." Pages 99–119 in *The Hebrew Bible: New Insights and Scholarship.* Edited by Frederick E. Greenspahn. Jewish Studies in the 21st Century. New York: New York University Press, 2008.

———. "The Naptaru at Ugarit." *JCS* 60 (2008): 53-55.

———. "The Old Babylonian Term *napṭarum.*" *JCS* 46 (1994): 41–46.

Westbrook, Raymond, and Bruce Wells. *Everyday Law in Biblical Israel: An Introduction.* Louisville: Westminster John Knox, 2009.

Williston, Samuel S. *A Treatise on the Law of Contracts.* Edited by Richard A. Lord. 4th ed. Rochester, NY: Lawyers Cooperative Pub., 1990–2014.

Winfield, Percy H. "The History of Negligence in the Law of Torts." *The Law Quarterly Review* 166 (1926): 184–201.

———. *The Province of the Law of Tort.* Cambridge: Cambridge University Press, 1931.

Winitzer, Abraham. "Assyriology and Jewish Studies in Tel Aviv: Ezekiel among the Babylonian *literati.*" Pages 163–216 in *Encounters by the Rivers of Babylon: Scholarly Conversations between Jews, Iranians, and Babylonians in Antiquity.* Edited by Uri Gabbay and Shai Secunda. TSAJ 160. Tübingen: Mohr Siebeck, 2014.

Witkowski, Stanley R., and Cecil H. Brown. "Climate, Clothing, and Body-Part Nomenclature." *Ethnology* 24 (1985): 197–214.

Wright, David P. *Inventing God's Law: How the Covenant Code of the Bible Used and Revised the Laws of Hammurabi.* Oxford: Oxford University Press, 2009.

———. "The Laws of Hammurabi and the Covenant Code: A Response to Bruce Wells." *Maarav* 13 (2006): 211–60.

———. "The Laws of Hammurabi as a Source for the Covenant Collection (Exodus 20:23–23:19)." *Maarav* 10 (2003): 11–87.

Wright, Jacob L. *David, King of Israel, and Caleb in Biblical Memory.* New York: Cambridge University Press, 2014.

Wunsch, Cornelia. "Glimpses on the Lives of Deportees in Rural Babylonia." Pages 247–60 in *Arameans, Chaldeans, and Arabs in Babylonia and Palestine in the First Millennium B.C.* Edited by Angelika Berlejung and Michael P. Streck. LAOS 3. Wiesbaden: Harrassowitz, 2013.

Yadin, Azzan. *Scripture as Logos: Rabbi Ishmael and the Origins of Midrash.* Divinations. Philadelphia: University of Pennsylvania Press, 2004.

Yadin-Israel, Azzan. *Scripture and Tradition: Rabbi Akiva and the Triumph of Midrash.* Divinations. Philadelphia: University of Pennsylvania Press, 2015.

Yaron, Reuven. *The Laws of Eshnunna.* 2nd rev. ed. Jerusalem: Magnes; Leiden: Brill, 1988.

Zimmerli, Walther. "Die Eigenart der prophetischen Rede des Ezechiel: Ein Beitrag zum Problem an Hand von Ez 14 :1-11." *ZAW* 66 (1954): 1–26.

Zimmermann, Reinhard. *The Law of Obligations: Roman Foundations of the Civilian Tradition.* New York: Oxford University Press, 1996.

Index of Ancient Sources

Index of Modern Authors

Index of Subjects

CPSIA information can be obtained
at www.ICGtesting.com
Printed in the USA
FSHW021447110222
88228FS